HIJACKING CATASTROPHE

9/11, Fear and the Selling of American Empire

HIJACKING CATASTROPHE
9/11, Fear and the Selling of American Empire

edited by Sut Jhally and Jeremy Earp
foreword by Howard Zinn

ARRIS BOOKS
An imprint of Arris Publishing Ltd
Gloucestershire

First published in 2004 by

Arris Books
An imprint of Arris Publishing Ltd
12 Main Street
Adlestrop
Moreton-in-Marsh
Gloucestershire GL56 0YN
www.arrisbooks.com

ISBN 1 84437 040 2

Printed and bound in Canada by Webcom Ltd

To request our complete catalogue, please call us at **01608 659328**, visit our web site at:
www.arrisbooks.com, or e-mail us at: **info@arrisbooks.com**

CONTENTS

ACKNOWLEDGMENTS

We thank the staff and interns of the Media Education Foundation for all their efforts in producing this book in a timely manner. Andrea Wozny and Shara Dunn worked tirelessly over the past nine months to get these interviews transcribed. In addition, we would like to thank Lynn Comella, Viveca Green, Ronit Ridberg, Erica Silva, and Andrew Killoy for their copy-editing work under extremely tight deadlines. We also extend our deep gratitude to our interviewees, who gave generously of their time and expertise.

FOREWORD

by Howard Zinn

There are, indeed, justified fears. But there are also situations, usually created by governments, where a population is aroused to uncontrollable violence—from lynchings to wars to genocide—by the manipulation of irrational fears.

History is full of atrocities committed in an atmosphere of fear created for political purposes: the launching of the Crusades against the "infidel"; the massacre of Armenians by the Turks in 1915; the attacks on Jews and Communists in Germany after the burning of the Reichstag in 1933.

The witch hunts of 17th-century New England were based on fears aroused against mystical and unseen horrors, and were useful in consolidating the power of the Puritan fathers. The mutual fears of whites and Indians of each other, some rational, some irrational, led to massacres on both sides.

After the American war for independence against England, the new nation, in the presidency of John Adams, used the building up of alarms about revolutionaries and foreigners to pass the Alien and Sedition Acts, restricting freedom of speech and allowing the arbitrary deportation of non-citizen immigrants.

Sometimes individual rulers of other countries become fearsome symbols to terrify the citizenry into supporting a war. In 1917, in the United States, the German Kaiser became such a symbol. This, along with the alarm generated by the sinking of American ships by German submarines, made it easier to mobilize the population for war, and to imprison those who spoke out against the war.

At the end of World War I, the discovery of a bomb planted at the house of Attorney General Palmer was used to justify the detention and deportation of thousands of non-citizens.

Cataclysmic events often served to create an atmosphere of fear, in which war became more acceptable, and constitutional rights could be ignored. Thus, in 1898, the explosion of the battleship *Maine* in Havana Harbor, with hundreds of American sailors killed, led directly to the invasion of Cuba in the Spanish-American War. And in World War II the surprise attack on Pearl Harbor became an occasion for fears of Japanese sabotage, even invasion, and resulted in the rounding up and imprisonment of over 100,000 Japanese-Americans on the West Coast.

A few years after the end of World War II, the most fearsome of such cataclysmic events occurred: the discovery in 1949 that the Soviet

Union had succeeded in building and testing its first atomic bomb. This raised the tensions of the "cold war" to its highest point, in which a hysterical fear of the Soviet Union spread quickly across the nation, encouraged by the government and the mass media.

It was in this atmosphere that children all over the country were taught to crouch under their desks to save themselves from the effects of a Soviet atomic bombing. This was the time of "McCarthyism," when the Committee on Un-American Activities was carrying on its inquisitions against academics and prominent figures in the entertainment world.

In this period, too, Ethel and Julius Rosenberg were sent to the electric chair, millions of Americans were put on government lists as suspected Communists or supporters of radical causes, and every revolution in a Third World country was seen as part of a world communist conspiracy.

The creation of the "Red scare" enabled the government to call for larger and larger military budgets and to build its stockpile of nuclear weapons far beyond any possible "deterrent" value. There were regular alarms, based on false claims of a "bomber gap," in which the Soviet Union was presumed to have a superior bomber force, and then a "missile gap."

Internal intelligence reports indicated that the Soviet military buildup was in fact far behind that of the United States, but these were ignored because the scare factor served the purposes of an aggressive foreign policy and a profit-seeking military-industrial complex.

Today, fears of "terrorism" play the same role that fear of "Communism" did during the cold war. The cataclysmic event of September 11 was as real as the explosion of the battleship *Maine*, or the burning of the Reichstag, or the existence of the Soviet Union. But as in those cases, it has been used to create an irrational hysteria, to justify government policies whose roots go far back in the history of the nation— policies of expansion, military intervention, and repression of dissent.

The current expressions of these policies are the bombing and invasion of Afghanistan and Iraq, the establishment of more military bases in the Middle East, an enormous increase in the military budget, and attempts to chill free expression by ignoring the protections of the Bill of Rights.

In the following pages, the reader will find a series of extraordinary ruminations on this issue: the relationship between September 11 and the extension of the American empire.

INTRODUCTION

by Jeremy Earp and Sut Jhally

As the official stated reasons for the war on Iraq have dissipated—no weapons of mass destruction, no imminent threat, no links to the 9/11 terror attacks—mainstream discussion has been limited to issues of intelligence and intelligence failures. Far less attention has been paid to what many experts argue are the real reasons for the war and occupation: control of dwindling resources, an intimidating demonstration of American military power, and a radical neoconservative philosophy that openly extols the virtues of a new, accelerated drive for American empire.

The interviews collected in this book were conducted for a documentary film (also entitled *Hijacking Catastrophe: 9/11, Fear, and the Selling of American Empire*) that examines the neoconservative roots and political effects of the Bush administration's response to the 9/11 terror attacks. Government insiders and more than twenty prominent political commentators place the emergence of the so-called Bush Doctrine and the war in Iraq within the context of a two-decade struggle by neoconservatives to radically increase defense spending and to transform the global post-cold war order by means of military force. Our intent in making these interviews available in book form, as with our intent in producing the documentary, is to provide an accessible analysis of the ideas and motives that are driving US foreign policy at this crucial moment in American history.

Taken together, these interviews clarify three primary subjects: the Bush administration's actual reasons for going to war with Iraq; the manner in which the administration sold the war to the American people; and the domestic and international consequences of the administration's dramatic transformation of US foreign policy in the wake of 9/11.

Several of the interviews focus on strategic plans drawn up by neoconservative foreign policy hawks after the cold war to break free of the existing elite consensus about America's role in the world. By calling for sharp increases in military spending after the fall of the Soviet Union, the neoconservative dream was to project and extend unchallenged American military hegemony into the 21st century. Defense strategy plans authored in the early 1990s by Paul Wolfowitz, Richard Perle, Dick Cheney, and other associates of neoconservative think tanks such as the Project for the New American Century (PNAC) contain two key historical facts that have gone virtually missing in today's charged political climate: first, that the 9/11 attacks were almost identical to the pretext these plans theorized would be necessary to justify a new military build-up; and second, that plans to go to war with Iraq and gain a military foothold in the Middle East were drawn up well before the 9/11 pretext surfaced. As PNAC chillingly, and prophetically, put it in September 2000, a full year before most Americans had even heard of Osama bin Laden: "The process of transformation, even if it brings revolutionary change, is likely to be a long one, absent some catastrophic and catalyzing event—like a new Pearl Harbor."

In the process of examining how this revolutionary agenda slipped into the mainstream with virtually no public debate, a number of these interviews move from policy to politics to examine how the administration used the mainstream media to justify the Iraq war within the emotional trauma of 9/11. Central to this examination are the media processes by which Saddam Hussein came to replace Osama bin Laden in the Bush administration's political rhetoric, and how ordinary Americans have been persuaded to remain silent while their civil liberties get eroded at home and a new American empire asserts itself globally.

By looking closely at how the Bush administration has exploited post-9/11 fear and anxiety to sell a controversial neoconservative agenda under the guise of the war on terrorism, we also focus specifically on how the administration has attempted to deflect attention away from the substance of its policies by tapping into a virtual archive of masculine archetypes and American mythology—an archive with deep roots in the American imagination and deep connections to popular American definitions of nationalism, patriotism, and what it means to be "presidential." One of the book's recurring themes is how understandable fears after 9/11 fed the cultural power of these political tactics—in the process shutting down critical thinking and debate while manufacturing public consent to policies that often work against popular mainstream interests.

The neoconservative vision of American empire has moved from the fringes of right-wing think tanks to shape the Bush Doctrine of pre-emptive war and the National Security Strategy of the United States itself. But debate about the wisdom of this vision has barely registered in the mainstream. For most ordinary Americans, "empire" remains an abstract and meaningless phrase. The interviews collected here are intended to clarify the nature and everyday effects of empire: its reliance on perpetual war; the undermining of democracy and civil rights in the name of security and safety; the rise of official secrecy, propaganda, and the glorification of war and militarism; the dismantling of the last remnants of the welfare state as the cost of war is borne by the poorest and most vulnerable sectors of American society; exploding deficits and debt to finance huge increases in defense spending and foreign military adventures; and the mounting loss of life as the young men and women of the American armed services are called to fight for a hollow cause and an agenda that have been insulated from public examination. Such examination is vital as Americans start thinking about the 2004 Presidential elections—a crucial watershed event in American history.

Tariq Ali is a longstanding editor of *New Left Review* and has written more than a dozen books on history and politics. His latest are *The Clash of Fundamentalisms: Crusades, Jihad, and Modernity* (Verso, 2002) and *Bush in Babylon: Recolonising Iraq* (Verso, 2003).

SJ: Are the invasion and occupation of Iraq something qualitatively different in terms of empire, or is it business as usual?

It is difficult to say in relation to the American Empire what "business as usual" is because this is an empire with a very checkered history. It's an empire that began in North America. The internal expansion of the United States was the result of violence: violence against Native people, violence at some crucial stages against migrant populations that were moving here. Something few people know is that more Italian immigrants were killed in Louisiana than blacks at a certain period in American history. So this violence was also used to unite the country. The American Civil War, which according to the most common view was fought to liberate the slaves, was essentially fought by the northern ruling elite in order to unite the country by force. There is this history, then, which is internal to the formation of this country, its structures, and its culture.

And then the US spread outward with the Monroe Doctrine into Latin America. There's a very good book that was written by General Smedly Butler after he retired from the United States Marines, which I always recommend to people and to which I refer in my own work. Smedly Butler was the most decorated US Marine general in history. General Douglas MacArthur admired him greatly and a big barracks in Okinawa is still named after him. Smedly Butler wrote a book called *War as a Racket*, and in this book he wrote, "All my life I have worked in the US Army. Now that I have retired, I have had time to think about what I was asked to do." And he basically said that the US Marine Corps and the US Army were used as hit men by the US corporations to go and conquer large tracts of Latin America to make these countries safe for Brown Brothers, etc. Then he lists all the big corporations of the last years of the nineteenth century and early years of the twentieth that invaded Latin America or Central America dozens and dozens of times. It's a very moving book by a serious general who suddenly realized what he did. He compared himself and the Marine Corps to Al Capone. He said what Al Capone did in a few districts in Chicago, we did all over a continent and all over the world.

I make this point to stress that there is a basic continuity in US policies over the last two hundred years. The point at which the US became a world empire was determined by events in Europe, primarily World War I. The US decided to go into that war after February 1917 when the first revolution in Russia had taken place. There was a fear that revolution would spread everywhere, thus challenging capitalism and the rule of capital. That's when the US made its first intervention on the world stage and became a world power. Since that time, the US has moved inexorably toward their role as a major world player because of their strength, economically, and then, increasingly, militarily. After World War II they were accepted as leaders of the capitalist world, and their leadership was never challenged during the cold war period.

But the US is an empire that has had its ups and downs: you have reforming presidents, aggressive presidents, presidents who say, "Now is the time to consolidate our victories—let's not do anything too dramatic." Then there are others who feel it is time to move forward again. The Bush administration and its personnel decided that it was time to move forward again. Now, this is an argument that was developed at the time when Bush Sr. was President, by an Afghan-American ideologue, Zalmay Khalilzad, who worked for Bush Sr. I'm summarizing his argument very boldly, but he essentially said that now that there are no cold war enemies, how do we preserve US hegemony in the world? We had everyone behind us because we were fighting communism. Now we have no one to fight, in that sense, so how do we preserve US hegemony? His answer was that we have to use force to preserve US hegemony.

The US had done this before, but during the cold war the ideology was different: the US was not the one who used force. The common belief was that force was used against them and they were basically defending themselves. This was not true, but that was the argument. In a world where Russia is capitalist, where China is capitalist, and where there is only capitalism, the threat is economic; the threat is to America's place and position as the dominant power in the world and this position is heavily dependent on economic control, so we have to use force to maintain our place. This argument has been bubbling away behind the scenes ever since.

In my opinion, the intervention that Clinton and Albright carried out in the Balkans had very little to do with humanitarian intervention, and a great deal to do with imposing the United States in that region and not letting the Europeans handle the conflict. When that happened, few people realized it, but they—Clinton and Albright—desperately wanted that war. Milosevic was prepared to concede virtually everything prior to that war, and then the US went in and upped the stakes by saying, "Okay, we want the right to enter your country and do whatever we want to that country, not just Kosovo but Serbia." Naturally, he couldn't accept that. I remember Clinton explaining the war to the American people and saying that we are going in there because we need to do it to protect our economy, which was weird. And people said, "Protect our economy by going to Kosovo?" But Clinton was thinking strategically: we have to go there and build bases. And they built the largest helicopter base in Europe, which is in Kosovo, and one of the largest US military bases, which is in Tuzla, Bosnia.

So this is a process, and if you read some of the books written by realist historians of the present, they point out very clearly that it is the Clinton administration that started the process of new interventions. The Bush administration, however, has taken it to a new height. They've moved beyond that because they were very lucky. They were lucky in the sense that 9/11 happened when they were in power. We can debate until the end of eternity what the Democrats would have done if they had been in power. Would they not have invaded Afghanistan? I think they would have gone for it. There was no opposition to the Afghanistan war, which was supported by everyone, so it wasn't a particularly unilateralist thing. The entire Security Council supported that. There were German troops sent in. Lots of Europeans were on board for that. The split between Europe and America came with Iraq. So until then, Bush was no different from any other president.

But the interesting thing is that the ideologues surrounding Bush and the policymakers behind the scenes—this hard-core group of right-wing American conservatives symbolized by Dick Cheney, Donald Rumsfeld, Paul Wolfowitz, Richard Perle, and Condoleezza Rice—actually discussed at the National Security Council and meetings surrounding it: "How can we use 9/11 to re-map the world and to get our way wherever we want?" This is now being documented, as well as the fact that there was a big debate at the National Security Council after 9/11 about whether to go first to Afghanistan or Iraq. It is actually quite staggering because contrary to the lies told to the American people, Iraq had absolutely no connections with 9/11. Al-Qaeda was despised by the regime in Iraq, which was a secular regime, not interested in religion, as such. So they delayed the invasion. They went into Afghanistan first, and then they decided to go for Iraq. Now why did they decide to go for Iraq? That's the interesting question.

I think the basic reason was not economic. I have never believed that oil was the single most important motivation, because they have access to enough oil in that region. If they were desperate for oil, they could have done a deal with the Saddam regime. In 2000 and 2001 they were buying oil from Iraq through intermediaries anyway. It was being sold to them, so it wasn't a question that the oil flow was going to be stopped. No, I think there was one basic reason for the invasion and occupation of Iraq and some subsidiary ones.

The major reason to take Iraq was a display of imperial power. They knew this was a weak army, and they also knew it had no weapons of mass destruction. If they had had weapons of mass destruction, they would have thought very carefully before they went in. They were sure there was nothing there and they knew they would easily take Iraq. And why do it at this particular point was to show the Arab world, to show Europe and the Far Eastern block—China and the Koreans—who was master. I think that was the basic purpose of taking Iraq.

Of course, an important secondary motive was to appease the Israelis, because you have a Likudist faction at the heart of the Bush administration. These are people who represent the most die-hard elements in Israeli society, and the Israelis were after the Saddam regime for some time. They wanted to take it out because they felt it posed a potential challenge to them. The Iraqis and Syrians were the only two regimes that hadn't done a compromise settlement with the Israelis. They knew that Saddam was giving a lot of money to the Palestinians, and why shouldn't he?

The day after Baghdad fell, Arial Sharon, the war criminal in charge of Israel, said to the Palestinians, "Now I hope you Palestinians will come to your senses. Your great protector has fallen." His remark showed absolutely no understanding of the dynamics of that struggle or the reason why it takes place. He's had his answer from the Palestinians more than once since that time, but that was the principal purpose of taking Iraq.

Where it's gone completely wrong for the US is that they weren't expecting resistance. The administration was not prepared for it, because the quislings, collaborators, frauds, mountebanks that they listened to—Iraqis either on their payroll or desperate to be on their payroll—had told them they would be welcomed with sweets and flowers. That is what the idiot Kanan Makiya told Bush when he went to see him at the White House, "Don't worry, it will be a liberation for the people." Well, the people obviously didn't regard it as such and this handful of Iraqi neoconservatives stationed in the United States gave the wrong advice to the Bush administration. The US soldiers in Iraq are now sending back desperate messages: "We are hated by the people here. They don't like us; they look at us with angry looks; they are embittered."

The section of the American population that has the best information about the situation are the soldiers serving in Iraq, because they see the truth and the reality of the occupation every single day with their own eyes. So whatever Fox television or the US armed services radio networks tells them, if it clashes with their own experience, they believe their own experience. That's the big difference between the bulk of the US population and the segment of it that is serving in Iraq. This is why you occasionally see angry letters, angry interviews, and angry e-mails when the soldiers are allowed to be on television. They're very sharp in what they say because of their own experience, and I have always argued that experience is the best teacher of a mass of people; they learn from their own collective experience. They don't learn through books or through great video shows. All of these are important, but what teaches people is their own experience. And I think what is happening in Iraq will finally come home to roost sooner or later.

SJ: What do you mean it will come home to roost?

It will come home to roost in the sense that even if the occupation succeeds in restoring some semblance of normality, it will explode in five, six, seven years time. That is why in my new book, *Bush in Babylon*, I explain the history of resistance in Iraq to the British Empire, which both created the country and faced resistance from almost the first year. The British managed to occupy Iraq for three decades, which may seem like a long time, but each decade was punctuated by resistance movements and finally a revolution. The British were booted out, and I think similar things will happen again if the occupation lasts that long.

The problem for the United States is the following: either they stay in there for three decades, which is going to create havoc at home because the American imperialists—contrary to what some people think and unlike the colonial empires of the 19th and 20th centuries—do not like to be occupiers themselves, they do not like creating their own network.

They prefer to find local people to do their dirty work for them. That has basically been the way in which they have ruled. Whether they are members of oligarchies, whether they are military dictators, whether they are elected politicians, which used to be rare in the old days, these are the people the US likes to do their work for them.

The problem with this occupation is that it is taking place in an epoch of the Washington consensus and neoliberal economics. So war is the other leg of neoliberal economics. This is an empire that walks on two legs: one is the Washington consensus and all of its institutions, including the IMF, the World Bank, and the WTO, all of which impose a particular sort of economy on the whole world. And where that doesn't work they go to war to create it. Well, if they're trying to create it in Iraq, which they are trying to do, they are not allowing so far any Iraqi companies to come forward or Iraqi merchants. What they are doing is encouraging American companies to go in and to do even the most elementary tasks there. The one Iraqi company that's being encouraged is not an Iraqi company; it's a joint venture by Ahmad Chalabi, the leading puppet in Baghdad, and his nephew, together with an Israeli company. That will go down really well in Iraq. In a very short amount of time, they have succeeded in isolating themselves from almost every segment of the Iraqi population. And I don't think it's going to work. The minute they withdraw their troops, the puppets they leave behind will be toppled. It's the same in Afghanistan. This newfangled colonialism is not going to work.

So what are they going to do if they keep their troops in? There will be growing anger and despair. It is interesting that the troops they send to Iraq are from the poorer sections of American society. The bulk of the army consists of Latino and black soldiers, many of whom have joined because they have no money and they need a job. Others have joined because they feel this is the only way they might actually get to go to school and get the education that they've been promised. Others have joined because they're not citizens. There are green card segments of the army that feel they might get citizenship this way. People are joining the army for different motives, largely economic. But this will be very different if casualties go up and they have to introduce some form of draft, at least to create a reserve army. If this happens, people will stop joining, saying, "Why should we join the army to be killed?" But if the recruitment goes down, then they will have to introduce a draft, which, horrible though it is, is more democratic. It says to the population that this is your war, not just our war. You've backed the leaders who are making this war, now go and die for them. That concentrates minds, which is why they are resisting this option and will carry on resisting it, because they know what the draft did during the Vietnam years. Bush knows what the draft did, because he avoided it.

None of the people in the Bush administration fought in Vietnam. They all found different ways to avoid it. All the senior people avoided it, with the exception of Colin Powell, who is in the army and who covered up one of the worst massacres in Vietnam, the My Lai massacre. But the others found ways of deferring it. So this is a leadership which, by and large, doesn't know what it is like to actually be serving in the military. They are remote and isolated, just like the Ba'ath politicians they are trying to topple.

SJ: What advice would you give to Americans as they think about the 2004 Presidential election?

I would say that it is not in your interests to have a regime that is waging infinite war. They have occupied Iraq, there are heavy casualties, and mainly working people suffer because they go and fight. The economy is not doing very well. If—and this is a very big "if" because the Iraqi resistance is making it difficult—the United States were to try to take Iran or Syria, they would need a draft for that. It could not be done with the present number of soldiers.

And I would say to American citizens: think very carefully before you vote. Are you going to vote for more war, which is what you'll certainly get with this regime? If this regime is sanctioned or is given the sanction of public approval at the next election, they will take it as a mandate to wage more war. However, I would also say to the American people: Don't trust the Democrats. Certainly get rid of this regime, but make sure that the Democrat who is elected is invigilated—is watched and is put under heavy pressure from the day he or she comes to power, because the Democrats have led the country into war many a time.

Essentially you have to think about the world we live in and how that world should be remade. And if you think it can be remade through war, what you're basically doing is encouraging more terrorists, more terrorist attacks, and more American lives being lost. Very little of this is reported, but in a country like Greece, the cradle of European civilization, 90 percent of the population is bitterly anti-American. You go into an island like Rhodes and you will find all the McDonalds destroyed. Anything vaguely smacking of Americanism has been destroyed. There's a very dear friend of mine who teaches in New York, and she went to a conference in Rhodes and her husband died on the beach. He had a heart attack and died. Both she and her husband were staunch anti-war activists. Her husband died and she found it difficult to get help and she said lots of people came and said that's all you Americans do, either go and kill people or cry yourselves. She was shocked, but of course understood. She explained, "Look, America isn't just one country. There are large numbers of us who oppose the war."

But the image of the United States that people get is essentially an image of official America, because the other America is rarely heard abroad. And the image they get is of American power and how that power is used. And the only force in the world capable of at least controlling that power is the American people when they go and vote in elections. So naturally, my advice would be to get rid of Bush. I think that would be a defeat for the war policy that they've adopted after 9/11, and it would at least open up a debate about what the administration is going to do. But whether or not they succeed in getting rid of Bush depends also on who the Democratic candidates are, and, let's face it, they are not a very inspiring bunch.

None of the Democratic candidates in my opinion has come up with a policy to mobilize the people. None of them has really campaigned against the provisions of the Patriot Act, how civil liberties are being affected, how people are being picked up off the streets, and so forth. None of them has done that because they're scared and none of them has come up and said the only solution to deal with terror— real terror, not imagined terror—is to try and reach a political solution in the Middle East because the most burning issue is the Israeli/Palestinian conflict. When one of the Democratic candidates, Howard Dean, said this, he was forced to retreat. He suggested that we must not just support the oppressor, but we should also look at the views of the oppressed, and for this he was punished and vilified and he retreated very, very rapidly. And then he supported the Israeli bombing of Syria. In my opinion, Democratic candidates like this, even the most so-called progressive among them, are not going to be very successful. As is gets closer to the elections, they have to really take Bush on every front, and they're not doing that. And if they fight the electoral war on the battleground determined by the Republicans, I think they might lose.

SJ: Americans don't like to think of themselves as an "empire." What would you say to them?

I think the first thing that people have to understand is that they are an empire, and that the United States is now in a unique position on a global scale. It is the only empire in the world. This is something that has never existed in the history of humanity before. You have never had a situation, or at least for thousands of years, when one empire has dominated the world. There have been tough empires, powerful empires, but they have never been unchallenged. This is the first time that you have a single empire, and if people don't believe the US is an empire, they should travel and go and see how the rest of the world is run by this empire, and the different mechanisms that are used to dominate and control. I think because the United States is such a large country with such a diversity of flora and fauna that most people don't like leaving it. They can find whatever they want in the United States. But the fact that only a minority of US citizens even have passports is indicative and symbolic of the isolation, and because a bulk of the population is isolated from the rest of the world, a handful of politicians can tell them what that world is like and drag them behind the war chariot whenever they decide to go to war. I think that it is extremely important that American people should get a different view of the world. They should travel; they should go and see what is going on in Palestine. I think a lot of very ordinary, decent American people would be shocked at the scale of the oppression that takes place in that one tiny place in the world. They should go and visit parts of Africa. They should go and see what's happening in the Far East to get a picture of the real world.

But once you understand that you are a citizen of an empire, you have certain responsibilities, and one of these responsibilities is to remain constantly vigilant and alert to see if the politicians are lying to you; to expose their lies; to march against their lies; and to challenge them at every possible turn and moment. For that you need a very alert citizenry. If you have a population that is not informed, then how can you say it's a functioning democracy? Surely democracy requires the broadest and most diverse means of information. If you simply give people one opinion day after day after day, what is the difference between you and a one-party state?

Every time I come to the States and watch the network news programs, which are awful, and then switch to Fox TV, I see a really gross propaganda channel for the administration and its system. It is so crude, pandering to the lowest common denominator and the basest instincts of people. And it's this situation which is very frightening to me. It is this situation that creates a population that doesn't know what is going on in the world. The fact that American citizens can think that the defeated Iraqi regime had anything to do with 9/11 makes the rest of the world laugh. If you talk to Europeans, even right-wing Europeans, they say, "Are you serious, do people in America really believe that Saddam Hussein had anything to do with 9/11? You must be joking." I said, "No, no it's a fact." But the US is the only country in the world that believes this. Here you have the world's most powerful empire with the most advanced technology that exists in the world, with the finest research universities in the world. The elite are educated and they know the truth, but you have a large mass of the people who are deliberately kept ill-informed or misinformed by the politicians and the media networks. That creates a big, big problem for the exercise of democracy. That's the level we're at now and this, I think, is very dangerous for democracy. In the interests of diversity and genuine democracy, one has to challenge this. If an American said, "But we aren't interested in politics," then say, "You pay the price if you're not interested in politics." That's the danger. You have to be interested in order to exercise control over your politicians.

SJ: What is your sense of the opposition to the Iraq war? Do the millions on the streets across the world make a difference?

The demonstrations that took place on February 15, 2003 were probably the largest anti-war manifestations in the history of the world, and they took place everywhere. And I don't think Europe was that different from the United States, incidentally. It's true in some parts of Europe—Italy and Greece most specifically—that you had massive turnouts. I mean 3 million people marching in the streets of Rome is quite amazing, and 80 percent of Spaniards are against the war. I think it was essentially a very decent impulse on the part of millions of people that this war was wrong and shouldn't be fought. Large numbers of people who came out for those demonstrations both in North America and in Europe were people who had never been out on a demonstration before and many of them actually thought they could stop the war just by their numbers. When they found they couldn't, they got very demoralized. But that mood still does exist. The question is how can it be harnessed, and I think a lot will depend on the resistance inside Iraq itself. Once a war has begun there is always a dialectic, a relationship between the resistance in the occupied country and an anti-war movement in the countries that have occupied it. So, we will see what happens. I am confident that if the occupation carries on for another six months or a year or two, you will have the growth of an anti-war movement again. Probably not as big as the demonstrations of February the 15th immediately, but something that could be more solid.

I think it's a massive task that confronts people who are opposed to the empire and its military adventures. It's not an easy thing, so it would be foolish to pretend that there's a simple answer to it, but basically the American public has to be convinced that this is wrong, and they're only convinced when they suffer. Unfortunately that's the reality. That's what created the big anti-war movement during the Vietnam years—when the causalities simply became unbearable. And who knows what's going to happen now. But certainly what one has to say is that official politics does not represent any segment of this movement.

During the Vietnam War, you had a handful of senators— Fulbright, Wayne Morse, and a few others—who were constantly attacking the Vietnam War on the floor of the Senate. Fulbright conducted hearings of the Senate Foreign Relations Committee that were broadcast live on the networks every night and all over the world, confronting the people in power and questioning them. That has ceased to happen. Curiously enough, the collapse of communism and the end of the cold war enemy has made democracy very bland, and the diversity that used to exist in democratic states during the cold war seems to be dying away, both in the media and in official politics. So for instance, if you look even in Britain today the differences between center-left and center-right aren't so great, and in the United States this has always been the case. Increasingly, then, you see young people alienated from political processes because they feel they can't change anything. So fewer and fewer people are now turning out in Europe because the same Americanization process that is taking place economically is affecting the politics of this country.

Against this trend we have to assert democracy from below, with alternatives, however small and weak they are, to provide different networks of information. That is much more advanced in the United States than in Europe, because people in the United States know the extent of the problem and the role the media plays. They are also preparing themselves to launch alternative things and this is why you have local radio stations, community TV stations, and a growing network of alternative centers of information. In Europe this has yet to happen, but it needs to happen. Of course the Internet has been a big boon in this process, but only a minority of people use it. It is not the case that every single person has access to this on a global scale. So the tasks for an anti-war movement are much different compared to what they were in the '60s and '70s. Somehow, they have to go much, much deeper to get at the truth and I think they will.

South Hadley, Massachusetts
October 17, 2003

BENJAMIN BARBER

Benjamin Barber is an internationally renowned political theorist and has written seventeen books, including *Jihad vs. McWorld* (Ballantine Books, 1995), *The Truth of Power* (Norton, 2001), and *Fear's Empire: War, Terrorism, and Democracy* (Norton, 2003). He is currently working on *The Decline of Capitalism and the Infantalist Ethos*.

JE: Can you talk about Bush's pre-emptive—or preventive—war strategy as a response to 9/11, and whether you think it can succeed in making the US more secure, as it is apparently designed to?

Although for the past 200 years the United States has, from time to time, intervened absent an aggressive attack on it, it has stayed with the theory and practice that a nation has a right to go to war only in the name of either self-defense or what is sometimes called an imminent threat, which is to say that if armies are massed on your border or airplanes are headed for your target cities you have a right to go to war. Short of that, no nation has a right to go to war when it has not been directly attacked. That principle was actually encapsulated under Article 51 of the United Nations Charter by the United States. It says, in effect, the only right a nation has to go to war is in the name of self-defense.

Now what happened on 9/11 is that the president and his administration decided that, given the changing nature of armaments, the nature of terrorism, and the fact that it wasn't states but individuals—what I call malevolent NGO's—that were involved in the attacks, and given that the stakes were so high, they could and would no longer wait for what they called the proof of attack from a nuclear bomb. We cannot wait, President Bush said, for a mushroom cloud to prove that the United States is under attack. Following that, they acted in accordance to the doctrine that was announced after 9/11 by Condoleezza Rice, the new preventive war doctrine. That doctrine said, in effect, that the US now reserves the right to go to war on its terms with a nation or society of its choice based on a perceived threat, and it can do that to prevent a possible strike against the United States.

This might seem sensible with respect to the character of terrorism and the nature of these new weapons. But in fact it moves the United States—for the first time in its history—outside the compass of international law, away from Article 51 of the United Nations Charter, and essentially says that the United States can make war at a time and place of its choosing, against enemies that it declares its enemies, based on its own perception of what the threats are. That's obviously deeply dangerous to international law, and it creates a precedent that this nation cannot afford to live with. Imagine if India and Pakistan said, "We will decide when the other is our enemy." Imagine if China says Taiwan is a threat and applies this doctrine. Imagine South Korea saying North Korea is a threat or vice versa. If other nations adopted a preventive war strategy as their own precedent, we would have a world of constant war, anarchy, and lawlessness.

JE: Some might argue that 9/11 showed us that this is a world that's already constantly at war, that anarchy and lawlessness already exist, and that we need to act forcefully to prevent terror from hitting home again. Is this preventive strategy something that could potentially work to combat terror?

Critics have worried that preventive war may be illegal, that it may put the United States outside the compass of international law, and that it may even be immoral. But in an age of terrorism, the real question is: does it work or not? And I would argue that the central defect of preventive war as an instrument of the war on terrorism is not that it's illegal—although that's pretty awful—but that it doesn't work. It hasn't worked and it cannot work. The problem that the administration is having, not just in Iraq but also in Afghanistan, is living evidence of the failure of the preventive war strategy as a counterterrorist strategy.

If the government of Afghanistan had been preparing to use weapons of mass destruction against the United States, or if the government of Saddam Hussein had been preparing to use weapons of mass destruction against the United States, one might say that a preventive strike by the United States prior to actually being hit might be seen as justifiable. But the problem is that the target of counter-terrorist measures is terrorism and terrorist organizations. As Secretary of Defense Donald Rumsfeld said right after 9/11, the problem America faces is that our enemies are not states; they have no leaders, no exact address to which forces can be sent. They have no conventional targets that can be taken out. In this sense, our enemies are invisible, non-state martyrs that I call malevolent non-governmental organizations (NGO). Al-Qaeda is a non-governmental organization, and taking out Afghanistan did not take out al-Qaeda. On the contrary. Sometimes the analogy that's used with terrorists is that they're like cancers on an immune-deficient body politic. And an extreme way to deal with cancer is to kill the patient so the cancer dies as well. But terrorists are much more like parasites than like cancer, and when you kill the host, you don't kill the parasite; the parasite simply moves on. The Taliban are gone, but al-Qaeda lives. Osama bin Laden is still on the loose. Mullah Omar is still on the loose. And even if these men are captured, their operatives will simply have spread to other parts of Southeast Asia and other parts of the world. You might say that Afghanistan is to some degree free of terrorists right now, but the mountains between Afghanistan and Pakistan are littered with terrorists. There are terrorists now in Indonesia, in the Philippians, in Kenya, and of course, once again, in New Jersey and Florida as well. Terrorists can move where they will, like a good NGO.

So targeting and taking out states, even states that nurture and sponsor terrorism—and we know there is little evidence that Saddam's regime was actually sponsoring and nurturing terrorism, but let's assume for a minute that there had been evidence—taking out Saddam does nothing to take out the terrorists. All the evidence we have to date is that terrorism has actually flourished in the face of the American attacks on Afghanistan and Iraq, which have been the best recruitment tools they could have. In fact, Iraq today has become a magnet for terrorists from around the world who are flocking there in the hope of killing a few Americans. So, the problem with preventive war strategy is that it targets not terrorists themselves, but those states that have at best a loose connection with them. And even if there's a close connection, taking out the state does nothing to take out the terrorists.

Moreover, we've done it unilaterally. We've done it by ourselves in a way that interferes with the international cooperation and multilateral policies that make legal police and intelligence cooperation possible. It's through intelligence-police, Interpol, and juridical cooperation that we actually have had some success in rounding up terrorists. But the unilateral strategies of war on Afghanistan and Iraq can actually undermine that multilateralism and make cooperation less, rather than more, likely. Prior to the strike in Iraq, we were cooperating with the intelligence services of Syria, Libya, Sudan, and Iran. Once the war started, and still today, there is far less cooperation. We've actually made the kind of international, multilateral cooperation that leads to good intelligence results and good international police results less possible as a consequence of these wars.

JE: You've talked and written extensively about approaches you feel would work better to prevent the kind of terror we saw on 9/11. You've talked about the old doctrine of deterrence, and about something you call "preventive democracy." You've countered this administration's rhetoric about an "axis of evil" with your own demand that we address an "axis of inequality." Can you say something about these concepts, specifically, why you think they would be more effective in real, pragmatic terms than current policy?

It's striking to me that the President said after 9/11 that we cannot afford to let terrorists strike us first; that we have to pre-empt and prevent further attacks by strikes on those who sponsor or nurture terrorists, when for more than 40 years the United States had as its explicit policy that it would accept a first nuclear strike against America's cities before it struck back at the Soviet Union. We agreed, in other words, to give up 50 to 60 million casualties in a dozen leading American cities rather than abandon the legal norm of striking only in self-defense. That was the policy of Democrats and Republicans from the beginning of the cold war to the end of the cold war. Yet President Bush argued that a deterrent strategy, one that had worked against the Soviet Union, should be abandoned because of a single terrorist strike against a couple of cities. In personal terms, and in the terms of the families and the cities involved, these were obviously horrendous, tragic, and egregious strikes. But on the larger historical scale, in terms of American power and presence in the world, they were like bee stings on a grizzly bear; they were of no real danger to this country.

Terrorism has only one weapon and that is fear. And the weapon of fear is intended to terrorize. The strikes themselves did little damage. The fear that followed, incited in part by an administration trying to defend America against terrorism, played a much larger role than the original strikes themselves. If we are going to counter terrorism, I think the way to do it is not to insist that we will strike first wherever we see there might be a terrorist group gathering, but rather to take on their weapon, which is fear. You take on the weapon of fear by refusing to be terrified, by refusing to be awed.

When the President used "shock and awe" as the term to describe the first air strike in Iraq, he was actually playing into the terrorist game, because he was trying to meet fear with fear, terror with terror. They think they can scare us, wait until I'm through scaring them. I imagine when he said shock and awe, somewhere in the mountains above the border between Pakistan and Afghanistan, Osama bin Laden was saying, "Damn, I wish I had thought of that; that's exactly the term: shock and awe. That's what I was trying to do to the United States." And that's, of course, what the United States was trying to do back.

But fear and terror are terrorism's means. Fear is terrorism's turf. America's turf is democracy, the open society, pluralism; it is an unwillingness to be scared into submission, scared out of its liberties, or scared out of its multiculturalism. And the danger since 9/11 has not been the damage of the 9/11 strikes themselves, but the damage we have done to ourselves on the way to trying to "protect" ourselves against terrorism. And here I do have an alternative strategy, because I think the alternative strategy has to be a democratic strategy, and it is one that I call preventive democracy, rather than preventive war. It is a commitment to democracy inside America, which means that we don't allow ourselves to be scared into giving up our liberties, our open immigration policies, and the ban on profiling. We don't allow ourselves to be scared into not traveling or scared into a declining economy. Instead we insist on ongoing civic engagement. We insist on remaining an open, multicultural, democratic society. That means taking on things like the Patriot Act, the Total Awareness Information Act, and the attempt to raise the bar on immigration, which has made it so difficult now for friends of America to get into this country. It also means supporting democracy elsewhere in the world. Right next to the axis of evil—and I agree with President Bush, I think we can talk about an axis of evil—you will also find a less visible axis of inequality, an axis of desperation, an axis of hopelessness, an axis where millions of people live on the margins of western civilization and economic opportunity. You can be sure that if a parent celebrates the martyrdom of a child of sixteen who dies with a suicide bomb strapped to him, that this is also a parent without hope in the future; it is a parent who no longer believes in possibilities for their own children. That suggests to me a society in desperate need of rectification and change, and it's there that we ought to be placing our efforts.

Had Bush wanted to signal his understanding of democracy, the day that Baghdad fell he would not have put a Humvee in front of the Energy Ministry, the heavy industries, the oil pipelines, or the defense ministries. He would have put a Humvee and an M-1 Abrams tank in front of every school, every library, and every museum in Baghdad in order to say, "The future of democracy is here; the future of this country depends on schooling." But that's not what we did. Although the President talks about democracy, preventative democracy isn't really what our policy has been about. So if we're looking for an alternative to preventive war, then we might look carefully at preventive democracy and what that can mean, not just in Iraq and Afghanistan but around the Third World, around the Muslim world, and, by the way, right here in the United States, a place where education remains secondary and the building of prisons is primary. Last year in Oregon, school ended three weeks early because there simply wasn't money to fund public schools. In the US we continue to starve education, and that has the same crippling effect on the future of the United States that the absence of schools has on the future of democracy around the world.

JE: Can you say a little more about the fear factor here, about your claim that this administration has countered fear with fear?

The politics of fear that this administration has deployed in trying to respond to terrorism has itself, in some ways, been much more dangerous than terrorism itself. And this administration has itself been responsible, inadvertently to be sure, for inciting the very terror that it was the terrorist's purpose to incite in America. Think about the color-coded terrorist warnings—yellow, orange, up and down. The government's been giving anonymous warnings—probably only to protect its own rear end against accusations that it didn't give proper warnings—that say: somewhere next week or the week after there will be an attack in a mall, or maybe it will be a bridge, or could it be a school; but anyway, watch out. Those kinds of warnings actually play right into the terrorists' goal of trying to incite fear. Donald Rumsfeld has said that, given the choice between persuasion on the one hand, and a gun on the other, like Al Capone he always prefers persuasion plus a gun to persuasion by itself. That suggests a mindset that's really dangerous to America.

The other side of the politics of fear is the politics of engagement. Let me say to those Americans who think, "Well, the government does well to warn us and to put us on our guard." Terrorism is real and you can't pretend it's not. The real answer to fear, however, is engagement, citizenship, activity. Think of coming across a car accident and you're a spectator. When you're a spectator, your stomach's in a knot. You watch, you get more and more afraid. But when you're engaged and you try to pull the people out of the car, when you're involved in resuscitating the patient and getting them to the hospital, it's quite different.

I think the people most without fear on September 12 in America were those people working at Ground Zero. They were in the greatest danger, actually, but they were actively engaged—the firemen and the medical officials and the cops who were working there first to find the victims and then to find remains and clear the site. They had a civic task, they were engaged, and they weren't afraid of anything. American citizens after 9/11 said to the President, "What can we do to become engaged and take some responsibility?" President Bush, unfortunately, said, "Go shopping. Go back to the mall. Go back to your normal lives. We'll take care of it." Spectatorship is an invitation to fear. Citizenship is how we fight the politics of fear. The politics of citizenship, the politics of engagement, of taking responsibility, is a much better way to deal with terrorism than hunkering down, being spectators, and allowing the government to rob us of our liberties and our multiculturalism, all in the name of protecting us.

JE: You're talking about one definition of America; the Bush administration often seems to be talking about another. You mention in your latest book that there's a tension between Bush's Bible-thumping, Manichean rhetoric on the one hand, and a deeper American strain that runs through people like William James and Melville, people with a more ambiguous, pragmatic sensibility than black-and-white, good-and-evil thinking. Can you talk about these competing senses of America?

We Americans always appeal to America in defending our ideology and our positions, and it's not a surprise that President Bush and his colleagues talk about a certain America to defend their policies. I think they get America wrong. And I won't cede to them their desire to own America or the idea that if I don't agree with them then I'm in some sense un-American. They talk about a moralizing America that's better than other countries. They talk about an America whose leaders get up on white horses and strap on their six-guns and go out and fight the bad guys and come back again. They talk about an America defined narrowly, not broadly. An America defined by sovereignty and independence, not its interdependence with the rest of the world. But there is also another America. It's there in Thomas Jefferson. It's there in Lincoln. It's there in Walt Whitman. It's there in Emerson. It's there in Langston Hughes. It's there in Toni Morrison. It's a multicultural America. It's an America that's defined not by its separation from the rest of the world, but rather by the way it embodies the multiplicity and variety of the world. It's an America that is part of that world. It's an America that flourishes only as the world flourishes and when the world flourishes. That is, I think, an America equally powerful, if not more powerful, than the narrow, parochial, walled-off America that Bush wants to tell us is our America.

JE: You've also written about the splits within the foreign policy establishment, and within this administration, between hawks and doves. And you've tried to reframe those terms a bit. How did you do this and why?

We have traditionally talked about those who are realist, pro-war types as hawks, and those who are kind of idealistic peaceniks as doves. I'm not sure that's the ideal way to talk about the new split in Washington and in this country, because I would argue that the new split is not between hawks and doves, but rather between eagles and owls. And let me just define those terms. Both of them understand the necessity of war. Neither of them are pacifists. But the eagles believe that we have a right to strike now, preventively, pre-emptively, quickly, and in a unilateral way. They are hawkish, but they are hawkish as unilateralists, and I think that in their own way they're idealist, because they think America still is back in the nineteenth century, that it can deploy its armies unilaterally as a sovereign force to take out our enemies around the world. The owls, though they're also hunters, are wiser. They come out at night when the day is over and they have a longer view of things. And I think they recognize that the eagles are actually idealists wishing for an old world where the tough guys can take out one another in open combat, man against man, a kind of *High Noon* on Main Street with Gary Cooper being played by President Bush, and the bad guys being played by Mullah Omar, Osama bin Laden, and Saddam Hussein.

But the reality is that military force deployed by nations with large armies and air forces actually represents a sort of asymmetrical force when put up against terrorism. Modern wars are asymmetrical and we've seen that in Iraq. There was no Iraqi force capable of withstanding the force of our military onslaught: the air force, the army, and the marines. The US marched across Iraq in a few days and took out the Iraqi armies. But now they find themselves up against guerrillas, terrorists who come out at night, people shooting from the darkness, people planting mines at the side of the road. For those kinds of assaults America has no symmetrical military answer.

The other problem with a purely military response to terrorism, even when the response is symmetrical—and I've suggested that really the response can't be symmetrical because the forces are asymmetrical—is that part of the war that we're fighting is not a military or even an economic war, but a cultural war. And what I think we don't understand is that many of the people who support terrorism or who look the other way or celebrate when America gets hurt, fear not so much an American occupation, not so much the hegemonic American economy. There are also those who worry deeply about the cultural impact of Americanization, the cultural impact of an aggressive, secular, materialistic culture. The problem the United States faces is that there's a powerful cultural element to their fear.

People in the Muslim world are deeply offended by and angry at what they see as an aggressive, secular, materialistic culture that threatens to undermine their religious values and corrupt the traditions and legacies of their culture, which they so dearly prize. Think of the mother in Damascus, the mother in Tehran, a mother in Sri Lanka or Pakistan. She has two great fears. One fear is that her children will not have the opportunity to enjoy the economic prosperity of the West, the advantages and opportunities of globalization and international trade, and of being part of world markets. And her other great fear is that her children will be welcomed by these markets, become corrupted, and lose their religion and values. To much of the world, we represent McDonalds, MTV, the Chicago Bulls, television, Disneyland, Nike, and all of those wonderful advantages of the virtual and actual malls that define American shopping and the possibilities of prosperity. To many people in other parts of the world, this represents a threat to their indigenous cultures, a threat to the pluralism and variety of their own societies and, above all, a threat to their religious beliefs. We should understand that. Because even here in the United States there are many Protestant fundamentalists who don't send their children to public schools because they're so frightened by what they may encounter out there in the public culture, which is the culture of Hollywood, the culture of Madison Avenue. The same is true for many of us. Few of us would trust our own children to watch anything they find on television 24 hours a day. Few of us would trust our children to go on the Internet and deal with anything they found there. Such is our increasingly commercialized and pornographic and aggressively materialist culture. And in some ways, this may be a greater threat to peoples in the Third World than our armies or our dollars or global trade itself.

In my book, I call this threat McWorld; it is Jihad versus McWorld.

The threat of a spreading McWorld is what saps their cultural strength, undermines their religious integrity, and corrupts the values that their children hold dear. In the long-term, this may be the largest problem we face in trying to bring democracy to the rest of the world, because if people think that democracy means McDonald's and Disneyland, and not the right to govern themselves in their own way in accord with their own values, then they will come to see democracy as part of the problem rather than part of the solution. It's up to us to separate democracy from McWorld—to separate democracy from the mall, democracy from privatization, and help people understand that democracy means the right to embrace their own values and their own culture and not to imitate ours.

JE: Despite, or maybe within, this global commercial spread, you say in your book that you find a source of hope in all of this as well—a counter-current in the kind of connectivity that recently enabled global protests and organizing on a scale never seen before. Can you talk more about this?

One of the saddest and, at the same time, most hopeful features of the current times is the fact that up until now globalization has mostly been about the globalization of our vices. We globalize crime. We globalize prostitution. We globalize the drug trade and the weapons trade. Terrorism itself is a kind of global anarchy imposed on nations. We globalized capitalism, jobs, and financial investments in ways that recreated the predatory capitalist conditions of nineteenth-century America. But we have yet to globalize democracy, citizenship, civic culture, and all of those things that, within the United States and Western Europe, have in a way softened capitalism, taken its rough edges off, regulated it, and helped make it part of a democratic order.

One of the exciting things to me is that we live in a period where we are beginning to see the globalization not just of terrorism on the one hand and capitalism on the other, but the potential globalization of citizenship, the globalization of civil society, and the globalization of civic institutions. There's an organization called Civicus that is a kind of umbrella group for international NGOs like Doctors without Borders, the International Red Cross, Green Peace, Human Rights Watch, and Transparency International. They have as their goal ongoing cooperation not among governments, but among citizens, not among state institutions, but civic institutions.

To me, that holds powerful hope, and once again that is why preventive democracy and not preventive war will be in the long term what saves America from terrorism and makes a world that is as safe for the entire world as it is for America. No American child can sleep safe unless kids in Damascus, Beijing, Malaysia, and in Africa sleep safely. Freedom is now a single thing for everybody around the world. Americans cannot be free if others are enslaved. So internationalism, global public opinion, and interdependence are not the aspiration of utopias, but a mandate of realism. The realists today are the internationalists. Utopians are the folks in the White House who think that one nation can still create a Pax Americana and rule the world by dint of their own sovereign will. The age of independence, the age of sovereignty, is over. We live in an age of interdependence. When we embrace it, when we democratize it, we will live in a world that is both safe and free for Americans and for all others.

JE: What's your response to those people out there who may disagree with this President's policies, but who nonetheless think this election—and electoral politics more generally—are irrelevant? That it doesn't matter. What do you see as the stakes involved in November 2004?

At every election we are faced with the question of whether it really matters, whether it's important to vote, and whether there are any differences that count. There are always differences that count, if not in policy, then in judicial appointments; if not in judicial appointments, then in environmental policy; if not in environmental policy, then in attitudes toward foreign policy. Of course it matters, and it matters in ways that may be invisible today, but will become visible tomorrow. There are many who thought it didn't matter in the last election who won, Tweedle-Dum or Tweedle-Dee. But the fact is, the appointments not just to the Supreme Court, but to the Federal bench—where there are several thousand appointments that a President might make in four or eight years in office—matter. The efforts made to save the environment and prevent it from being exposed to greater dangers, for which future generations will pay the price because decisions being made today cannot be unmade ten or twenty years from now if the damage has been done, those matter. Those types of decisions are vital. So yes, it counts, and it counts big. And it really doesn't matter whom you vote for. But if you argue that it doesn't matter, so don't bother to vote, you've really forfeited your own liberty.

I have another message on that, though. We worry, of course, about our leaders and about who is in the White House, the Supreme Court,

Congress, and the Federal State House. All of this is important, but citizenship is not just about voting. In this country, we have a tendency to think that voting is all about leadership, and every couple of years, whether it's the State House or the Presidency, we say, "Where's the man on the white horse who can save us now from the last dope who we put in." But part of that is a kind of white horse syndrome, a notion that democracy is nothing more than voting for the leadership and then leaving it to them to govern the country. Democracy is about self-government. Democracy is about engaged citizenship. Democracy is measured ultimately not by the quality of its leaders, but by the quality of its citizens, and too many Americans sit around worrying about who's going to be in the State House and who's going to be in Washington without thinking about their own responsibilities and their own engagement locally, nationally, and globally. And people say, "Well, what can I do?"

Someone like Jody Williams, who created the Landmine Treaty, shows what you can do. Everybody in an NGO shows what an individual can do. People in the civil rights movement showed what citizens can do. Citizens can do a hell of a lot. The term of every citizen is a lifetime, not two years or four years. You have a lifetime to do that work.

America might be a healthier place if we focus less on who the next governor or president is going to be and much more on our own responsibilities, on our own need to participate in every aspect of the civic and political process. Taking on more responsibilities, ourselves, would put less pressure and less responsibility on our governors. So yes, we have to vote, we have to choose; that counts. But that's not the last or only step. That's the first step toward citizenship, and citizenship means governing ourselves on a regular basis, and being engaged in not just political, but civic, activity all the time. There are all sorts of things we do that are political that we don't even recognize as being political.

JE: I'd like to close by asking about your own personal reaction to 9/11 as it unfolded. What did it mean to you? And since then, what's your reaction now to Bush's mantra that he'll never forget 9/11?

Like George Bush and almost everyone who lives in America, and I suspect like many people around the world, 9/11 was a powerful event that I will not forget. I doubt that anyone who had any exposure to it at all, whether on TV or by living in New York, will forget it because it was perhaps one of the most decisive events of our time. I was in

Washington. My family was in Manhattan. I was about a half a mile away from the Pentagon and they were about a mile away from Ground Zero. So we each experienced it, and we talked briefly on the phone until the phones went out. I got a train back to New York that evening. Penn Station had already closed, but there was a train bringing police and reserves to New York and I managed to get aboard and come to a closed, locked-down Penn Station. I walked home to my wife and my daughter at about 11 o'clock at night, watching from New Jersey as we came across the wetlands, looking across and seeing the smoke and the glow still coming from what used to be the World Trade Center.

I'm a born New Yorker, so for me it was a powerful personal event. And yes, I will remember as the President remembers. I think the question for all of us, though, is what we remember and what we do with the memories? What is the lesson? What does it tell us? What does it teach us? For the President, it teaches the lesson of the axis of evil. It teaches the lesson that America has enemies—secret, dangerous enemies who have to be taken out. It teaches the lesson that we can never be weak; we have to flex our muscles at every turn. It teaches the lesson of a Pax Americana: if sovereignty no longer protects us, then we have to extend sovereignty around the world and create a Pax Americana. That's one kind of lesson. It creates a politics of fear. A politics of insulation. A politics that closes down America's borders and raises walls around America. And I fear that that is the lesson that many Americans, and certainly President Bush, have drawn. Draw up the wagons, raise the walls, and get ready to take on the bad guys anywhere they are. Send the troops anywhere the enemies are and destroy them.

There's another lesson, though. Of course my first reaction to 9/11 was fear, anger, rage, and vengeance. Of course, I wanted to go get the folks who did this. I think all of us had that reaction. But my second and more permanent reaction was to say, God, the world is small. Things that happen in Karachi and Damascus and the Congo and Nigeria are reflected in what happens here. The forests that burn in Brazil, the tropical rainforests that are taken down in Indonesia to make way for malls there, have an effect on the air we breathe. Diseases in Hong Kong and Africa, HIV and SARS, come to America. I go to my Massachusetts home in the summer and I worry not about a Massachusetts virus, but a West Nile Virus. We live in an inter-dependent world.

For me, the lesson of 9/11 was one of mandatory interdependence. We've got to find ways to deal with terrorism together or we will all be consumed by it. We have to find ways to live together or we will die together. We have to find ways to be free together or no one will be free. To me, that was the enduring lesson of 9/11. And if that's the lesson we take with us, it may be a lesson that, for all the horror and pain of 9/11, was a useful lesson, one that pushed America into the world embracing its interdependence with the world and making it a partner of the world, rather than a time in which we said to the world, "Join us or else," which is what President Bush said. Instead, it would be a time when we said, "Now the moment has come for America to join the world."

New York City
November 6, 2003

Medea Benjamin is co-founding director of Global Exchange and for over 20 years has supported human rights struggles around the world. She is author of eight books, including *Bridging the Global Gap, The Peace Corps and More* (Seven Locks Press, 1989), and the award-winning *Don't Be Afraid, Gringo: A Honduran Woman Speaks from the Heart* (Perennial 1989). In 2000, she ran for the US Senate as a Green Party candidate and in 2003 co-founded Code Pink: Women for Peace.

SJ: From the viewpoint of security, do you think that the activities of the Bush administration since 9/11 have made Americans safer?

Well, I look at this from the point of view of a mother. I have two children, I want my children to live in a safe world, I don't want any more September 11's to happen, and I look at everything this government has done post-September 11 and I think, "Not much more you could have done to make us less safe." I feel scared when my kids get on a plane like they just did at Christmas time. I feel afraid for my daughter, who now lives in New York, and I feel that the aggressive cowboy policies of the Bush administration have taken away any sympathy that there was toward the United States at the time of the great tragedy of September 11, and made us more insecure. I think that if you care about the security of your family, the security of your community, the security of your country, you'd have to be appalled by this administration. Every poll that's been done, whether it's been done by the Department of Defense, or by organizations like PEW, or by Gallup polls shows that people like us less today than they liked us on September 11. So you'd think that Americans would be scratching their heads and saying, "Did we do something wrong?" Invading Afghanistan and then Iraq and this kind of arrogance and disregard for the lives of other people around the world—that hasn't made us safer.

Nor has this whole idea that other people's lives don't matter very much... The fact that thousands of Afghans, innocent Afghans, were killed when we invaded that country mattered to a lot of people around the world because they saw it every night on their TV stations. They saw innocent villages getting bombed, entire villages getting destroyed. And the same is true when we invaded Iraq—people saw on their TV screens, whether you're talking about the Arab world or in Europe or in Canada, they saw innocent people getting killed. We didn't see that in this country. And so there is this ignorance in the United States. We hide the fact that we killed many more people post-September 11 than were killed on September 11. Innocent people. Women and children. But the fact that it's not showing on our TV screens means Americans don't know, and so they don't really understand why it is that we're less secure now than we were on the day of September 11.

SJ: Why is the idea of permanent war and pre-emptive strikes dangerous for Americans at home?

Well, this idea of perpetual war, permanent war, this idea that the US indeed has the right and responsibility to go change whatever regimes we don't like, means that people—first of all in countries that we designate as either the "axis of evil" or "enemies"— are living in perpetual fear. Talk to people who live in Iran. Talk to people who live in Iraq. They are in constant fear. This kind of aggression makes the whole world less safe. The idea of pre-emptive strikes really, as the secretary general of the UN says, can lead the world into total chaos because it is then a justification of any country—whether it's India or Pakistan or Russia—to go into a neighboring country and go to war because you think that country might attack you. It is a kooky idea that you can just say, "Oh, I might be attacked and so I'm going to attack this other country." The whole idea of pre-emptive strike is a great threat to the rest of the world. It has made the rest of the world live in more fear and I think in addition to fear there is anger, because nobody likes the bully. You know you look in any schoolyard and the kids say, "Oh, you know, that guy, he's the big tough guy and he beats everybody up." People don't like the big tough guy— they might fear the big tough guy—but they don't like him. I think that for many millions of people around the world, even people who like America on one level—because people do love our music, our culture, our movies, our sports. They like a lot of things about the United States—but when they look at government policy, I think it has made many people around the world fear the United States, and also be angry at the United States. It is much better policy to be loved than to be feared, and certainly the policies of this administration have not made us loved.

SJ: So what should we be doing?

Well, we can stop going around the world imposing our will, but there are many other things we can do to be liked around the world. It continues to be true that we are the most miserly country when it comes to giving aid abroad. People think we give so much aid to those countries. If you look at the actual numbers, we give the least amount of money of every single industrialized nation for things like health care, education, things that would actually make people's lives better. You want to be loved in the world? Help people around the world. I can see transforming the $87 billion that we just dedicated to Iraq, $60 billion of which was for the military. You know what we could do with that $60 billion to make people like us in Iraq? You know what we could do to really build schools and health care systems? We could even use half of it here at home and still have plenty to go around. So what we have to do is totally redo where we spend our money, what we spend our money on. If we want to be a country that is well loved around the world, let's start with cutting the military budget. You can't spend $400 billion on the military and still think that we can have programs that benefit people's lives here at home and be generous to the poor countries of the world overseas. You can't have both. You can't have the guns and the butter. And this administration has increased the level of the military budget beyond the dreams of previous conservative administrations and has put money into things like new nuclear weapons, like the weaponization of space. All that has to be cut. And you know what? That would make us actually safer at home.

SJ: You have also visited Iraq as part of delegations of military families. Could you tell us about that?

The most amazing thing about going to Iraq was that I was with families whose loved ones were either serving in the military or had died in Iraq. And what was so profound about that trip is that these military families got a chance to see first-hand that their loved ones were in danger every single day, that every single member of the US armed forces who we saw is desperate to come home. All they talked about was wanting to come home. The son of one of the members of our delegation said to his father, "Dad, they hate us here. They saw us first as liberators and now they see us as occupiers and they hate us. They want us to go home, and we want to go home." One woman saw her daughter for the first time in three years, because her daughter had been stationed in Germany and then was deployed to Iraq. This woman on our delegation saw her daughter on one of the military bases and her daughter was holding a big AK-47. She broke down and cried seeing her daughter and she said, "If I had the money to put my daughter in college, she would be holding a book instead of a gun. She shouldn't be holding a gun." None of these kids should be holding guns. They should be back in the US, in college, studying.

What's happening in Iraq is a disaster for the Iraqis. When you see people who hated Saddam Hussein, whose families suffered tremendously under Saddam Hussein, and they actually look you in the eyes and say, "Things were better then," and tell you now that they hate the Americans, we are doing something terribly wrong. It's not just that they don't have electricity, and they don't have phone communications, and the sewer system has fallen apart, and everything the US destroyed during the invasion is not being rebuilt. Or that we're bringing in these Halliburtons and Bechtels and engineers being paid $1,000 a day while highly professional Iraqis are standing on the street corner with no jobs. It's not just that. It's the way the US is functioning there, the way they are knocking down people's doors in the middle of the night, scaring women and scaring children and dragging off the men in the family and putting them into the very prisons that were Saddam Hussein's and not giving them access to lawyers and not giving them any charges. And the Iraqi people are saying, "This is democracy? This is the democracy that the US came here to impose on us?"

SJ: You recently debated one of the neocons, Richard Perle, on PBS. What did that experience teach you?

What is so shocking about these neoconservatives is that they are living in a bubble. An absolute bubble. They have no idea what is going on in the world and what the results of their policies are. And they are trying to convince themselves, for example, in Iraq, that their policies are working. I had a chance to debate Richard Perle on television and the thing I kept stressing was, "Richard, get out of your office and come with me to Iraq. That's all you have to do. And we'll go anywhere you want. Any city you want, any street you want, and just talk to an ordinary Iraqi and you will see a totally different reality." I go to the people when I'm in Iraq. The US administration in Iraq is ensconced in Saddam Hussein's old presidential palace and they are living in the same kind of bubble Saddam Hussein lived in when he wouldn't let anybody near him to tell him the truth about what the people were thinking. The US government people are doing the same kind of thing. They don't go out on the streets without bodyguards, they don't go out on the streets and talk to ordinary people. People like Richard Perle who are making policy in this country have absolutely no idea of the results of their policy on the ground.

SJ: So how have the neocons gotten away with this so far?

The main thing that this Bush administration has going for it is the fear factor. That is it. The fear factor allows them to attack Afghanistan, allows them to attack Iraq, allows them to contemplate other countries, allows them to put billions and billions of more dollars into the military and take away money from key programs here at home. It allows them to take away the most basic rights of Americans that were enshrined in the Constitution and the Bill of Rights. This is being done before our very eyes—things like the ability of Americans to keep the government out of the most private issues, of financial information, access to the client and lawyer relationship—these kinds of things are being broken before our very eyes. When the US now has the ability to come into your home and search your home without a warrant, has the ability to pull you off an airplane without telling you why—all of these things should be of the gravest concern to Americans, and yet it's being done under the guise of fear. "We have to do this because the terrorists are lurking behind every door."

SJ: You were in Iraq when George Bush made the "bring 'em on" comment. Could you tell us how the troops reacted to that?

First of all, this was coming from a guy who never fought himself. You should have seen the reaction among the troops when they heard that. They were saying, "What is that about? Bring on the attacks? We're the ones that are out here, on the streets, doing patrol, that are the targets. How could he be saying that?" And they started to question Bush and they started to question Rumsfeld and say "This doesn't make a lot of sense, saying bring on more attacks against us." This could only be coming from people who never fought. We have to remember that the guy in charge of the White House is what we call a chicken hawk, a warmonger who never fought. He can dress himself up all he wants in his military gear, and show up on aircrafts and present himself with a turkey in front of troops... this guy never fought a war, and he is presenting himself as someone who is supporting the troops, supporting our freedoms, though what he is doing is putting troops in jeopardy and taking away our freedoms.

During the run-up to the election, we are going to see a lot of images of George Bush as the cowboy. George Bush as the guy who's going to get out there and protect us against the terrorists who are hiding behind every tree. We've got to deconstruct those images and we've got to say that this is not a game. This is not "cops and robbers." This is not the way to make ourselves safe. And I would particularly appeal to women to say that we don't need a cowboy running this country. We need someone who understands that the only way to make us safe is to be part of a world community, is to be loved by a world community, is to put our money into things that help our children, that make our world a better world, not a cowboy who's going around the world shooting up other countries, other people, killing other people's children. That's not going to make us safe.

SJ: Are you hopeful about the next election?

What people in this country have to understand is how dangerous this administration is, how much it has put us at risk here at home by alienating millions of people around the world, and how dangerous it has been for people overseas. It is a threat to the global community, and this is a time in history in which we've got to organize and say, "We won't allow another four years of this administration." I just shudder to think what another four years of this administration would do to us. This is a time for people to get out and talk about the Bush administration as a danger to us. And we can talk about it on many different levels. We can talk about what the Bush administration has done to the environment, what the Bush administration has done cutting budgets around the country, what this has done to our educational system, what this has done to our civil liberties. While they are wrapping themselves in the flag, they are actually shredding the Bill of Rights, the Constitution. We can talk about what this administration has done to our standing in the global community by saying no to the Kyoto Accords, no to the International Criminal Court, no to the international institutions that are being built to make us safer as a global community. From so many different perspectives we can talk about it, but we have to unify in one thing: This administration has to go. We have to organize. I'm not a Democrat, I'm a Green, and I recognize that it doesn't matter at this point. This is a time to unite people who are Libertarians, people who are Greens, people who are old-fashioned conservatives, who never believed that we should be trying to "nation-build" around the world. For us all to come together and stop the neoconservatives, stop the Bush administration.

We have a real opportunity ahead of us. I think the Bush administration has gotten itself into something that is indeed the classic definition of a quagmire. I don't think that the Iraqi resistance is going to stop. Meanwhile the Bush administration is trying to hide the fact that every day US soldiers are being killed. It's trying to keep those pictures of those flag-draped coffins from being shown on our TV screens. I don't think that the US people are going to continue to tolerate this. The administration has had to cut back its plans to invade other countries like Syria, has had to start talking to other "evil" countries like North Korea and Iran. This is our opportunity to say that we won't tolerate US soldiers being killed everyday. That we won't tolerate billions of dollars being spent on killing people in places like Iraq and Afghanistan. That we won't tolerate putting so much of our resources into this war machine. And the way to say we won't tolerate this is to make sure that come November 2004, Bush is not in the White House.

San Francisco
January 3, 2004

NOAM CHOMSKY

Noam Chomsky is Institute Professor at the Massachusetts Institute of Technology and the author of more than 90 books on linguistics, philosophy, intellectual history, international affairs, and US foreign policy. His recent works include *9/11* (Seven Stories Press, 2003), *Pirates and Emperors, Old and New* (South End Press, 2003), and *Power and Terror* (Seven Stories Press, 2003).

JE: We've had revelations from inside the Bush administration itself, from people like former Secretary of the Treasury Paul O'Neill and counterterror head Richard Clarke, that there was some kind of predetermined agenda pushing the invasion of Iraq—an agenda that predated 9/11. Do you see such an agenda at work in current US foreign policy?

They've told us, loud and clear, so we don't have to speculate. The National Security Strategy of September 2002 announced the agenda for world domination in a very brazen fashion. Actually, the principles that it expressed were not novel. You can find precedence for them in the Clinton administration, the Kennedy administration, and back to World War II. But those were different. It was the same principles, mainly that the US should have global domination, and should have the right to use force at will, without international authorization or credible pretext, in order to ensure its domination. That's an old principle. However, it was announced with unusual brazenness and force in the National Security Strategy in 2002.

This was a very public announcement—'This is the way that we're going to run the world'—and the world was immediately put on notice. To make a doctrine credible, as the term is used in diplomacy, you have to carry out what are sometimes called "exemplary actions" to show that you really mean it. The invasion of Iraq was virtually announced at the same time as the new National Security Strategy. And it was understood around the world, and in foreign policy circles here, to be an illustration of the fact that the US administration will use force at will for achieving its ends—in this case, gaining a major foothold in the central oil-producing region of the world. And it will do so without pretext or authorization. The UN was treated with open contempt. The UN Security Council was openly informed that it could either be relevant and endorse what the US was going to do, or it could be, as Colin Powell described it, "a debating society." World opinion didn't matter. International opinion didn't matter. Domestic opinion didn't matter. They were just going to do it.

JE: Were there other indications around this time that they were bent on pursuing, so openly and so aggressively, this unilateral bid to intervene in the world, with or without allies?

That was only one of a number of actions taken at exactly the same time in the fall of 2002. There was a series of actions at the United Nations and other international negotiations to block, and in fact terminate, negotiations on arms control treaties, treaties banning bacteriological warfare, efforts to bar militarization of space, and so on. In fact, the US announced at the very same time that it was sharply expanding its space militarization program to move, as space command put it, from control of space to ownership of space. That's consistent with the National Security doctrine, which says that the US will not only use force at will, but will prevent by force, if needed, any potential challenge to its domination. So in the case of space, that means moving from mere control to ownership.

The reason for the extreme hostility and fear that quickly rose all over the world was that the invasion of Iraq was understood to be an action taken to demonstrate that this program for global domination by force and the crushing of any potential challenge was meant to be taken extremely seriously. The same was made even clearer, in some respects, by the reaction to the failure to discover weapons of mass destruction. The most important aspect of that was not that they revealed intelligence failures, or lying, and so on. That's all true, but of marginal significance. The real importance was that it changed the doctrine. The doctrine had been the official doctrine in September 2002: that the US will use force to prevent any government that is developing weapons of mass destruction that might, they claimed, threaten us. We will use preventive military force to block that. Well, after the failure to discover any trace of weapons of mass destruction programs, the doctrine was changed to the declaration that the US will be free to use force against anyone who has the intention and ability to produce weapons of mass destruction. Well, everyone has that ability. The local Cambridge high school has the ability to construct weapons of mass destruction. Intention is in the eye of the beholder. So, that's essentially an announcement to the world that everyone is on notice. That if we don't like something you're doing, if you're interfering with us, then we will feel free to use our overwhelming military force to ensure that you conform to our will. That's the doctrine. It couldn't have been stated more clearly.

JE: In what other ways did this program—what's now called the Bush Doctrine, but what was formerly known as the Wolfowitz Doctrine—in what other ways did it reveal itself and evolve?

It was sharpened by further developments. For example, in the buildup to the war, there was division in the world. There was almost overwhelming popular opposition to the war. I don't think you can find a case like it in history. The international Gallup polls, which incidentally were not reported here, showed that there was almost nowhere in the world where you could get even 10 percent support for the program that Bush and Blair were pushing in light of military intervention. But governments did differ. There were governments that went with the overwhelming majority of their population and refused to join in the attack. There were other governments that overruled an even greater majority of the population and took orders from Crawford, Texas, instead of paying attention to the 80 percent of their population.

And it was very interesting to see the reaction here, not just in the administration, but in the media among commentators and so on. The distinction was between the "bad guys," who were from "old Europe," which was taking positions in accord with perhaps three quarters of its population. They were the "bad guys." And then there were the "good guys," like Berlusconi, who were overruling even a larger majority of the population and following orders from Washington. That's a very striking demonstration of the attitudes toward democracy on the part of the administration, the media, commentators, and others. The hope for democracy means doing what we say. It doesn't mean paying attention to, say, 80 percent of the population. And that message is very hard to miss. It's a real tribute to American intellectuals that they have been able to miss the meaning of that.

To make it even more dramatic, the figure in the administration who is regarded as the grand visionary leading the crusade for democracy is Paul Wolfowitz. He expressed very clearly his attitude toward democracy in the case of Turkey. Turkey was bitterly attacked in the United States, across the board, even in the liberal press, because the government took the position of 95 percent of the population, instead of doing what they were told to do by Washington. Wolfowitz, however, went even further than that. He publicly condemned the

Turkish military because they had not intervened to prevent the government from adopting the position of 95 percent of the population, and he ordered them to apologize to the United States and to agree that from now on they will act to help the United States. That's democracy, as understood by the grand visionary who is bringing democracy to the world and the Middle East.

Maybe the American media and American intellectuals prefer not to see this, but the rest of the world does. And that's why you have these remarkable poll results in Europe, which are really quite shocking. The United States is ranked right alongside of North Korea and Iran as a major threat to world peace. In fact, the only country that's considered a greater threat to peace in Europe is Israel, and if you think about that, it's not Israel that's a threat to peace. Israel is a small country. It's the US backing for Israel that's a threat to peace; otherwise, it's not a threat.

If you go to our neighbors in Latin America, who have more experience with the exercise of American power than anywhere else in the world, the figures are also shocking. If I remember correctly, it's around 87 percent opposition to US policies throughout the hemisphere. And as you get closer to the United States, the opposition is greater. In Mexico, I think it was around 95 percent or something like that. Brazil was similar. Those are very striking figures, and they're just in the last few years. They're a reaction to the programs that were announced and implemented by the US, and it is kind of interesting that the administration is being compelled to back down. The world is not that easy to run and, as they've discovered, even Iraq is not that easy to run—although it looked as if it should have been the easiest military occupation in history. But it isn't, and day by day the administration is backing down from its more extreme positions and trying to put cosmetic changes on them so that they can still continue them, but under some other rubric.

Just today, the lead story in the morning papers is that the US and the CPA, the governing US authority ruling Iraq, are agreeing to the demand of the Iraqis for a more democratic process. The US has been strongly opposed to any kind of democratic process in Iraq. They want to make sure they can run Iraq. The Iraqis are objecting, and the objections are so strong that the US is now trying to back down and, as the press put it, find a way to make it look more democratic— crucially, to look more democratic. But they have to do something to make it look more democratic because of the overwhelming opposition of Iraqis to the imposed system. So now they're trying to get the UN to play some cosmetic role in making it look democratic.

JE: Can you say something more about the role of Wolfowitz in all of this?

Well, they're also probably going to back down from the extremely vindictive Wolfowitz position. He's one of the most extreme reactionaries in the administration. He demanded that they put forth a declaration stating that only countries that supported the US military effort will be able to apply for contracts and participate in the rebuilding of Iraq. That's absolutely outrageous, and they're apparently being compelled to back down from this position because the rest of the world just doesn't fall over and say, "Okay, kick us in the face if you feel like it." And that's happening on issue after issue.

The US does have overwhelming military domination of the world and its military force has no remote competitor. But in other dimensions that's not true. In terms of economic power, it's one among several approximate equals. Asia and Europe are roughly comparable economic powers. The same is true in other respects. And even smaller parts of the globe are not that easy to run just by force. The Andean region, for example, which is part of the backyard of the United States, which it expects to be able to dominate just by threat and military coups and so on, is now pretty much out of control, from Bolivia to Venezuela. It's falling into the hands of popular force, which the US is having difficulty controlling.

The invasion of course was a walk over; they wouldn't have ever attacked if they hadn't known Iraq was totally defenseless. It is amazing that the war took more than three days. But that was nothing. The problem was controlling it afterwards and the problems that have arisen in that effort, which are severe, have caused a retraction in the aggressive thrust of the administration. If it hadn't been for that, my guess is that by now there would have been an intervention. In the end, there still may be, but the chances are less likely. The nature of the policies is not obscure. They're stated with considerable clarity.

JE: One of the things we're trying to clarify is what, at base, is motivating this administration's foreign policy. There is a question about how ideological this administration is, how political it is, how realist it is. There are different interests at work, perhaps simultaneously. When you're saying there's a retraction right now, are you saying that this represents the silencing of the most extreme elements of this administration? How do you read this, and what would you identify as the key motivations driving US policy right now?

I think the retraction is due to the failure of extremely aggressive and arrogant policies, which the more extreme members of the administration—Rumsfeld, Wolfowitz, Cheney, and the others— assumed would easily work. Well, they didn't easily work. So they have to back down and modify tactics. You have to live in the world, no matter how extreme you are. As for the ideology behind the administration, I think there are undoubtedly variations, but it's pretty straightforward. Internationally it's what they describe: global domination through force, if necessary, and the crushing of any potential challenge, a disregard for international institutions, and so on. That's the international policy. But domestically it's even more important. They are dedicated to dismantling the progressive achievements of the past century. Through the past century, there have been large-scale popular struggles to try to protect people from the ravages of market forces and from growing corporate power, which have been very destructive. And a lot of things have happened— progressive taxation, Social Security, the New Deal measures, some minimal medical care and developing new schools, and so on and so forth. The administration is dedicated to dismantling all of that.

JE:: What kind of conservatives are these?

They are not in favor of a small government. These are not conservatives. In fact, the federal expenditures rose more quickly under the Bush administration than they had in twenty years since the Reagan administration. It's pretty much the same people in charge: those who believe in a very powerful and intrusive state, one that works to the benefit of the rich and powerful. What happens to the general population is kind of incidental. This administration is drawn mostly from more extreme elements in the Reagan and Bush I administrations, and it's even more dedicated to that goal. They want to dismantle everything: the limited medical support system, Social Security if they can get away with it, schools. By now we are practically at a flat tax level, and if they could shift the burden even more to the eighty percent of the less privileged, they will do that. Most of these policies are sort of in motion, and are being put off for a few years. They will come into play in another three or four years after they have an electoral mandate to pursue them more intensively. But I think that program's pretty clear and not at all hard to discern.

One of the best analysts of it is right in the *New York Times*, Paul Krugman in his regular columns. You don't have to go to the left, dissident circles to find an analysis of this because it's so obvious. They simply want to dismantle the progressive legislation, which comes from popular struggle. It's never given as a gift from above. They want to dismantle it and turn the country into a utopia of the masters. And they could hardly be more open about it.

JE: Why is there not more significant opposition to this open disregard for and dismantling of these programs? These are popular programs. In your view, is it a matter of total distraction, the fact that people have been diverted and just aren't paying attention? Does it have to do with something Karl Rove and Bush's other political operatives understand about fear?

A traditional way to control a population is by frightening it. It wasn't invented in the United States. It's commonly used. Take, say, Germany in the '30s. We should remember that Germany was the peak of Western civilization at that time. The peak. It was the peak in the arts, in the sciences, in literature; the main achievements of western civilization, to a large extent, took place in Germany. If you wanted to study in physics and if you were in the United States in the '30s, you went to Germany. This was a cultured, civilized, advanced society. They were driven into bloodthirsty maniacs to carry out some of the worst atrocities in history by fear. They were frightened. They were afraid that German civilization was going to be destroyed by the attack against it by the Jews and Bolsheviks. Yet this is not the only case.

The same tactics were adopted here. People don't like the comparison. But if they don't like it, they should change things, not object to the fact that it's true. The Reagan administration, for example, was able to carry out programs, not as extreme as this administration, but similar. So during the Reagan years, for most of the population, maybe 70 or 80 percent, real wages stagnated or declined, household wealth may have actually declined, but it certainly didn't grow. And for a small sector of the population, there was extreme wealth. That's why the editor of the *Wall Street Journal* can describe the Reagan years as the "seven fat years"—they were, for him and his friends, but not for maybe 80 percent of the population. How did they stay in office when, if you look at the polls, their policies were strongly opposed? How'd he get elected?

Well, just take a look at what happened. Every year they pushed the panic button. First there were Libyan hit men running around Washington seeking to assassinate our brave leader, the cowboy, with the White House surrounded by tanks to protect him from Libyan hit men. And we took care of that. Then there was Grenada, which you could barely find on a map. The nutmeg capital of the world was building an air base that they were going to use to bomb the United States, so we had to cower in terror before Grenada and invade Grenada, after which Reagan said, "We are standing tall because we succeeded in overcoming Grenada." I think it was something like 6,000 Special Forces who got 8,000 medals for their achievements.

In October 2002, when Congress passed legislation authorizing the President to use force because of the threat to the security of the United States posed by the government of Iraq, that caused most of the world to break out in laughter. But virtually no one pointed out that that Congressional declaration was just a repetition of a national emergency declared by President Reagan in 1985. He called a national emergency because of the threat to the security of the United States posed by the government in Nicaragua, which was only two days driving time from Arlington, Texas, and where these monsters were waving their copies of *Mein Kampf*, as Secretary of State Schultz put it, threatening to overcome us. And that declaration of national emergency was renewed annually. The next year was Libya again, they were threatening us with disaster, and so the United States bombed Libya. The Europeans were appalled. What happens in the Mediterranean matters to them. They were trying to call off these lunatics.

At the Tokyo Summit in 1986 or 1987, the Reagan administration circulated a paper saying to Europeans, either you will go along with us or else. Go along with us, or the crazy Americans will take it over and do it their own way. And they frightened Europe into acquiescing to their precedence. Meanwhile, this continued year after year with one or another threat.

Recall how George H. W. Bush won the election: it was by playing the race card. Either vote for me or black criminals will rape your sister. That was the main feature of the election, which raised him in the polls. In 1989, they called for another phase of the drug war. Hispanic narco-traffickers were going to destroy us unless we did something to protect ourselves from this massive assault. In a couple of weeks, fear of drugs rose from practically nothing to a top issue in peoples' minds.

Crime, drugs, Libyans, Nicaraguans, Grenadans, Arab terrorists— they're all attacking us from all over the place. Therefore, we have to cower in fear under the umbrella of power. The brave cowboy will save us from all of this.

When Karl Rove pulls the same tricks now, he's just replaying a familiar record. Every commentator should be pointing out that every one of these things is just a replay of a very familiar formula. You can ask about the reasons, but the fact of the matter is it's a very frightened country and this goes back long before the Reagan administration. For whatever reason, there's a lot of fear in the country. Fear of outsiders, fear of crime, fear of welfare mothers, fear of blacks, fear of aliens, fear of all sorts of things. And it's easy to stimulate that kind of fear, just as it has been in other countries. Germany is a striking example because it was, in many ways, the peak of Western civilization. It didn't take long for Hitler to be able to convert Germans into raging maniacs. And that goes back in our history, too.

During World War I, the United States was a very pacifist country, and most people had no interest in becoming involved in an internal European war. It's a very reasonable reaction. But the Wilson administration created the first major state propaganda agency and corporate committee on public information. Orwell would have loved that. The state propaganda agency did succeed in turning the country into raging anti-German fanatics to the point where the Boston Symphony Orchestra couldn't play Wagner; they wanted to destroy everything German. It's a technique that works, and Rove and his guys made it very clear that this was going to be the primary program of the administration. They're not keeping it a secret.

Just take a look at when the Republican Convention is taking place. By pure coincidence, it's taking place in New York City just before another anniversary of September 11? Pure coincidence has nothing to do with it. They made it clear in both their words and in action that they're going to try to control the population by fear.

And it's worldwide. The United States is extreme, and it's extremely important because of its enormous power, but just about every power system in the world exploited 9/11 as a technique of repression. Russia used it as a pretext for intensifying their massive atrocities in Chechnya. Now it was defense against terror. China did the same thing in its western provinces, increasing repression against the Muslim minority, under the threat of terror. Israel did the same thing in the occupied territories. Now they're fighting terror, not just taking peoples' land and water. Indonesia did the same. Across the board, the more democratic countries, almost all of them, developed some kind of repressive legislation to discipline their own populations. Here, it was called the Patriot Act. These don't have much to do with terror—maybe nothing to do with it—but they have a lot to do with disciplining your own population. Power systems will exploit their opportunities. They have to achieve that result. They'll exploit an earthquake for that purpose, and something like 9/11, well, that's easy. I say, yes, it had an effect on the United States, a dramatic one. And a similar one elsewhere.

JE: Let's close with the election. How would you respond to people who say that there are a lot of structural forces at work here, that generally presidents are figureheads, electoral politics is passé. Is there something in what you're saying about this administration that marks it as different, that calls this kind of thinking into question? How important do you think this election actually is?

These are matters of judgment. The institutional factors are overwhelmingly important and the spectrum of policy choices is pretty narrow. That's why you can find precedents for the National Security Strategy in the Clinton, Kennedy, and other liberal administrations. The Clinton administration, in its regular defense presentations, stated quite openly that the United States, if necessary, would resort to force unilaterally to protect markets and resources. Actually, if you think of what they said, it goes beyond the National Security Strategy. They didn't even talk about a threat. With the Bush administration, it's a pretend threat; with the Clinton administration, it was straightforward: it was to control markets and resources.

So, yes, you can go way back and find precedents, but there's a group in the White House right now that has a very narrow hold on political power. They hold political power by a thread. And they happen to be an extremely arrogant, dangerous group of reactionary statists. They are not conservatives. They're deeply reactionary believers in a powerful interventionist state. They want to dismantle any form of progressive state action. The government is there to serve the rich and the powerful, not the population, and they're extreme in their willingness to brazenly and openly use force and the threat of force to achieve their international objectives. I think that's extremely dangerous. Another four-year mandate for a group like that could lead to actions that are not only dangerous but will be close to irreversible. So in my opinion, it's unusual in that respect.

Cambridge, Massachusetts
January 16, 2003

Kevin Danaher is co-founder of Global Exchange and the author of many books, including *Corporations Are Gonna Get Your Mama: Globalization and the Downsizing of the American Dream* (Common Courage, 1997), *Globalize This! The Battle Against the World Trade Organization* (Common Courage, 2000), and *Democratizing the Global Economy: The Battle Against the World Bank and the IMF* (Common Courage, 2001).

SJ: In your view, what are the neoconservatives in this administration trying to accomplish?

If you go back and you look at the history of empires, you will find that people come to power who have a more desperate view of things—a more desperate ideology—in empires at apogee and just after apogee, because they are about to go down or are going down. Look at the economic statistics of the US balance of payments: there's a deficit that is up to about five trillion a year; the US federal debt is three times the federal government debt, which is three times the size of all the world government debt combined; and we lost three million industrial manufacturing jobs in the first three years of the Bush administration. In a lot of ways US power in the world is collapsing. Neoconservatives are trying to compensate with military might and muscle for what they're losing in terms of economic control. The United States is now buying more computer equipment and electronics from China than China is from the United States, and these are just some of the indicators. You could make a list that was pages and pages long and, in fact, people have done so. What neoconservatives are trying to do is extend the life of the American empire—US influence in the world—through brute force, because they couldn't manage to do it by economic means. They're going to fail, though, as we see when we go into Iraq expecting to be welcomed with flowers and open hearts, and instead we get welcomed with car bombs and rocket-propelled grenades and dead American soldiers.

SJ: Does it matter who wins the next election?

It certainly makes a difference who wins the election. On the one hand, there's a structure to this system: corporations dominating the policy-making, whether it's the Republicans or Democrats. On the other hand, come down from the level of abstraction and add nuance, and clearly on environmental issues it's better to have Al Gore or Howard Dean than to have George Bush. Bush has proceeded to undo not dozens but hundreds of environmental regulations and I guarantee that if the American people knew about this, the overwhelming majority of them would be against it. If you polled people about the destruction of environmental regulations, it would be about 75 to 90 percent against the Bush administration. So the administration has to do it in secret, and this is why I'm not impressed by the sentiment that Bush is so powerful, and that the Bush administration has so much power. They have the power to kill people, and they have the power to drop cluster bombs on Iraq and drop bombs in Afghanistan. To me, that's not the way you run an empire.

Empire actually destroys the democratic process because the empire is in the interest of a small minority. Big transnational corporations account for about 5 to 10 percent of the economy. All United States exports only account for 23 percent of the economy, so they're sacrificing 77 percent of US economy—which is small stores, local trades people, local restaurants and services—for the 23 percent that is the big global transnational. The problem is that transnational corporations do not have roots in any particular place. They will go anywhere in the world to make more money and that's their economic strength: they can shut down a factory here and move it to China. That's also their political weakness, though, because we can go out there in the local community and say, "Look, Wal-Mart doesn't care about your town. They're going wipe out all that small mom and pop sector." Walk down the street in Colorado, and there are all of these closed stores and so you ask local people, "What happened?" and they say that a Wal-Mart moved in. So now there's a movement to stop that and, in hundreds of hundreds of towns, local people have stopped these big box stores.

There are a huge number of people who are open to a different message that totally contradicts the neoconservative message. Once people understand that these guys have no less of an objective than destroying the US Constitution, there are going to be a lot of NRA members with guns in the gun racks on their living room wall who will support this movement to change the nature of policy-making in Washington. Policy-making is currently designed to suit big transnational corporations, not local communities, and if we can't sell that to people and explain it to them, then we're pretty bad educators and organizers.

SJ: How are neoconservatives going to destroy the Constitution's basic principles?

Well, they've whittled it away already. Take the Fourth Amendment—illegal search and seizure—they can now come in your home without any kind of court order, warrant, or whatever. To keep us on terror alert orange, or whatever the particular fear factor is for that day, they can come into your home or my home, plant listening devices, take documents, photograph documents, tap the phone, not tell you about it and get away with it. Is that what our ancestors fought a revolution against King George for? Is that why our ancestors died and fought the civil rights movement, sacrificing their lives for the right to vote? So that the right to vote wouldn't matter? So that the President gets chosen by one vote on the Supreme Court?

Excuse me, I don't think the Supreme Court should choose the President; I think the people are supposed to choose the President. Go out and ask citizens of America what the electoral college is and see if you get any knowledge at all of the regional process that selects the President. And let's guess whether those electoral college members were the electors or not and above average in income or below average in income. Everyone knows the answer! It's a skewed system; it's a rigged system; and there's going to be a movement to get back to the basic principle that the country was founded on, namely sovereignty. Sovereignty means ultimate political authority, ultimate political power, and sovereignty under our system resides not in Congress, not in the White House, and not in the Supreme Court, but in the people. The fourth branch of government is supposed to rule over the other three. George Bush is a public servant and he lives in public housing; it's nice public housing, but it's public housing nonetheless.

Jim Hightower's idea is that members of Congress should be like NASCAR drivers: they should wear jumpsuits with corporate decals proportional in size to how much money that corporation gave to that member of Congress. Public servants like police officers and firefighters wear uniforms, and members of Congress should wear uniforms too. They get paid a higher salary, of course, but if you give me a hundred fifty thousand a year, I'll wear a clown's suit. I'll wear what uniform the people tell me to wear, and there should be transparency. Sovereignty resides in we the people, and these politicians work for us; they are public servants and we should be able to remove them from office with great alacrity if necessary. Those basic principles will never die; they will never be destroyed.

This movement is building new layers and penetrating lower into the youth generation that's coming up. These kids are fired up. They are half my age, have twice the energy, are creative and are coming up with all sorts of ways to build a movement. As a result, I see the neoconservative thing as a holding action; conservatives are holding on by their fingernails and the main card they have to play is violence. Violence and fear and ignorance and hostility and racism, and you can't build a future off of that. It's very weak lumber to build with—it's rotten lumber.

SJ: What are the implications of so short-sighted a view?

All of our petroleum should be treated very carefully and used only for specialty plastics and composites and things that really have to have petroleum, not just for burning in a car. There are plenty of technologies that would be much wiser for that—hydrogen fuel cells, for example—and that technology will be developed and the countries that get themselves in position, like Toyota, for example, saying that by 2012 they're going to transition all of their drives, drive trains to alternative technology. Ford and General Motors, the US companies, they could have done that, but they didn't because they have so much monopoly power. They influence the US government. They control the legislation. So there's a structural blockage. Their political power and influence allow them to avoid necessary changes they'd make if they were really smart and thinking 50 or 100 years down the road. They're thinking as far as next quarter's profit law statement, so they're going to lose in this struggle, the US economy is going to collapse—it's coming, the US balance of payments deficit is 5 trillion a year. In 2002 it was 4.9 trillion—half the US GNP. The US GNP is about 11 trillion, and the US federal government debt is seven trillion dollars, three times the size of *all* Third World Debt. I'm not even counting in that mandates like Medicare, retiring government personnel, retiring military, Social Security. You add that in, that's another 25 trillion, so there's a debt these guys have created in Reagan I, Reagan II, and Reagan III. And what is debt? Debt is reaching forward to future generations, taking their wealth, and spending it.

The only way the US government and the Federal Reserve can counteract that is to raise interest rates to attract money back. This is what the IMF and the World Bank have always done to Argentina and Brazil and all of these Third World countries. And what does it do? It favors bringing in international money but shuts down your local mom and pop economy, because the store that wants to expand in the neighborhood can't afford the interest rate. You want to buy a home, you can't afford the mortgage; you want to buy a car, you can't afford the interest because the interest rates are high. So you favor Wall Street but screw Main Street, and once that happens, you're going to have a grass roots rebellion against these clowns like nobody's ever seen.

SJ: In your view, are the neoconservatives driven by religious beliefs, in addition to political motivations?

I think they talk a bigger religious game than they really believe. If you really believe in an all-powerful God, an all-seeing, all-knowing creator of all things visible and invisible, as they used to teach us to say in the Catholic church when I was a kid, you wouldn't kill people, you wouldn't go out dropping cluster bombs into Baghdad, you wouldn't go breaking into people's homes in Iraq and putting the men on the ground with bags on their head and handcuffing their hands behind their back, while their women and children look on. If somebody did that in my house, what would my attitude be after they said, "Oh sorry! Wrong house! You're the wrong guy!"? I think that I'd be carrying just a tad bit of resentment toward them, and if I had a gun, I might even be willing to go out and shoot at them. If somebody invaded the United States, the very people who support Bush would be the ones fighting that foreign presence, so why shouldn't the people of Iraq be fighting the US presence in Iraq?

Bush wants World War III. What these guys want the world to be like is Israel and Palestine: fighting, killing everyday, building walls, murdering, and bombing. Is that really where we want to go? That's where they're taking us. When 9/11 happened, they used it as an excuse; they weren't responding to the incident of September 11, 2001, and we still don't know what actually happened. We do know that the Pentagon, the people responsible for protecting our airspace, is holding out documents and information from the Congressional committee assigned to investigate this. They're refusing, even though they're public employees and we own all that information. But bracket that and look at the response: they took 9/11 as an opportunity to do military conquest of the planet, rather than to find out who actually did this. Let's put them on trial, put them in jail, get all the governments of the world to support us in a criminal justice methodology—not a war methodology—a criminal justice methodology, and say these guys are criminals.

SJ: What's the danger to ordinary Americans in treating Osama bin Laden as an Islamic warrior fighting to bring down the United States rather than as a criminal?

They're not warriors. Bush defined them as warriors, but I didn't see them as warriors. If you're killing innocents, you're not a warrior. A warrior is somebody who goes out and fights other warriors, not innocent civilians. On the streets of New Jersey, where I come from, bin Laden would be considered a punk. Instead of putting these guys in their proper position of being punks, though, you elevate them to the status of warriors equal to the world's superpower. It's really dumb, because now you help them.

Bush and his people may know this; this is not something that only critics and people on the left know. They know this, and it's okay because they have to create a credible threat. If they're going to lock down America and do military conquest of the globe, they can't have the American citizenry questioning the policy. The American citizenry has to be scared stupid and that's their project: to make us scared stupid.

My problem is that I've been to Washington, DC, and stood in the middle of the night out in the Jefferson Memorial and read the inscriptions of Jefferson's quotes that are hammered into the marble. If you look up inside the rotunda at the favored quote at the highest point in the building—you have to turn around backwards to read it—it says, "On the altar of God I pledge undying hostility to any government restriction on the free minds of the people."

The free minds of the people are the bedrock of democracy; these people in power right now are trying to destroy the free minds of the people, and with it the Constitution and everything else we hold dear about our political system. Flawed as this system is, it's still an historical achievement. We were the first nation state to establish the principle that sovereignty, ultimate political power, resides in the people, and that's a fundamentally radical concept. And these guys don't like the implications of it for their maintenance of minority wealth and power, and they're out to destroy that. But they will fail. I guarantee you that they will fail.

SJ: What's your take on the election?

Whatever the outcome of the next election is, whether Bush gets reelected or the Democrats take the White House, the system is bound to change in a rapid and radical direction. It's going to move away from dictatorship of the few and away from an economy that destroys nature to a real democracy where there is real participatory community control and an economy that is in harmony with nature. That will happen; this is not a prediction. This is going to happen because nature is the home team, and she always bats last. Global warming, the depletion of the soil, the poisoning of the underground water, extreme weather events, the glaciers melting, the polar ice caps melting, all of that is coming. The oil and the petroleum will run out out over the next 30 or 40 years. There'll be a confluence and a massive die-off, billions of people, and that's going to shock people out of apathy.

Dante said the hottest parts of hell are reserved for those who in times of moral crisis maintain their neutrality. You don't have to decide if they're bad guys, just maintain your neutrality. The ground upon which you stand to maintain your neutrality is getting thinner all the time by increasing inequalities, social crisis, and the environmental crisis. There is stark evidence up in front of our faces, so how big can the blinders be? The blinders can't be extended indefinitely, and when people see the all these signs of social inequity and the horror of environmental destruction, they will choose to get involved in the paradigm shift. You can see it right now in all of the statistics—organic agriculture growing, wind energy, solar energy, recycling—all of these different manifestations, none of which is a revolution. But all brought together, it's revolutionary. We're on the cusp of an historic transition to a new kind of global citizen where people actually feel the meaning of what it is to be a global citizen and to take responsibility for the planet. That consciousness is out there now and it's being strengthened within this grassroots, people's globalization movement. And it will be victorious; the only question is how long it is going to take. That's all: how long is it going to take? It will happen.

San Francisco
January 3, 2004

MARK DANNER

Mark Danner is staff writer at the *New Yorker*, professor of journalism at the University of California, Berkeley, and the author of four books, including *The Massacre at El Mozote: A Parable of the Cold War* (Vintage, 1994) and *Beyond the Mountains: The Legacy of Duvalier* (Pantheon, 1993). His latest book is *The Road to Illegitimacy: What Really Happened in the 2000 Florida Vote Re-count* (Melville House, 2004). He has written widely about the war in Iraq for the *New York Review of Books*.

JE: In an interview you did with PBS a month before the war started, you talked about how you were not quite sure who was then winning the battle of ideas in the White House. It was still up in the air: was it going to be the realists, Bush Senior's people, Powell, or was it Rumsfeld, Wolfowitz, and the hardliners? I'm just wondering if you've seen any change in that, any evolution, in terms of that internal struggle, nine months into the war?

I think we're used to talking about government as one thing. We'll say that the Bush administration does this, or it does that. And of course, government includes a great number of people, thousands of them jostling each other and fighting each other, particularly about controversial positions, which the war on Iraq was. So the struggle over what that policy is going to be doesn't end.

The war itself was a victory, certainly for the neocon vanguard of the administration, the most prominent members of which are in the civilian levels of the Pentagon, the upper levels of the Pentagon. But the fight is still going on. Different people define the war and its purposes in different ways. You have the neocon faction that stated publicly that the war was a necessity for building democracy in the Middle East, for responding to the threat of 9/11 and the threat of terrorism by redeveloping the region. So it's an ideological goal. But you also have a lot of people who I think got on board the bandwagon, as it were, for more traditional realist reasons. Rumsfeld might be one of those. Cheney might be one of those.

It's hard to define these people very specifically, but traditional realist reasons would be that the Persian Gulf is a necessity to America's economy and to America's foreign policy. It's a vital national security interest, and it will never be secure unless Saddam Hussein is removed and the threat of Iraq is removed from the mouth of the Persian Gulf. Those people may have shared, to some extent, the goal of democracy, but it wasn't primary for them. The war, the difficulties of the war, especially the aftermath of the initial battles in March and April, have to some degree undermined the prestige of those who pushed the war for ideological reasons, and I think it gave more power to the so-called realists. That is, the people who were skeptical of these broader ideological goals and the notion that you can transform the Middle East, that you can transform Iraq, and do it all on the cheap—that you didn't need a great many soldiers, you didn't need a long occupation, and that American troops would be greeted with flowers and candy. All of these things have proved to be untrue, which is, of course, what many realists, as I'm calling them, had said from the beginning: that war would be a very difficult thing and we should have relatively modest goals.

I would say that now, nearly a year after the war began, it seems to me that the neoconservative vanguard that pushed for this war is somewhat in retreat. That doesn't mean that the battle is over by any means, and of course, all of this depends on the overlay of politics as well: what's attractive to the American people. We are about to enter an election contest that may require a kind of revitalization of that neoconservative rhetoric about freedom, democracy, and transforming the Middle East, all of which is very useful politically because it's very clear, broadly drawn, and dramatically stated. And it dovetails very well with a traditional, American populist ideology about what the US should do in the world: it should spread freedom and destroy dictatorships. This is what Truman used when he put forward the Truman Doctrine as well, which is familiar from American foreign policy history. So I don't think the game is over. I think the neoconservatives have suffered some serious losses but all of them are still in place, all of them still hold the jobs they did at the beginning of the war. The mistakes that they've made, some of them very, very prominent mistakes, haven't resulted in anybody being fired or anybody being removed from their job.

JE: You're talking here about neoconservatives. Who are these guys? How are they different from traditional conservatives, and where did they come from?

When you start talking about neoconservatives, or the sadly more prominent term, lately anyway, paleo-conservatives, you get into levels of intellectual history of the last 30 or 40 years. Neoconservatives are often called liberals who have been mugged by reality. The first generation of them were intellectuals on the left during the '50s and the

'60s, and many of them became more conservative in the late '60s or early '70s in reaction to what they viewed as the excesses of the left. When they saw the New Left of the late '60s, when they saw the loss of American prestige after the defeat in Vietnam, they became conservatives. Many of them are prominent Jewish writers who had major connections to Israel. This doesn't include all of them by any means, but some of the more prominent ones include Irving Kristol, the father of William Kristol, who is now the publisher of the *Weekly Standard*, the major magazine in this movement, and Norman Podhoretz, who is the father-in-law of Elliot Abrams, who is now in the National Security Council.

This is the heart of the first generation of the neoconservatives. They were Jewish lefties, some of whom went to City College, City University of New York, were Trotskyites, were very much on the left during their young adulthoods as figures fighting for a better America. In the late '60s, they then decided that the left had gone berserk; it had become anti-American and they became conservatives—"neo" because they didn't grow up as conservatives, but they changed to this side of the political spectrum. Many of them formed groups like the Committee on the Present Danger, for example, of the late '70s, which essentially said that the United States was understating or underestimating the threat of the Soviet Union. They formed committees that essentially criticized the Carter administration for being too leftist and too soft on the Soviets.

When you get to people like Paul Wolfowitz, the deputy secretary of defense, and Richard Perle, who is on the Defense Policy Board, both of whom were associated with the Reagan administration— Wolfowitz at least—and the first Bush administration, you're talking in a way about a second generation of neoconservatives. Both of them, I believe, are associated with Senator Henry Jackson of Washington, also a very key figure for the neoconservatives. He was a Democrat but very much on the right on defense issues.

These intellectuals and politicians essentially came from the Democratic Party. Many of them became Republicans, and what I think is essential about them is that they bring to the right the kind of revolutionary politics that began on the left. And you see that string when you look at the notion of bringing democracy to the Middle East. That is the way to solve the problem. The way to confront the problem of terrorism, for example, is not by simply containing it, but by going to the root of the problem and causing a democratic revolution in the

Middle East starting with Iraq. And you see in that kind of answer something that's very much not in the conservative mainstream. Conservatives obviously want to conserve; they're not generally for revolution. Yet this is a project for neoconservatives that really is a revolutionary project in the Middle East.

You also oftentimes see very close connections to Israel. And one of the reasons probably for this change in the late '70s and early '80s, when many of these very strong supporters of Israel moved to the right, was that they felt that a weak democratic foreign policy, a policy that coddled the Soviet Union, was in the end going to be bad for Israel, because it was not going to protect it from countries that were then very close Soviet allies, including the Syrians and the Iraqis, for that matter.

Now you get, as I said, into layers of complexity that go into American intellectual history, post-war history, rather intricately. You also have in the background of Paul Wolfowitz a connection with Albert Wohlstetter, who was a defense theorist and very influential within US government after World War II, and who was also connected with theories of rollback, which is another level of this argument. After World War II, the consensus policy of the United States foreign policy was set out by George Kennan, an intellectual in the State Department and later an ambassador to the Soviet Union and Yugoslavia, who developed a policy called containment. The notion of containment, crudely summarized, is that the Soviet Union exists, is a strong state rival of the United States, but is built on certain contradictions. Its political system cannot be permanent, and the United States, to defeat it in the cold war without fighting an actual hot war—which nuclear weapons had made too dangerous to contemplate—must surround it, contain it, keep it from acquiring more allies, keep it from expanding, and essentially contain it by the use, I think, of discrete counterforce, which was one of the phrases. Keep it from expanding and eventually it would collapse. This was the policy of the United States, put in very crude terms, and it lasted for about 50 years.

Those who supported rollback essentially felt that this policy was immoral. That is, the United States, built on a notion of freedom and the idea that all people are born with certain inalienable rights, could not adopt a policy that essentially accepted an immoral Soviet Union as part of the world. The United States had to have a policy that had, at its heart, the spreading of freedom, the bringing of freedom to other countries and other peoples. And at the heart of this had to be the notion that you would roll back Soviet advances and that you would free the people who were under Soviet tutelage and in Soviet imprisonment, like Eastern Europe, for example. So you saw the struggle over the broad lines of American foreign policy in the early '50s.

I'm going into this in depth because you see this kind of philosophy springing out as if it had been in an underground stream for 40 years. Now in the second Bush administration it springs out of the ground: the US is obliged to spread freedom around the world; the status quo is in some way immoral. 9/11 essentially gives us an opportunity to spread freedom in the Middle East, for example. We have to respond to this kind of threat and this kind of opportunity by spreading the American ideology, by spreading democracy to those benighted peoples who don't have it.

And I think the reason why you have to look at this historically is because when you look at America's reign as a great power, which is essentially a half century long, this is quite a radical notion in its foreign policy. It breaks with policies that have been upheld by Democrats and Republicans for more than a half century. It has appeared before in these rollback proponents in the late '40s and early '50s, but it has never held sway the way it has in the first two or three years of the Bush administration. So I think it's important to see that, though it has precedence, it's quite far to the right on the political spectrum.

JE: A number of the supporters of this war have shifted their rationales for invading Iraq now that no weapons of mass destruction have been found. We hear now that it's about removing the dictator and spreading democracy. What's interesting to me about this reversal is that it allows the neocons to answer a central left critique of this war: the charge that the US is hypocritical for going in now because America was once in bed with Saddam. The neocon response seems to be to agree with this, and to turn it against the left. They're saying, "You're right, but that was exactly the problem. We need to correct the past sins of the US and bring some morality to American foreign policy." So this can get confusing, in light of what you're saying. Doesn't this mark a neocon connection with the goals of the left, given that there's this moral strain running through both mindsets?

Well, one of the neoconservative arguments, a tactical argument, if you will, for the war in Iraq, is, "Hey, you can talk to us about how the United States supported Saddam for a decade, you can talk to us about how when he was using weapons of mass destruction, gas weapons on the Kurds, for example, we were supporting him. And you're right, that makes us sound like hypocrites. However, isn't it better to reverse that course and change to a policy that is morally sound, rather than simply pointing to this immorality in the past?" And that, it seems to me, is partly their argument.

Now, when I say "tactical" it is because it is essentially a response to what is a very effective argument against them, which is how can we, the United States, go to war against Saddam Hussein using the argument that he has attacked his neighbors when, in at least one of those attacks, the main one, which was against Iran, the United States supported him? That's a difficult argument to respond to and I think on the neoconservative side there's a tendency to simply say, "Yes, the United States did support him and that was wrong, but the only way we are ever going to wipe that slate clean, or at least start to, is by doing the right thing now."

I think the broader question has to do with the Middle East. If, indeed, you're serious about a democratic revolution there, then there are many countries that the United States has enormous influence with—the Egyptians, for example, to whom we give $3 billion in aid a year; we essentially float their government—that one would think that in our foreign policy, without a war, we could have enormous influence without actually invading the country and overthrowing the regime. And there's been no move that I've noticed toward a democratic revolution in Egypt or other places where, as in the Gulf regimes, too, the United States has enormous influence. Nothing is being done there to advance these neoconservative goals.

With regard to the notion of morality, one of the reasons why many in the Middle East can't take seriously the policy that the United States advances, the policy of triggering a democratic revolution in the Middle East, is because when they look at the region they see the autocracies there, they see the despotisms there. What they see are regimes that are supported by the United States. In the view of many people, the despotism in the region could not exist without US support, so the notion that the United States has to come in with guns blazing to cause a democratic revolution is a fantasy.

They look, for example, at the Saudi regime and say, well, this regime would not exist without the strong diplomatic and military backing of the United States. It's the most powerful autocracy in the Gulf. It dominates the Gulf. Since World War II, the United States has supported it implicitly and has been absolutely necessary for its existence. One of the more prominent people in the region who thinks this is, of course, Osama bin Laden.

The entire strategy of al-Qaeda, certainly after 1991, starts with a recognition on their part that the regimes that they view as traitorous, treasonous, as fake Muslim regimes—and they would include Mubarak's regime in Egypt and the Fahd's regime in Saudi Arabia—can only exist because of US support. If that support were cut off, those regimes would fall. So they consider the United States to be the far enemy, and Mubarak and the Fahds and others to be the near enemy. Because they'd had little success destroying the near enemy and destroying those regimes directly, they decided late in the '90s that they would attack the United States. If they could force the US to withdraw from the Middle East and withdraw its support for those regimes, they could then weaken and eventually overthrow those regimes.

So you have an irony here: the stated policy of the United States administration is to spread democracy in the Middle East, and the stated policy of the opponent, al-Qaeda, led by Osama bin Laden, is to force the US out of the Middle East—in the process destroying those autocracies that al-Qaeda feels are only there thanks to US support. It's a rather perfect opposition, in a way, and it is, as you point out, rather difficult to understand.

JE: If you read Richard Perle, for example, or William Kristol, they're very clear about the need for the United States to create and project the perception of strength, the perception that the US can and will use military force whenever it decides to. And that's a little different from spreading democracy. Can you talk about this, this near obsession with force? They're very, very clear about this.

I think what might be called the obsession with force, or the need to use demonstrative power, is very much part of this administration's philosophy. The second Bush administration, clearly after 9/11, made some assumptions about the need to show that the US would respond vigorously and violently to an attack on its territory. You see this tendency from the first days after 9/11. If you read Bob Woodward's book and other accounts, you know that in the meetings of the inner sanctum of the Bush administration, the attack on Iraq was brought up on almost the first day, even though there was no evidence whatsoever that the Iraqis had been involved in this. Of course there still is no evidence whatsoever. And I think, in a funny way, it's a mistake, or simply beside the point, to argue that there's no connection between 9/11 and the Iraqis, so why are we attacking them? As if the administration believes that there is a connection. They've used the idea of a connection publicly without stating it, but they've given the impression that there was a connection to build up support for the attack on Iraq, and they've done that very adroitly.

But I don't think in the inner sanctum of the administration there's a strong belief that Saddam was behind the attack on the United States. Instead, there's a notion that the United States has to show a forceful, strong, and violent response because it was attacked, and because in the region, in the Arab world in general, there is a need to see force. As someone put it recently in the *New York Times*, an officer on the scene in Samara, I believe, "You know, the Arab mind, they only respect force." It's a very crude way of putting it, but I think there is a notion that you can deter further attacks and you can project your power only by showing a strong willingness to use it. This is where the neoconservatives, if you will, certainly join forces with realists and others in the administration—you have to respond forcefully; your prestige and authority are carried by a violent response.

If you look at the late stages of the Vietnam War, particularly during the Nixon administration, Henry Kissinger would use the word "credibility" again and again. That is, we can't run from Vietnam because it will harm American credibility. I think he meant a number of things by this. Some of it had to do with the nuclear deterrent. Some of it had to do with American alliances in Europe and Asia, and how they would be harmed by a perceived willingness of the US to run away from a commitment. On the left and in the center as well, this was pooh-poohed, this notion of credibility.

But for the neoconservatives, and the conservatives, I think, in the Bush administration, they see the late '70s as proof positive that they were right about this. They see a litany of foreign policy disasters: the fall of the Shah, the fall of Somoza, a general US retreat around the world, wars in Angola, and Mozambique, and problems in Southern Africa. All of these things were caused, in their view, by the American willingness to run from Southeast Asia. They would probably add to that a number of other things, but not publicly, because they happened during the Reagan administration, including the departure from Beirut in 1983 after the attack on the Marine barracks. Then there was the flight from Somalia after the attack in '93, which killed eighteen Americans in Mogadishu. To them, all of these things show to

America's enemies that the United States is not willing to prosecute a war and to stay where its interests were perceived to be at risk.

These actions, these fearful, cowardly actions by US leaders, opened the way for the challenges of the '90s, including Saddam's invasion of Kuwait, for example, in which he referred repeatedly to the fact that the Americans were not willing to lose 10,000 dead in a war—look at Vietnam. He stated this publicly, I believe, to April Glaspie, the ambassador in Baghdad, in their one meeting. So the neocons and other conservatives essentially respond to these events by saying, "We've been attacked. What this region understands is force. What it understands is American willpower, and the demonstrated American will on the ground." They seem to believe this very strongly.

I think that's why many of the arguments that say, "Look, Saddam was not behind 9/11. Why are we attacking them? Why are we attacking Iraq?" are somewhat beside the point because, to this administration, this attack, this brazen attack on the United States on September 11, 2001, demanded that the US as the imperial power go, as Fouad Ajami has put it, to the heart of the Arab world. I think that many of the people in the administration, Don Rumsfeld, for example, whatever their views about the possibility of spreading democracy in a lasting way, do believe that indeed you have to go to the heart of the Arab world and show this kind of vigorous response to the challenge that 9/11 represented.

JE: What would you say to Americans about what's wrong with this position? Is the administration's philosophy, in your view, fundamentally flawed, or are we just in the beginning stages of something that might eventually succeed in making us more secure?

I think there's a disconnect between the stated goals of the Bush administration in the Middle East, and their willingness to commit resources, not only resources like military force, troops on the ground, money, and so on, but also political capital, to the achievement of that goal. You're seeing it right now in Iraq. There's a very grandiose ambition to change the Middle East, to transform Iraq into a democracy. But there's a reluctance to admit the cost of such a policy and to commit the resources necessary to achieve the goals that have been stated. You see it in what was set out as the goal in Iraq before the war by President Bush and others, and then the actual commitment of troops and money, the reluctance to state frankly to the American people that this was going to be a long occupation. The refusal to give any sort of estimate of the money that would be involved. The denial that it would require troops there for years. When General Shinseki, then the Chief of Staff of the Army, said that it would take several hundred thousand troops, he was fired. He was shut up and then essentially fired.

I guess you could argue that the administration itself underestimated what would be required. I would say that many of these people—having grasped to their breasts this glorious goal to bring democracy to the Middle East—when they were presented with what the bill would be, they essentially refused to admit it. They realized that the beautiful goal that they had developed, if you were honest about what it would take, would become a lot less beautiful. Therefore, they were not honest about what it would take, as far as money, as far as lives, as far as military equipment, as far as the part of the army that you would have to devote to it. They denied all of this, so they could sell it.

What's wrong with that, you might ask? Don't governments understate the costs of things all the time so they can sell them to the people? And you'd have a point. I think that's true. They do underestimate it all the time. The big problem with this policy is that you have a deficit of support for something that was advertised to the American people as easy and that has become hard. Now that Americans have realized that it's hard, the political support is waning very quickly. It went up with the capture of Saddam. It will now go down again with the continual deaths.

I think the reason that support is so fragile is because the president and the political leadership of the country were not candid with Americans and were probably not candid with themselves in putting forward not only what they wanted to achieve, but also what it would cost. That's my essential objection to them. Now, why is that serious? It is serious not only because American political support is fragile as a result, but also because when you look at these people in Iraq who are fighting the United States, the people who go out every day and place bombs by the side of the road so that when a convoy goes by they press a button and they kill Americans, the people who take pot shots at American troops, the people who are using the shoulder-fired missiles to shoot down American helicopters, people who are putting the car bombs together and blowing up the UN and other targets in Iraq, what exactly are they attacking? What is their target?

I would say, as an American colonel said to me in Baghdad, their target is American will. That's the target. That's what they're trying to destroy. Clausewitz said that to win a war you have to identify the center of gravity of your opponent and then destroy it. When I asked this American colonel what the center of gravity is for the rebels when they look at the United States, he said, "It is American will."

Because of the reluctance to be honest about the cost of what the US is attempting in the Middle East, American will, as the central target of the opposition, is very badly defended. The way you defend it is to build it up through political capital. The president has to explain to the people why this is necessary, why the sacrifices that will have to be made to achieve this policy are necessary. And George Bush, to my mind, never did that. So my major objection is this disconnect between what they want to achieve and what they're willing to spend to achieve it. And I don't see in that simply dishonesty, a central political dishonesty, which happens all the time. I see in it a great deal of risk because this is a guerilla war.

JE: Looking forward to the election and how 9/11 may factor into it, you mentioned terrorists undermining the will of Americans. Would you make so bold a statement as to say that Bush's use of 9/11, his exploitation of the fear it generated, is itself an attack on American will?

That's an interesting question. I think the Bush administration has been singularly successful in one area, which is the political use of the war on terror. They've been very effective in building their own political support in intimidating the Democrats, who have traditionally not been strong on national security, at least in the last three decades or so since Vietnam, and arguably since the loss of China in '49, if you really wanted to argue the case. One should remember that on September 10, 2001, George Bush was looking at a pretty difficult fall. He was looking at budgetary difficulties. A lot of problems had accrued to him because of his tax cuts, because of the problems in the economy and so on, and 9/11 was a revitalizing event for him. There's no question about it, politically. I mean, it sounds perhaps bad to say it, but it is true. They've been extremely effective in using the war to bolster his popularity, to put him forward as a wartime leader and someone who can protect the American people. So, in a way, 9/11 was a boon to him.

To say that he's exploited it in a way that's weakened American will is, to me, going a bit too far. I think he's taken some risks, particularly with the war in Iraq, that have left the United States open to dangers that it needn't have been opened to. 9/11 began a struggle, or at least underlined a struggle, with al-Qaeda that had been going on since the mid-'90s, and certainly since the late '90s. It put this struggle front and center in American foreign policy. Three thousand Americans were killed on American soil. Now, the decision was made within the administration to take this event and to take this struggle against al-Qaeda, and make it into a full-fledged struggle between good and evil. That is, al-Qaeda, and the war against terror as it was phrased, were raised to a struggle similar to the one against communism. And the doctrinal lineaments of American foreign policy after 9/11 are very similar to what they were after 1947, after the Truman Doctrine. There's a very strong precedent for this in American foreign policy history: you take a relatively isolated event, in '47 it was the insurgencies in Greece and Turkey, and you make it into a symbol of a worldwide struggle between good and evil. Why do you do this? Because American foreign policy has to be based on popular will and this is a very easily understood way to discuss these matters. It is the US, the good nation, struggling against evil.

The important thing to remember here is that one didn't have to put it in these terms. One didn't have to say, "If you're not for us, on our side, you're on the side of the terrorists." That was not a necessary response. That was a chosen response. Now, the advantage with this, as with the Truman Doctrine, is you put things in very easy terms for people to understand. The disadvantage, I think, is that you mischaracterize what's going on, which is an important disadvantage. I mean, you're essentially saying that this is a worldwide struggle against evil, which, to my mind, it isn't. It's a struggle against an organization of perhaps 5,000 to 10,000 people that arose during the war in Afghanistan and that came about in a particular place, at a particular time. It is a formidable group. They're well-trained. They're very dedicated. But they do not represent the entire world of evil, and this is not a worldwide force fighting the United States. And the United States will essentially defeat them. I don't doubt that. To me, the mistake of the Bush administration has been to glorify this into something that it is not, and to take actions based on that glorification that were imprudent. And the war on Iraq, in the end, was imprudent, because it was a war that was not necessary. It didn't need to be fought. It was a war to remove a threat that was not imminent in any way. Iraq was a fading power. It certainly wasn't a vital threat. And this war detracted and distracted from the real fight, which was in Afghanistan and South Asia.

In the US, particularly under the Bush administration, we are very accustomed to speaking of the United States as the most powerful state that has ever existed in the history of the world. The US has the greatest army, the greatest military force that has ever existed. The difference between the power of the United States and the rest of the world is a greater difference than has ever existed since the time of ancient Rome. You hear those statements made all the time, and I happen to think that it's complete rubbish. I don't think it's true. I think power has to do not only with whether you have certain kinds of gadgets that kill people, but whether you have the will to use them, and whether you have the democratic support to project that power. Under Clausewitzian terms, you multiply actual power—technology, men under arms—by will. That's how you get a state's power. The United States, under those terms, is not the greatest state that ever existed or the most powerful nation that ever existed.

The United States is now overstretched militarily. As a recent General Accounting Office study revealed, come March the United States will not have sufficient troops to replace those in Iraq. The Army is overstretched. The country has a permanent trade deficit that is greater than any in the history of the world. Our economy is based on a very fragile footing, when it comes to foreign trade and the level of our production versus what we're buying from abroad. So the notion that the United States has such a superfluity of power that it can do whatever it wants in the world, is simply wrong. And in those terms, the idea of invading Iraq now, to me, was a misconceived policy that distracted from things that were much more important to the United States in other parts of the world, particularly South Asia. And it also risks leaving in place of what was a terrible autocracy, but was at least very stable, a failed state in which al-Qaeda and others will be able to grow, to build recruitment, and to use as a base for further attacks on American troops. So, I think, on many levels it was misconceived.

JE: A lot of people have made the case that elections aren't really where you make change, that electoral politics is corrupt by definition, and that these guys, the Bush administration, may be a little bit more of an accelerated form of the regular corruption, but no big deal essentially. You have to take it to the streets and do it differently. Do you think that there are major stakes involved in this election?

I think that this election could be the most important in the last half-century. Now, that sounds hyperbolic and maybe it is, but to me, particularly when it come to foreign policy, the Bush administration represents a kind of radicalism that we haven't seen in American foreign policy before, period. Certainly not in the post-war period. I think it's a kind of radicalism that members of the first Bush administration recognize and have tried to tone down. I'm talking about the former National Security Advisor Brent Scowcroft, former Secretary of State James Baker, and others. This administration's foreign policy is dramatically different from anything we've seen before in an American government since World War II. For that reason, I think this election is enormously important. Because whoever the Democratic nominee is, I think it's inevitable that that candidate will stand for a return to a less radical, more consensus-based, more alliance-based foreign policy.

It is nonsense to say that this election won't make much difference. One could talk at length about the domestic issues at stake and those are also extremely dramatic, but on a foreign policy level this election, to me, is life or death. Let me put it this way: any Democrat who is elected in 2004 will inevitably be faced with cleaning up a certain number of messes that the Bush administration has left in its train. In particular, they will be faced with trying to fix relationships with old allies like the French and the Germans, and with rebuilding relationships with new allies like the Russians, and to some degree the Chinese, that have been damaged in the last three years.

Those who say that elections don't matter only have to look at the year 2000, when 547 votes in Florida determined that George Bush was elected and gave us a foreign policy that I think was dramatically different from what a Democratic administration would have given us after 9/11. I think a Gore administration would not have invaded and occupied Iraq. I think a Gore administration would not have destroyed relationships with some of our oldest and most important allies. I think a Gore administration would have built on alliances, both lasting alliances like NATO and treaty alliances like Kyoto and other international treaties, to expand a web of relationships that have benefited the United States for the last half-century. So had 547 people voted differently in Florida, or had any number of other contingencies come about that didn't, the United States would be in a very dramatically different position today internationally. I think there's no question about that.

I also think that 9/11 probably would have ushered in a rather dramatic change in energy policy in this country. It would have been very difficult to achieve, but I think that the former vice president's political sympathies and political history suggested he would have brought to bear or tried to bring this to bear as a response to what happened on 9/11. So I think that elections make an enormous difference and I think that the 2004 election could and will make an enormous difference. I think the stakes are extremely high.

New York City
December 26, 2003

Shadia Drury is among the world's foremost scholars on the history, philosophy, and politics of neoconservatism. She is the author of the acclaimed book *Leo Strauss and the American Right* (St. Martin's, 1997). Her newest book is *Terror and Civilization: Christianity, Politics, and the Western Psyche* (Palgrave Macmillan, 2004). Professor Drury holds the Canada Research Chair in Social Justice at the University of Regina in Saskatchewan, Canada.

JE: You and others, Seymour Hersh of the New Yorker, *for example, have talked about the influence of the political philosopher Leo Strauss on key neoconservatives within the Bush administration. Can you just give me a brief sense of the Strauss lineage?*

Abram Shulsky in the Pentagon, who was responsible for intelligence and for making the case for the war in Iraq, studied directly with Leo Strauss. He has said that what he learned from Strauss is that deception is the norm in politics. The other key person, of course, is Wolfowitz. He was a student of Alan Bloom's at Cornell and he is arguably the most famous of Strauss's disciples. He is very much behind the Project for the New American Century, and is one of the leading neoconservatives and one of the chief architects of the war in Iraq.

JE: Who was Leo Strauss, and what are some of the basic principles of his political philosophy?

In the most basic terms, Strauss was someone who was extremely affected by the Holocaust. He was a Jewish intellectual who had to leave Germany during the war. I have great sympathy for Strauss because he had to leave Germany and start up school with a scholarship at a very sophisticated college with a brand new language. He had to basically start learning English from watching soap operas. I consider him to be a victim of the Holocaust.

But he is also a victim in a second way. He was a victim in the sense that he was completely, intellectually preoccupied with the Weimar regime and how Hitler came to power. He was under the impression that it was because of liberal democracy that Hitler came to power. This was his model of liberal democracy—he thought that it was the most dangerous kind of regime, and he basically equated it with the victimization of the

Jews and the victimization of Socrates in Athens. He was terrified about what the majority, the inferior many, the vulgar many, have the potential to do to the superior few when they get too much power. If we were to think of someone who is afraid of liberal democracy, someone who believes that there should be an elite that can manipulate the images on the cave and control the masses, that's the simplest way I can describe his philosophy.

JE: Can you say a bit more about Strauss's view of democracy?

What he learned from his experience is that because Hitler came to power in a democracy, democracy—and in particular a liberal democracy—was extremely dangerous; it was the most dangerous regime that you could possibly have. What he set out to do was to show how you could escape from the kind of situation that arose in Germany and from the horrors of Europe. He wanted to save America from her own love affair with liberal democracy, and he thought that he could do this by cultivating an elite—a conservative elite—that would ultimately undermine the liberal elements of American democracy.

JE: Strauss is said to be one of the intellectual fathers of neoconservatism. Can you clarify what neoconservatism actually is?

Neoconservatism, simply understood, sees itself as a movement that is socially conservative and economically liberal. That is the general interpretation of neoconservatives. But I actually challenge this understanding, because it's a self-understanding that is not very profound or deep. When you look at it more closely you find that even though they see themselves as economically liberal because they are championing capitalism as opposed to socialism or communism, they are actually children of corporate capitalism, and corporate capitalism is extremely compatible with hierarchy, discipline, and authority; it is extremely conservative. It is not in any way compatible with liberal democracy, with liberal individualism. But the images of liberalism and the images of the self-made man are images deeply rooted in our collective psyche and our collective consciousness. The image of the self-made man who pulls himself up by his bootstraps, out of absolutely nothing, and emerges out of the womb almost completely fully formed with all his talents extremely cultivated, as if he owes nothing to society—that is deeply rooted.

We use that image, but in fact, when you examine it more closely, what exactly is corporate capitalism? Corporate capitalism basically turns individuals into herds. It forces individuals to be herded into large office buildings. It forces them to be herded into large factories. Capitalism is highly anti-individualistic, if we think of liberalism as individualistic. So if all we think of liberalism as capitalism, well fine, then they can call themselves liberals; but that's a minimalist conception of liberalism in my view.

JE: Do you see elements of Strauss running through the ideological vision of the Project for the New American Century, the neoconservative think tank that a number of influential members of this administration were affiliated with before Bush came to office?

The Project for the New American Century basically outlines the whole neoconservative foreign policy, which is one of American world domination. Their vision, as laid out in some of their key documents, actually contains elements of idealism as well as elements of realism. What I mean by this is that neoconservatives are not a homogeneous group. Some of them are realists and some of them are idealists; some of them are religious and some of them are secular. But they are all united in their hostility to a liberal, secular society, and they're all united in an aggressive foreign policy for different reasons.

When you read some of the documents published by the Project for the New American Century, in particular Rebuilding America's Defenses, you see words like "military readiness" and Star Wars, which is a new plan for American armed forces in space. The whole document is intoxicated with American power and the belief that Americans should be able to fight several wars—they call them theatre wars—at different places in the world all at the same time. They outline the foreign policy of the neoconservatives, and that foreign policy is nothing short of world domination. With the Soviet Union out of the way, they see a great opportunity for America to use her unparalleled military might to control the world and to spread American values and principles.

JE: When you say that their foreign policy vision is both realist and idealist at the same time, what do you mean by that?

It's politically realist in the sense that power is everything. Now that we have power we should be able to dominate. We should allow our principles and our values to rule the world. But at the same time, while it's saying that power is the be all and end all, justice is irrelevant in international affairs, because international affairs is a jungle. People like the Europeans are concerned about justice and about US unilateralism, but this document completely throws off any concern with justice or unilateralism or multilateralism.

The story of Gulliver and the Lilliputians is a perfect analogy of just how the neoconservatives see foreign affairs. In *Gulliver's Travels*, if you remember, the palace of Lilliput is on fire and Gulliver comes to the rescue by urinating all over the palace. Well, the Lilliputians are totally appalled by this sacrilegious, irreverent conduct, and they're very mad at Gulliver. But at the same time, they realize that Gulliver has not only saved the palace, he has saved all of them. So the idea here is that there are different standards for the powerful and for the powerless. One of Allan Bloom's books, Bloom being a famous disciple of Strauss and a hero of many of the most influential neocons today, one of his books is actually called *Giants and Dwarves*. In it, he is fascinated with the story of Gulliver.

The point is that the powerful can do things that are supposedly beneficial to everyone else only if they can spread their own values and their own principles. There is a certain idealism operating there, because there's a conviction that American principles are good, that they are superior to everybody else's principles. If we use force, no matter how much injustice we may inflict on the world in the process, the assumption is that the world will, in the end, thank us, just as in the end the Lilliputians thanked Gulliver. So, that's the basic idea. In that sense, then, there's a combination of real political power and the powerful will do whatever they like. They don't have to act multilaterally. They don't have to take into account any consideration about the principles of justice. But on the other hand, there's this idealism that supposedly our principles are the superior principles and that the world will thank us in the end.

JE: I recall your saying somewhere that Strauss believed it would be tragic if his project were ever fully realized, because he understood that spreading American values carried within it the potential to soften people, to weaken them. Can you talk about this strange contradiction?

Strauss thought that the success of society really depended on an absolute, unwavering faith that America is better than any other place. At the same time, he didn't really anticipate that Americans would be so responsive to his message because of American exceptionalism, this idea that as a nation America is like no other. She's the lion that will light up the rest of the world. The idea of American exceptionalism made Americans extremely receptive to Strauss beyond his wildest dreams, and once you create a monster you can't always control the monster.

Strauss would have abhorred the idea that America would spread capitalism and consumer society around the world, because for him that was what Nietzsche described as the last man. What Carl Schmitt described as the trivialization of life. So for him, that wouldn't have been a particularly appetizing result. But of course, it's not likely that this project will succeed, that America will succeed in subduing the world and giving it its own brand of liberal democracy as understood by the neoconservatives. I mean, the project of the neoconservatives is to first reform America and then to export her to the world; to transform her liberal society, which they see as basically perverted. It leads to children out of wedlock; it leads to family breakdown; it leads to drug addiction. Not to mention it leads to nihilism and the death of God. What's being transported to the world is a capitalist economy, coupled with a very socially conservative society. It is not a society that puts the individual above the group or the community, but a society that gives priority to the community over the individual, and a society that gives priority to virtue over freedom.

This brings me to a very interesting phenomenon about the neoconservatives. As much as they abhor the Arab world, they're also extremely envious of the Arab world. They envy their religiosity, they envy their un-liberated women, they envy their high birth rate, and they envy their willingness to sacrifice themselves by rushing headlong to their death. Meanwhile, they think that liberalism makes people soft and unwilling and unable to fight and win wars. So for them, the real enemy is what the '60s represented: the Civil Rights movement, the women's movement, and President Kennedy, for example. The '60s were a time when American society was starting to open up. The era of fear of the McCarthy era was behind us. You have to remember that the neoconservatives were great champions of both Vietnam and the McCarthy era, and they continue to defend McCarthy.

JE: Can you say something more about the elitism inherent in his thinking, and whether this was reconcilable with his love of America?

Strauss really had a kind of contempt for the masses. He thought that they were mainly slothful and pleasure-seeking, and the only way to get them to sacrifice themselves for their nation and for their God is to create a sense of crisis, looming catastrophe, and impending doom. Only then, when their own self-preservation was severely threatened, would they rise to the occasion.

Politically speaking, neoconservatism has social dimensions, foreign policy dimensions, and economic dimensions. Neoconservatives are populists. They're not liberal democrats, strictly speaking. You have to remember that our liberal democracy is really a kind of democracy that has its source in two different traditions. One is the liberal tradition and one is the democratic tradition. The liberal tradition is really concerned with freedom: freedom for individuals to do whatever they please as long as they don't harm anybody. And liberals don't really care how that's done, whether you do it by constitutional monarchy or by democracy, which is about the rule of the majority. To me, neoconservatives are politically democratic but anti-liberal. They create a wedge between liberalism on the one hand and democracy on the other, because they see liberalism as problematic. They see liberalism as a threat. But in fact, without liberalism what kind of democracy would we have? We would have a democracy that is nothing more than the tyranny of the majority.

We have to remember that democracy is not a form of government that is without question. Without doubt, the best form of government has to be limited by the liberal tradition that has insisted on the rights of individuals, on the rights of minorities, on the limitations of executive power. That's what the liberal tradition has provided for democracy. That's the kind of positive limitation that liberalism has put on democracy. To me, the neoconservatives seem to fulminate endlessly about the crisis of liberal democracy, while at the same time creating the very crisis they're fulminating about, precisely by undermining the liberal aspects of our civil rights.

The Patriot Act is a clear indication of the undermining of civil rights, individual freedom, the primacy of individuals, and the rights of minorities. The neoconservatives basically abuse and exploit the vulnerable aspects of democracy—and democracy is very vulnerable to the tyranny of the majority; it is vulnerable to the rise of demagogues who will manipulate people though lies and through propaganda, and that's exactly what the neoconservatives do; they use populism as a kind of tool, as a ploy to destroy liberalism. Their goal seems very clear, and that is to convince people that liberalism and their freedom are what put them in danger. It seems to me that fear is the greatest ally of tyranny. If they can convince people that liberalism leads to licentiousness, to having children out of wedlock, to marital break-down, to a lack of security, and to terrorism, then people will readily give up their freedoms.

JE: Is Strauss's political philosophy relativist? Is the ground of neoconservatism an acknowledgment that there is no ground, that there's only power, that power is itself moral?

One of the things that I should explain is that most neoconservatives don't understand Strauss. Many of them haven't even read Strauss. What they get from Strauss is a certain spirit, a certain sense of crisis, a sense of impending catastrophe and looming doom that liberal society invites, that nihilism and the death of God are dangerous. Postmodernity has its roots in Nietzsche and Nietzsche basically says that there's no truth, everything is interpretation; and in fact truths are just disguised manifestations of the will to power. If all the claims to truth are disguised manifestations of the will to power, you could do one of two things: you could work to basically unmask and deconstruct power to show its complete groundlessness. Or you could decide to do the very opposite and say that this is a very dangerous situation that we're in. All myths have been exploded. What should we do? Maybe what we should do is not make things less secure and less safe. Maybe the thing to do is actually to spin the myth and the illusion, use your philosophical capacities to read the tradition on this instead of creating a certain amount of stability.

I essentially think that Leo Strauss and Alan Bloom were postmodern. They believed that Nietzsche was right, but that this was a very dangerous situation. So Leo Strauss thought of himself as a man who was at odds with his time. He was pretty much a man of his time, in the sense that he was a man who was terrified of skepticism but completely devoid of faith.

JE: You've written quite a bit about Strauss's belief in the "noble lie," about how deception is built into the very foundation of his political philosophy. You've also made connections between the noble lie and what you've seen from the Bush administration. Isn't it the case that politics, political rhetoric—whether informed by neoconservatism or not—always depends on certain kinds of deception? What's the difference you're concerned with here?

Strauss had a kind of postmodern interpretation of Plato about the noble lie. You could argue, I think, that no politics at all could dispense with lies. You have to lie to the enemy, and you certainly have to conceal certain things at all times for the purposes of security. It is one thing to talk about concealing certain intelligences and lying to the enemy, and it's quite another thing to talk about manipulating your fellow citizens on a regular basis. It seems to me that to say lying is a norm in politics is to undermine the very foundations of democracy itself. If democracy is going to have any claim to being a good form of government, it's precisely because two heads are better than one. It's precisely because people can use their reason and their common sense and that they can publicly deliberate. When you lie to someone you rob them of the opportunity to act as they would have had they known the facts. This is what governments do by lying to the people. They make the people into puppets for their ends. Puppets that are going to do their own bidding. They don't give people the opportunity to deliberate and to act the way that they would have normally acted if they had not been lied to.

So systematic lying is a form of manipulation that shows that the democracy has become corrupted. It's a profound corruption of democracy when people are simply viewed as a mass that is manipulated by an all-knowing elite that is convinced that they know the truth, that they alone have access to the truth. They can't possibly learn anything from the debates and discussions of others, because they're convinced that they know the right way for everybody else.

JE: You also write about Strauss's identification of three kinds of men. Can you explain this?

There are three types of men for Strauss: there are the wise few, the gentlemen, and the vulgar many. Direct rule of the wise was, for him, largely impossible, but the indirect rule of the wise was quite possible as long as you have the collaboration of the special breed of men that he called the gentlemen. For Strauss, the gentlemen were a class of men who believed in God, wanted honor, cared about morality, but weren't too smart. They loved war for sure, because war is a source of honor. They were really macho types in that sense, but not terribly bright. You don't want them to be too bright, because if they're too bright, they might not be so easily swindled by the wise. Now, the wise have to educate the gentlemen. They have to rule and guide them, and it's much easier to guide them if they're not asking too many questions.

The gentlemen are willing to go to battle. They want to fight for their country. They're extremely patriotic and totally uncritical of their country. In many ways, you could say that Strauss wanted the best opportunity for the wise to rule from behind the scenes and to manipulate the gentlemen. But that can only happen if those in power lend an ear to the wise. With the Reagan administration and the first and second Bush administrations, the Straussians flocked into government, precisely because they thought that these were the kinds of powerful men who would lend them an ear.

JE: What did you mean when you said in a recent interview that there's a certain "virile fantasy" running through the neoconservative worldview?

An important part of this social conservatism, of course, involved this whole idea of family values, which is a highly charged euphemism for keeping women at home and reducing them to their biological function. This is for two reasons. One, so that the world can be run by men, because only real men know exactly how the world should operate without the interference of women. Two, because the real world is filled with present danger, constant threats, and infinite enemies. We would therefore have to fight a lot of wars and we need women to become baby factories, because if we're fighting all these wars we're going to need a lot of soldiers. That is the realistic streak within neoconservatism. And there is a kind of virile fantasy in all of this; it's a kind of macho understanding of the world, and you see it very clearly, for example, in Robert Kagan's dismissal of Europe as this effeminate, soft, pampered place, whereas we Americans live in the real world: the world of power politics. Europeans, on the other hand, are just concerned about justice and multilateralism. Justice is for the weak. But this virile fantasy seems to me to be premised on a very perverse and debased conception of masculinity, violence, and domination. And that kind of masculinity is not going to last very long because eventually there will be enough countries in the world that will want to get rid of the macho America regime, including America's previous allies in Europe.

JE: What was Strauss's view of religion, and how is it relevant to the kind of religiosity we see in George W. Bush?

Strauss taught the neoconservatives that religion is the cement of society, and that without religion society would collapse. He was ultimately someone who believed that there was no foundation for morality apart from fear of hellfire and the afterlife, and that you couldn't motivate people to act morally otherwise. It's a kind of a great pessimism about human nature that dovetails with the religious mindset. Some of the neoconservatives are genuinely religious, but other neoconservatives are like Strauss. They see religion as a useful political tool. And when they look at the American founders, people like Irving Kristol, for example, think that it was a big mistake to relegate religion to the private realm. They believe that religion is a very powerful political tool.

You can see the force of this in the speeches of George W. Bush. He is constantly talking about how God loves America, how God is on the side of America, how her enemies are on the side of Satan. Interestingly, this is the same kind of biblical language and dualism that you find in Osama bin Laden, who sees America as the great Satan. So it's not something that is distinctive to Bush.

Bush recently said that Muslims and Christians worship the same God, and he's more right about this than he realizes. God really should be left out of politics, because politics is about plurality, it's about diversity, and it's about how people who don't agree about what metaphysical truth is can live together. What you have here is the idea that somehow God is on our side and our enemies are on the side of Satan. This dualistic vision of life radicalizes politics.

Bringing religion into politics is to wed God and the nation. Leo Strauss wouldn't exist if it weren't for Carl Schmitt and his conception of politics as being fundamentally based upon the distinction between friend and foe. This is the most fundamental distinction in politics, according to Carl Schmitt. Schmitt was a radical, right-wing German jurist, and Strauss completely agreed that the distinction between friend and foe was absolutely fundamental to politics, but he wasn't satisfied with Schmitt's position. In fact, he radicalized Schmitt's position. Schmitt said that politics should be separated from other dimensions of social life, such as aesthetics and morality. We should destroy the foe just because the foe is the foe, not because he's necessarily evil or ugly or economically damaging to us. Strauss didn't think this was a realistic posture. He thought that politics would be better served if, in fact, the foe were seen as being evil. If we attached religion to politics in order to see the foe as being against God, against truth, against justice, we could probably strengthen politics, and of course it will also strengthen the determination to destroy the foe. But that does not make politics more moderate. Quite the reverse. In this way, neoconservatism is extremely immoderate. The introduction of religion into politics makes it much less moderate than, say, traditional conservatism.

JE: What key distinctions do you draw between conservatism and neoconservatism?

As a liberal myself, I'm very sympathetic toward traditional conservatism, because I think every society needs a certain conservative temper. A traditional conservative is someone who basically prefers the tried to the untried, a person who has a certain respect for the existing traditions, who is moderate, who is conscious, who is wary of change. None of these qualities are qualities that the neoconservatives have. On the contrary, they overtly reject traditional conservatism, saying that it's dull and that it won't win elections. They might be right about that and they may ultimately believe that there is too much reconciliation with the present, because traditional conservatism tries to conserve the good that is in the present, where neoconservatism really has very little that they like about America that's in the present. Irving Kristol says that there is much to abhor about the American present, so he cannot possibly accept traditional conservatism and its present-mindedness. Newt Gingrich, for example, echoed something similar when he said that we have to start with a blank slate.

You see the same thing reflected in the Project for the New American Century: the idea that politics is like craftsmanship and that you can remake the world. You can reinvent the world in your own image. But politics isn't like that at all. It's not like building something or making shoes or making a house. With politics you always start with something that is already there: people, values, and tradition, for example. So politics is the art of the possible. That is what conservatism teaches us, and it's a lesson that the neoconservatives have rejected.

JE: For all of Strauss's love of America, is there something, then, inherently anti-American in his philosophy, in neoconservatism? And are the neocons who are in power now political radicals?

It depends on how you understand American. American is very complex. It's anti-American if you understand America, as most of us do, as fundamentally liberal in its foundations. In that sense, it's absolutely anti-American. If America is liberal and individualist then there is nothing about neoconservatism that is particularly American apart from its commitment to capitalist economics.

They are radical in the sense that they want radical change. They are radicals in the sense that they see politics as a form of making something out of nothing. They are, to be very accurate, reactionary, and I'm not using that as a general term of abuse. They are reactionary in the literal sense of wanting to turn the clock back on what they see as the liberal revolution of the '60s. If you listen, for example, to Bob Dole in the elections of 1996, he said he was going to build a bridge to the past. Of course, we know that Bill Clinton said that he was going to build a bridge to the future, and we now know what happened there. So they're reactionaries in the sense that they want to turn back the clock on the liberal revolution and they want to take America back to what they feel is a kind of romanticization with a golden age that they associate with the '50s—an age of deference, an age of fear, an age of McCarthy, and an age of nationalism.

JE: You talked earlier about neoconservatism and its relationship to fear, about this sense of constant awareness of danger and looming catastrophe. Can you expand on that in relation to 9/11?

9/11 was really critical to finding political leaders who will do the bidding of the neoconservatives, because the neoconservatives have been feeling a sense of present danger, of crisis, of looming catastrophe, but with no one else to share their sensibility. After 9/11, it was possible to get people to share their sense of crisis and their political sensibilities. Unfortunately, 9/11 also allowed them to proceed with their project, but the project had very little to do with real security for America. In fact, the whole war on Iraq is a war that has completely hijacked the concern with Osama bin Laden and the concern with real terrorism, which is a real threat. It has actually made Americans less secure rather than more secure, because now, of course, the terrorists are flocking into Iraq, because anarchy is very inviting for terrorists. As long as Saddam Hussein was there, he was the great enemy of Osama bin Laden and the fundamentalists. Anyone who understands anything about Middle East politics realizes that these two guys were enemies, but they might not be anymore. They may have united themselves against the colonial enemy.

Regina, Saskatchewan
November 26, 2003

MICHAEL ERIC DYSON

Michael Eric Dyson is an ordained Baptist minister and the Avalon Foundation Professor in the Humanities and Professor of Religious Studies and African Studies at the University of Pennsylvania. He is the author of ten books, including *Making Malcolm: The Myth and Meaning of Malcolm X* (Oxford University Press, 1996), *I May Not Get There with You: The True Martin Luther King, Jr.* (Free Press, 2001), and *Mercy, Mercy Me: The Art, Loves, and Demons of Marvin Gaye* (Basic Civitas Books, 2004).

JE: What's your view of the Bush administration's response to 9/11?

I think the Bush administration has exploited the sense of terror generated by 9/11 for its own political advantage. While saying that it's committed to not politicizing this issue, it has crassly politicized it on a number of different levels. Take the Patriot Act, for example, which of course is intended to somehow shore up the boundaries of American democracy, when in one sense it has repelled those very principles. What else are we fighting for in this war against terror except the ability to tell the truth as we see it as American citizens, regardless of the political choices we make or the ideology that we align with? So if the very point of fighting the war on terror is defending the possibility that we, as Americans, can speak up, we can't at the same time be angry at those people who see some funky relationship between domestic policy and foreign policy. We should not be told that we are un-American if we express these views. We saw that before. Martin Luther King, Jr. faced that in Vietnam; people who are progressive along the political spectrum have faced that time and time again when they've spoken up.

Likewise, the heightened sense of security and the colors we assign somehow suspiciously coordinate with parts of the domestic agenda that the Bush administration wants to see either focused on or de-emphasized. So when the debate is concentrated on the sluggish economy in the face of the Bush administration's inability to stimulate it, there have been curious and suspicious correlations of heightened forms of alert.

I think it's very important for us to see that the kind of fear-mongering that has occurred in the aftermath of 9/11 has been deleterious to American society, because it refuses to acknowledge that civil liberties are the lifeblood of American democracy. Now, we don't mean civil liberties to such an extraordinary degree that we just chuck out all concerns about this new era of terrorism. We don't mind going through extra checks at the airport to make certain that we are all safe here. Regardless of our ideology, our commitments, and our beliefs, we're willing to be safe. But we do mind chucking fundamental structures of civil liberties, and we do mind giving up freedom of speech and the ability to criticize the Bush administration. That kind of thing is totally ridiculous. And I think that kind of bullying has made people quite suspicious—and rightfully so—about the manipulation of American fear in the aftermath of 9/11.

JE: One of the things we're interested in with this project is the gender gap in American politics, specifically the male side of the gap, which very rarely gets talked about or examined head-on. Do you have any explanation for why white working-class men have moved steadily toward Republican candidates when we know that on most issues the Republican Party is not exactly friendly to the interests of these guys? Is there something the GOP understands, something the Bush political operation understands, about race and masculinity that shores up this gap?

I think there's a convergence of at least three issues here. I think there's the issue of race and the kind of identification that reflexively takes place with other white guys in control—even if they're white guys who you don't think are doing the best job. But the alternative is that other folk will come in and take over, and then we'd really be at a disadvantage.

Number two is the gender issue. These are white *guys*, so even if you're not part of the male movement, where you're beating the drums on the floors on the weekend, you're at least beating the tom-toms of a kind of militarism that reinforces this sense of security. There's a very gendered way in which the Republicans have ingeniously created the sense that this about "real men"; it's time for real men to step up to the plate. Enough of this namby-pamby stuff, because George W. Bush represents the reborn American male. He is one of us. He doesn't speak very eloquently; he was a C- student at Yale. I mean, the guy was drunk by his own admission until he was forty and got a job. He might not drive a pickup, except on his farm when he goes home to the ranch, but that guy's one of us. So there's a real visceral identification with him, even if you don't necessarily have the same circumstances as George W.

Thirdly, I think there's a class dimension here. I think the Republicans have ingeniously exploited the working class and working poor, but especially middle class white men, who feel that they're under assault. Affirmative action has beaten back the interests that they have. Women identify with it, black and Latino people identify with it, so in one sense white men feel under assault. This is an extension of the same kind of resentment that someone like Timothy McVeigh could tap into. I'm not suggesting that these people are fellow travelers with Timothy McVeigh, but there's no question that when even Howard Dean said that we have got to win back the Democratic Party for those guys out there who drive pickup trucks and fly the Confederate flag, that was Dean's attempt on the Democrat side to tap into the pool of resentment that the Republicans, by and large, have had their way with. So I think those three things together allow them to exploit their natural market.

JE: You're a Baptist minister. You've talked about Bush's religiosity, his evangelicalism. Can you talk about that a bit more, especially whether or not you see it infusing his policies and his political approach to problems?

There's no question that evangelicalism and Protestantism have had a significant influence on his own understanding of his foreign and domestic policy. I think he has a sense of divine calling to make sure that American values are protected. In one sense, then, there's a collusion between ideology and theology here, and we're not entirely certain that the theological would outweigh the ideological and, if it did, whether it would be any advantage, because the theological has been so deeply and profoundly informed by a sense of missionary zeal to join with the pursuit of empire.

There's an old story that many people tell throughout the world: when the Americans came they brought the Bible and we had the land. They asked us to pray and when we opened our eyes, they had the land and we had the Bible. That kind of missionary impulse, one that deploys theology and, in this sense, feeds evangelicalism, depends upon conversion. I have to get the message of Jesus to you, and in order to get the message of Jesus to you, I have to first convert you. In order to convert you, however, I have to tell you the truth about what I see is going on in the world. In that sense, there is a strict relationship between politics and religion; and in that sense, I think Mr. Bush has been profoundly and deeply influenced by this missionary impulse to go forth into the world and to preach the gospel of Americanism.

How this manifests itself culturally is pretty scary, because there's an "us versus them" mentality. There's this kind of Manichean distortion going on there. The idea that you are aligned with evil—the axis of evil—is about this evangelical rigidity. But what's interesting is that there are other dimensions of his religion that can be turned against him. Any good theologian and evangelical person could say, look, what about the notion of sin being in us and not just in them. How about the fact that all of us have fallen short of the glory of God. How about the fact, Mr. Bush, that when we think about evil, it's not just something out there, but something that we're tempted by as well. There's none of this in Mr. Bush's rhetoric, and unfortunately he has been able, I think in a quite ingenious fashion, to exploit not only his evangelical religious beliefs, but to do so in a way that, regardless of people's religious affiliations, they relate to. Right now, the black and white divisions in evangelical theology have collapsed. People are willing to suspend their skepticism and deny the legitimate fears they may have, and allow Mr. Bush to impose his religious views on us in very scary fashion, because they agree with him that this battle is black and white; it's between those people who are trying to destroy us and those people on our side. I think he has been able to take advantage of the fear that people naturally have in the aftermath of 9/11 and use it to push a religious agenda, sometimes in a subtle fashion and sometimes in a quite explicit way.

JE: People might say that they're really the same thing, that this is a God-fearing nation, was built that way, and any critique of Bush's religiosity, along the lines of the critique you just gave, is actually a critique of America. Do you see some counter-current, some other way of conceptualizing America without losing this religious impulse?

The mistake that many people often make is that they blur the history of American religion and American empire. For instance, if you take a close look at Thomas Jefferson and Benjamin Franklin, these are not Christians in the sense that we would understand Mr. Bush to be. This is not a Christian nation in the sense that people think they were promoting religion in its particular Christian form to unify the culture. Benjamin Franklin said, hey, whatever religion there is, if it is good for the nation because it brings us together and creates a kind of political consensus for us to be able to do our business, great. He was not promoting a particular version of Christianity. Thomas Jefferson, for that matter, might have had his *Reader's Digest* version of the Bible, but by the time he cut and pasted what he believed should be taken and extracted from the scriptures, most Christians would have been appalled. They wouldn't even recognize their Bible afterwards. So we've been hoodwinked by the some of the most right-wing members of the evangelical wing of the church to believe that this is a Christian nation, when it simply is not.

When we think about manifest destiny, even slave owners were going out into Africa. They were going to save these heathens from their own non-Christianity and bring them over here to, guess what, become slaves. So there's always been this collapse between American ideology and American empire. The expansion of American dominance in the world has always had a religious justification. I think we see this splendidly and clearly in Mr. Bush's attempt to subordinate his own foreign and domestic policies to his religious beliefs. It is a narrow slice of evangelicalism that has to be acknowledged; it's only one slice, because there are many more progressive people who engage in evangelical thought to challenge the powers that be and to put forth an argument against collapsing the Kingdom of God into any identification with the particular state that now happens to be America. This notion that America is God's choice is just outrageous and some would call it the sin of identifying the nation with God's will. That's just ludicrous, but unfortunately those voices don't get heard very much in this society.

JE: There are a lot of people out there who say there's no American empire, that this is a simplistic and gross misreading of the nature and history of empire. Can you explain why you say the United States is an empire, and explain what you actually mean by that?

When I say that this is an American empire what I simply mean to suggest is that the forces of domination give the nation a sense of justifiable outrage against the enemies of America. The positive dimension of American empire is to be the bully and the cop throughout the world, to impose a moral viewpoint on other nations in the name of a self-righteous perspective. What I mean by a self-righteous perspective is that we feel that given our protection of the principles of democracy, we are justified in making sure that anti-democratic principles throughout the world are opposed, and when we see manifestations of them it is our responsibility to wipe them out. So for me, empire is both the ability to impose your will on the rest of the world and the desire to do so in the name of a justifiable self-righteousness.

And let me tell you what else is interesting about empire. The brilliance of empire is to deny the fact that we are imperialistic. So one of the rudimentary conceptions of empire is the ability to have plausible deniability: we are not an empire; we're a nation that's interested in loving our neighbors. We're joining with other figures and other nations throughout the world. Plausible deniability is one of the most critical elements of empire. It is similar to the interesting dialogue about whiteness that's going on now: that when you're in a dominant culture and you're white, you're often not made to reflect on that whiteness. It is not until something challenges that—until blackness, brownness, redness, or another ethnicity begins to show what whiteness means—that you even acknowledge that a) you're white; b) you have privileges associated with that whiteness; and c) that you have to do something actively against this situation, otherwise you're extending the dominance of whiteness. Now, substitute empire for whiteness and you see how empire works.

First, you are already part of an empire when you have the ability to deny it, and second, plausible deniability is linked to extraordinary forms of privilege that are rarely questioned. Thirdly, since 1945, when we emerged as the primary superpower, we have felt justified in going out into the world and doing things in the name of those lesser gifted people and nations that didn't have the requisite power, skill, and military to defend themselves. For me, empire is about the concentration of power and the ability to impose one's will according to a moral vision.

Now is that different from what's happened before? Well, the circumstances have made it different. This is neo-imperialism. The US in a neo-empire. The circumstances of globalization have rendered discourses about empire in a different mode now because, for instance, you're living in a world that is much more intimately connected as a result of the Internet and the collapse of local economies. You now have multinational corporations and conglomerates, such as German companies owning American book publishing, so there's a kind of promiscuity, ideologically speaking, going on. In that sense, globalization has nuanced empire in different ways. But where it hasn't stopped the ability of America to constitute itself as an empire is that America has the military. It has the wherewithal to suggest, at the end of the day, that the bottom line is if we see something that we don't like, then we're willing to go to war to eliminate it. And this new doctrine of proactive intervention is not the isolationism that people worried about earlier. Now we're willing to go at it alone and willing to say that if we think something is a problem, then we're going to strike first.

JE: If you go to Bush's website, you'll find a number of photo albums dedicated to specific themes of his presidency and candidacy: foreign policy, national security, etc. One of these albums is called "compassion," and in virtually every picture Bush is shown posing with people of color, mainly African Americans. In none of the other photo albums do you see as many black faces, if any at all. What do you make of this collapsing of compassion with race?

What's interesting about Mr. Bush's identification almost exclusively of compassion with African Americans is that, on the one hand, their likely explanation would be that they're reaching out. Republicans have been accused of being insensitive to Latino and African-American interests and with not showing an ability to reach out. That's the positive, charitable interpretation. The negative, suspicious one, which is mine, might be that there's a kind of condescension there. Not only is there a kind of manipulation of race, but there's a kind of ghettoization and segregation of black people. Black people are good when we want to talk about compassion, and about reaching out to them in order for them to be better, so as long as we control the Republican Party and the means by which that compassion can be distributed. The problem with that is, of course, that it doesn't leave any wiggle room for those people to 1) dissent against the kind of compassion that is distributed to them, and 2) what it suggests is that black people don't have a legitimate interest in other areas of foreign policy and domestic policy.

When Martin Luther King, Jr. moved from speaking about civil rights and began to talk about domestic policies in relationship to poverty, or especially when he began to speak out against the war in Vietnam, there were people who felt he was overstepping his boundaries and bleeding beyond what is normally associated with the Negro. This politics of compassion reproduces that scenario. Once Dr. King began to become irreverent when he spoke out against the Vietnam War, he was no longer Dr. King—he was an irascible preacher who didn't have any expertise on such matters. In 1964 he won the Nobel Peace Prize, so that may have given him some moral authority to speak out against what he understood the war to be. So in that sense there is a continuation of a Republican manipulation of compassion that looks good, but underneath it is this kind of condescension that Mr. Bush has been a genius at manipulating. On the one hand, he looks as if he's reaching out to this valuable constituency, but what he is really doing is reproducing the ghettoization of them: you're good if we can use you for purposes of telling the American society that we're concerned about "the least of these." But to actually hear from the least of these, to hear dissent, to bear criticism, to allow them to speak out against the war in Iraq, won't be tolerated. So the manipulation of this politics of neo-compassion that the Bush administration has parroted, I think needs to be examined closely.

JE: How has Bush been on race, substantively speaking, in your view? Do you see his as markedly different from past presidencies in confronting issues of race in this country?

I'm sure if you were, as an African American, to live next door to Mr. Bush he would be kind. He would help you take out the trash and shovel your snow. I have no question in my mind that as a human being he's a good-hearted guy, but that doesn't make a hill of beans of difference when it comes to social or public policy. For Mr. Bush, on Martin Luther King's birthday a year ago, to announce his opposition in strong terms to affirmative action suggests that he is willing to manipulate the politics of racial compassion to his advantage. But he gives not a hill of beans for the interests of African-American people. His administration aggressively pursued anti-affirmative action policies in the brief it filed, standing with those people from the University of Michigan who wanted to turn back the clock, so to speak, on affirmative action. He took an aggressive stance against affirmative action, when he has benefited from every form of special pleading that one might imagine. Daddy had to call up the college to get you into Harvard and Yale, and then you brag about being a C-student. There's no denying that you speak the King's English but not to the Queen's taste. You're messing up every which way. Not only are your nouns and verbs not together, but they're divorced in very deliberate fashion so you can be seen as an everyman. People say, "Oh, his spoonerisms prove he is one of us." But if this had come from an African-American woman or someone from another ethnic group, it would have been proof that these people are not yet ready for prime time. So he is able to manipulate mistakes and use them to his advantage, but if black people were to make the same mistakes, they would be used to prove their essential unintelligence.

His own personal skills are enormous, but his social and public policies when it comes to race are atrocious. This is why, by the way, African-American people feel that we can be proud of Condoleezza Rice as a human being who has achieved a Ph.D. or General Powell as a general. But many people bellow out their belief that black people somehow should give them a break. "Aren't you proud of them?" Well, we're not proud of people who extend fascist policies; we're not proud of people who are in the White House, but who are incapable of preventing the president from speaking out on Martin Luther King's birthday against affirmative action. We're not proud of people who manipulate their race when it is convenient for them and who also say they're about transracial forms of democratic government. I think that Mr. Bush has seized ingeniously on Colin Powell and Condoleezza Rice as the figureheads for his racial policy. But like those figures, it has not meant anything substantive for the advancement of African-American people. I think in that sense he joins Bill Clinton's manipulation of the symbolic politics of associating blackness to his father's failure to do anything. In that sense George W. has ingeniously benefited both from the politics of Clinton and the politics of his father, and the combination has been especially destructive to black people.

JE: What would it take, in your view, for working class and poor white guys to see their economic situation not through the lens of race? You're talking about the brilliance of the Republican Party with tactics like the Nixon Southern Strategy, their deliberate appeal along racial lines to win support from poor and working class whites.

Martin Luther King, Jr. was jailed once in Birmingham and he turned to his white jailor and said, "You and I aren't much different. There's not a huge gap that separates us. You don't have control over the institutions that govern your life. You don't have a basic say in American democracy and yet the dominant forces of white supremacy manipulate you into believing you are my enemy." Unfortunately, that's a tragedy that hasn't changed. I think what we have to tell our white brothers who are working-class and blue-collar cats is that they are in the same boat as most African-American people, as most Latino people. You suffer from the economy, too. If you allow elite, white politicians to manipulate you into believing that your real enemy is the black guy that works beside you in a factory, where you're both inhaling toxic chemicals that will cause both of you to die early, as opposed to this elite figure in the American political echelon or corporate structure that is living off of your anxiety about this black guy, you're going to go down in defeat.

What we have to say to them is that we're in the same boat in terms of class and in terms of some of the cultural values that we share, even if we have different racial approaches to that. We need to convince white working America of this. It's interesting that we have a language and vocabulary for race in America but we don't have much of a vocabulary for class. What about poor or rich? What about having health care or not having health care? Then we would be able to break the numbers down and see the number of white people on welfare, the number of white people who are poor, the number of white people who don't control the government in ways that they'd like to see. How many white people say, "You want affirmative action, but why should your kid get an advantage over me?" or "You want reparations? Why should your kid get it over mine, when we don't have any economic wherewithal either." I say to them, "Look, it's not either/or."

What's amazing is that right-wing conservatives become Marxists when it comes to the issue of race. Ah-ha, you had better watch out, because those black people are taking money out of your pocket. How many black CEOs of major Fortune 500 companies are there? How many black Senators? How many black members of Congress are there? How many are there where it counts for white people's livelihood? Are they subject to black rule? So when white people back up and begin to make an analysis about how they have been manipulated by these white elites, there will be the possibility of forging a much stronger link between progressive working-class and blue-collar white, black, Latino, and red people, as opposed to the continued manipulation of the white working class by corporate elites.

JE: Let's turn to the Bush AWOL issue, the mystery and controversy surrounding his service, or lack thereof, in the Air National Guard during Vietnam. I'd like to know if you think that's a legitimate issue, because there are a lot of progressives who say that to question Bush on this issue is to reinforce the very militaristic rhetoric that people on the left typically reject.

There is no question that you can't have your cake and eat it too, so to speak. Mr. Bush has made hay about his record both implicitly and explicitly serving at a time of crisis. "I was there. I was on the front line. I'm your man." But it turns out that he really wasn't. And the reason we may have to make hay of that is not because it is reproducing this notion that masculinity is up for grabs. No, we're trying to have ideological consistency, and if you say manhood is about stepping up to the plate to represent, and then you stand in the on-deck circle and constantly don't step up to plate to take a swing, you ain't in the game. You're just a guy on the sidelines looking at the game, to use that baseball metaphor—and reinforce the idea of masculinity that we are discussing.

I do think that Mr. Bush has to be challenged on this. I think it is absolutely correct to do so, and that there's a relationship between that manipulation of masculinity and the codes of dominance through the military and the fact that you say you're the leader of the free world because you say you have military experience, and we find out you've been AWOL. You didn't really show up. There are holes even in the story that you put forth in the media. I was there... look I have memories of it... I remember that I was there. It's a kind anticipatory Alzheimer's, or maybe it's moral dyslexia. You're just reading it backwards.

What we have to say to Mr. Bush is, "Now you got to face the music." If you look at the troops, there are disproportionate numbers of black, brown, and poor white people serving in the military. I mean, if Jessica Lynch showed us nothing more it was the fact that many white people use the military the same way that black people have used it for years. They're trying to have a way up out of the ghetto. They use the military to catalyze their upward mobility. If that's the case, it's not an ideologically driven militarism that says, "I want to reinforce the American Empire and I'm your man or woman." No, it's about an economic downturn that does not allow people to find alternative measures in order to get a decent education and to find work.

JE: What does this election mean to you? Because, once again, there are those who lean left politically, as you do, who say the action is elsewhere, that we shouldn't get seduced into thinking that electing a Democrat will make any real difference, structurally speaking.

There's no question that there's something extraordinarily important about this election. We have to get on the street. First of all, I wouldn't even have my job at an Ivy League School had Martin Luther King, Jr. and Abraham Joshua Heshel and other concerned Americans not hit the streets and made sure the prerogative of democracy did not rest solely and exclusively in the hands of those people that were against our interests. Voting is concrete. It is necessary, and it's something that's democratic because every citizen can do it.

This is a very important election not only because of what I think Mr. Bush represents in his own political consciousness. It makes a difference because this is a battle about the way the world operates, who gets a chance to run it, and who has a chance to say so. Of course the candidates are not perfect. It's like when people tell me that they're not coming to church because there are hypocrites there. I say, "Well, there's always room for one more. Come join us." Those people who say that politics is terrible, well, come join us and you can be a part of it. Politics is about the arguments over the distribution of resources. That's what politics, at one level, is about. Don't think that it doesn't concern you. It concerns you if you are concerned about what kind of water you drink, what kind of air you breathe, or what kind of terrorists will be around you. It concerns you if you're worried about race, class, and gender. This is hugely important. We have to vote. And like they say in Chicago: Vote early and vote often.

Philadelphia
February 11, 2004

DANIEL ELLSBERG

Daniel Ellsberg is a lecturer, writer, and activist on the dangers of the nuclear era and unlawful interventions. He is best known for releasing to the press in 1971 what came to be known as "the Pentagon Papers"—a top-secret government study about the history of the United States involvement in the Vietnam War from 1945 to 1968. His trial, on twelve felony counts posing a possible sentence of 115 years, was dismissed in 1973 on grounds of governmental misconduct against him. His disclosures led to the convictions of several White House aides and figured in the impeachment proceedings against President Nixon. He is the author, most recently, of *Secrets: A Memoir of Vietnam and the Pentagon Papers* (Viking, 2002).

JE: You said in one of your recent interviews that this administration "lied us into war." I'm wondering if you can explain what that means. That seems a pretty strong charge.

You know, I'm not saying that they were very unusual in doing that. One side or another, or both, in any war, has generally lied very egregiously. In this case, I would say we've been lied into this as blatantly as we were lied into Vietnam. And I was saying that in the fall of 2002, at a time when we did not know how much they were hyping the evidence for WMDs, for weapons of mass destruction. I wasn't even referring to that. Bush fooled me on that one. I did believe, with all they were saying, that Saddam probably did have gas left over from the Gulf War, and did have biological weapons, and did have a nuclear weapons program, since our leaders said it so strongly. It seemed plausible. In light of that, I found it just incomprehensible that they were moving ahead toward invading, because my greatest fear, actually, in approaching the war was that Saddam would use biological or chemical weapons against us and that we would reply with nuclear weapons. That was my major fear.

Now, it turns out, that was illusory. He didn't have the gas or biological weapons. I didn't need to fear that, you might say. But while they were lying about their evidence of WMDs, they were also clearly lying in every other aspect of the war. The basic premise that Saddam represented the number one danger to American security and to world order was an absurd statement. I felt certain that they could not believe that. I hesitate here, with the regard to the President's beliefs, because it's hard for me to get inside Bush's head. I don't know what he believes. But I could not believe that Rumsfeld or Cheney or their subordinates felt that Saddam was the number one danger, nor that Powell did, and Powell actually said just that. This is a world in which al-Qaeda exists and could get nuclear weapons, but the whole idea that they're getting them from Saddam Hussein was the least likely avenue for obtaining them, given that there are some 30,000 ill-guarded Russian weapons, and that some of them have to eventually be for sale on the black market if the theory of the market means anything at all.

As a result of this war and the approach to this war, the need for a Third World country to have nuclear weapons to deter us has been impressed on a lot of people. To say that Saddam Hussein, after ten years of sanctions and the Gulf War, was any threat at all was basically absurd. The notion that with the end of sanctions he would get nuclear weapons and then be an extreme threat, unable to be deterred—that's an absurd statement. It's a matter of judgment. I couldn't believe the CIA believed these things, and when they did put out the statement to Congress through George Tenet, I was reassured at least that they had their feet on the ground. Tenet said that it was the judgment of CIA that Saddam could be deterred, would be deterred, even if he had such weapons, and that it was extremely unlikely that he would either use them or give them to any group not under his control, like al-Qaeda, unless he was attacked. Which is to say that an attack greatly increased, rather than decreased, the likelihood of our getting attacked by nuclear weapons or by weapons of mass destruction.

So the notion, then, that we were reducing our risk by attacking Saddam again seemed like an absurd judgment. And I was sure, in the case of most of these people, including Powell, that it was all a lie, a conscious lie, to justify war. It turns out that even the English notion of a WMD threat, the idea that they had chemical weapons ready to be used on just 45 minutes notice, was a tremendous hyping of the evidence, very flimsy evidence, ignoring the reservations of most intelligence analysts. Bush's famous sixteen words about the false report, the forged report that Iraq was trying to buy uranium from Niger, the reason that couldn't be dropped despite CIA reservations was that it was the only thing that gave the color of self defense and therefore legality to our pre-emptive, or preventative, strike. Without any chemical threat against our troops in the area, there was no excuse for ignoring a lack of support by the UN Security Council. Without these false claims, it would have been clear, as it is clear, that this was a purely aggressive, illegal crime against the peace. They were trying to give it some color of legality. In short, we were lied into war.

JE: Related to what you've just said about pre-emption and the interventionist policies of this administration, you talk in one of your pieces about the age of "indirect empire." You say that it's coming to an end, that the age of direct imperial occupation is what we're looking at now. Can you clarify what you mean?

Our empire has been mostly indirect—the exceptions being the Philippines and our imperial expansion across North America in the 19th century. Our influence abroad has been mainly indirect, achieved by picking the rulers, or assuring that the people who ruled these former colonial, Third World states, are to our liking and will serve our interests. If they don't, we get rid of them, in any number of ways, the most direct being assassination or military coups. Those are the main ways, but financial pressures can also do it, as can propaganda, bribery, etc.

Our regime change in Iraq, of course, was through a direct invasion and military rule. We seem rather slow as a country to perceive what the rest of the world can see very clearly, and that is that Americans are governing Iraq directly through a military administration. To be sure, we're also picking Iraqis who are supposed to have some influence, but they clearly don't. And so we have an occupation there of a country that does not want to be occupied and sees no real rationale for this occupation, glad as many of them are to lose Saddam Hussein as the ruler. And we're getting very little acceptance of the idea that we have a right to govern and to kill police and set all the rules and really turn all the laws. Virtually no one seems to be accepting that in Iraq, which was apparently quite foreseeable to the State Department, the CIA, and many people in the military, but was simply ignored by the civilians in the Defense Department and the White House.

JE: You've said, essentially, that lying is standard practice in American politics. The two arguments I keep hearing, on right-wing talk radio especially, are first that it doesn't matter that there were no weapons of mass destruction, because at least we got rid of a brutal dictator. And second, that deception and secrecy are sometimes required to protect national security. What do you make of these two different rationalizations for the necessity of democratic governments to lie or misrepresent the truth—the one because the end, in this case democracy, justifies the means, the other because our security is at stake?

What is the national security argument? How is this supposed to be helping our national security?

JE: Well, for example, they've blocked key components of the 9/11 investigation under the justification that some information, if released, will pose a security threat.

Ah, but that's the question of 9/11 and of al-Qaeda. We do have a threat from al-Qaeda, a serious threat. Whatever an investigation would reveal, al-Qaeda would be among our enemies and pose some serious threats against the United States. The idea of secrecy, from al-Qaeda, has some validity. But, in my opinion, I haven't seen any indication that it justifies the sweeping revocation of Constitutional rights in this country that this administration is bent on pursuing. There is a secrecy problem there. However, the notion that the struggle against al-Qaeda—to contain it and reduce the threat it poses, the so-called war on terrorism—the notion that this is the reason for the war on Iraq is one of the biggest of lies. The very crucial, supposedly factual, question of whether there was a clear link between al-Qaeda and Saddam was clearly without evidence at the time. And I was sure, by the way, that if they had evidence, we would have seen it.

So their lack of bringing forth any evidence that was not controvertible told me a year ago that that this was false, and in retrospect that seems to be the case. So I would say that the war against Iraq not only is *not* part of the war against terror, al-Qaeda, and other terrorist networks, but that it virtually *gives up* the war on terror. It substitutes for it and suppresses it, in the sense that I think it's impossible to think of reducing the threat from Osama bin Laden and al-Qaeda so long as we are occupying Iraq and killing civilian and non-civilian Muslims there. I think that can only serve the recruiting goals and the determination of al-Qaeda and Osama bin Laden. The idea that we'll really make progress in what we're trying to achieve while we're occupying Iraq is, I think, hopeless. Or so long as we are perceived, correctly, as really the sole support financially of the settlements in the West Bank and Gaza in Israel. So long as our support of Israel's illegal occupation in Palestine continues, I think it's fairly hopeless to think that we can pursue an effective collaborative war against terror.

So our national security, I would say, is threatened seriously by this invasion, and by our policy with respect to Israel under this administration. And every day the occupation continues, it's going to get worse. I'm sure it's going to get very much worse. I would say that Osama bin Laden—and I don't say this rhetorically—I would say he quite literally prays for the continuation of the George W. Bush regime.

Nothing could give him a better environment for achieving his objectives.

JE: You mentioned at the beginning of your response the massive revocation of civil rights that has accompanied these policies. I'm wondering, based on all you've witnessed in your lifetime serving a number of presidents, if the situation we're looking at now has any precedent for you.

As I look back on my service in the executive branch through a number of administrations, I recall very few individuals who had much appreciation of our democratic system or the Constitution. They had attitudes of contempt for Congress and neglected any possible restraint of law on what they were doing. None of that was all that different from what we're seeing now—except in degree. I do have the impression that Ashcroft, and for that matter Rumsfeld and Cheney, don't have any respect or understanding at all of any benefits from democracy. They see what they're doing as being for the good of the country, in a way the public could not understand. And if people don't understand it or accept it, they are to be ignored or suppressed.

I think this group's instincts for instituting a kind of police state here are, in degree, far different from anything we've seen before. Even though we were not governed before by people who were terribly concerned about what the people wanted, I would say there is a qualitative difference here. I think that with another big terrorist attack under this administration, we'll see a move toward becoming a police state, which we are not now. We're very far from being a fascist police state at this time, an authoritarian state of the kind we have installed and maintained all over Latin America and Asia and the rest of the Third World. But I think we will likely become that kind of state with another terrorist attack. I say this because, unfortunately, I think the instincts of this administration will lead them to have plans ready for such an attack, as I think they did before 9/11, plans for using public fear to close down civil liberties and to assure their own unchallenged rule.

Likewise, I don't see the resistance yet, certainly not in Congress or the mainstream media, on this issue. I see a lot of public activism, relatively speaking, against the so-called Patriot Act. But I don't think that impresses the administration. I don't see it supported in Congress, with one Senator, Russ Feingold, daring to vote against that act. That was terrible, but that was just after 9/11. I think that after another 9/11, the public will accept a tremendous closing down of civil liberties, just as the Israeli public clings to Arial Sharon disastrously in the face of the second intifada. It's not wise behavior on their part to cling to the strong man who is making matters worse, but I do infer that something very similar will happen in America—and relatively speaking, it has happened over the last two years.

JE: You mentioned in another recent interview that this administration shamelessly exploited 9/11 for its own gain. I was watching Richard Perle the other day, and he made a very different argument from the one you just advanced. His view, and you hear it in neoconservative circles very openly, is not that the administration used 9/11, but that 9/11 proved they were right all along. Their point seems to be that the terror strikes were an indication of precisely what can happen unless we build up our defenses and use force more willfully and proactively in the world. So in this view, 9/11 isn't a pretext, it simply proves the rightness of their foreign policy vision.

See, I can't quite figure out whether a guy like Perle, who is clearly intelligent, is actually saying such things and stupidly believing them, or whether he is simply being a propagandist and selling a dangerous and intolerable policy as best he can. I really don't find that easy to guess because I haven't met him. But the truth is that great stupidity can coexist in the same person with great intelligence, and that may be what's happening here. The fact is that 9/11, itself, shows a willingness of that entire administration, including Perle as a consultant on the Defense Policy Board, to ignore the threats that Democrats and some Republicans had been pressing on them with the greatest urgency. That was said to be one of the Clinton administration's last briefings with the incoming administration. They tried to impress on the Bush administration that Osama bin Laden and the Saudis were very dangerous and had to be dealt with. The administration spent a year ignoring those threats, at best, and they did this so egregiously that thoughts of conspiracy here are not in themselves insane. They're not off the wall. It's an explanation for what is otherwise very hard to explain.

Second, for ten years the larger scheme of Perle and Wolfowitz, and joining them Rumsfeld and Cheney, has been an attack on Iraq and a reordering of the Middle East. Has what's happened over the last two years shown that that was a good way to address the problem of Osama bin Laden, who has been there during most of that period? It's the opposite. To oblige Osama by killing Muslims on television, by bombing them extensively, to say that's a confirmation of the peril of Osama bin

Laden, of al-Qaeda, of 9/11, is a reversal of the truth. So I say, at best, that the perspective that led to this war is extremely unwise, the judgment reckless, uninformed, ignorant, not to be trusted. And that's true of this particular gang, starting with Perle, specifically. But, at worst, it means what they're accused of: a cynical willingness to achieve their imperial purposes at the cost of significantly increasing the danger of terrorism to citizens in this country. And that's what we're getting.

JE: You've used the term "elected monarchy" to describe what you've seen over the years as the growing, increased powers of the Executive branch. You say you're especially concerned about this with the Bush administration. Why?

The willingness of this president to say very blatantly, "I haven't decided whether to attack Iraq or not," at a time when we had neither UN authorization nor Congressional authorization—when he announced that he, personally, would decide—that was a simple negation of the Constitution. I think it's Article 1, Section 8 of the Constitution that says that in the absence of an imminent or ongoing attack, only Congress can decide whether to go to war. It was not for him to decide. And that not only showed a monarchical attitude on his part, but also an acceptance of that by Congress. Of course that is not unique. There were precedents for that. That happened with the Tonkin Gulf Resolutions, and with the Afghanistan war, where again only one member of Congress was willing to assert the Constitutional prerogative of holding hearings, debates, and then making the decision. Barbara Lee, alone, acted constitutionally and responsibly and in a non-cowardly way. But then a year later, 132 did vote against it in the House, and 23 senators voted against it, but not one senatorial candidate for president had the courage to vote against that unconstitutional delegation of power. It was clearly labeled as such by Senators Byrd and Kennedy, the two remaining senators who actually had voted for the first Tonkin Gulf resolution in 1964, delegating to the president the decision of going to war in Vietnam. They have regretted it for nearly 30 years; they were warning their fellow senators that they should not set themselves up for those same decades of regret.

JE: When you compare the Tonkin Gulf resolutions to this vote, do you see the lack of courage you're describing in both cases as in any way different? How does the fact that we were, indeed, attacked on 9/11 factor in here?

Well, the notion of a threat at home is of course not new to us. There always was a threat of a false alarm leading to an all-out nuclear exchange, a threat we were living with and which our policies were exacerbating and provoking day by day, year by year, and decade by decade. But the American public slept through a lot of that. They never did become very aware of our contributions, so they thought it was a threat that we were doing our best to avert, which was not the case, actually—we were provoking that scenario, and we were making it more likely, almost in the same way that Bush is increasing the chance now of terrorist attacks at home. But 9/11 did make concrete an actual attack, as if the Russians actually attacked our forces, which they never did during the entire cold war. If you think about it, our forces were never attacked by Chinese or Russian forces, from the beginning to the end of the cold war. Now, with 9/11, we have been attacked by an adversary at home in a significant way, and it can clearly be repeated, almost surely will be repeated.

The most we can do effectively is to reduce the risk of another such attack, to reduce the frequency of it and the impact of it by various measures, none of which we're doing. But the public in this situation seems to look for someone who presents himself as a strong man, who will take any measures, protect us by any means, and this is not wise or admirable behavior from our body politic. The chances of this species surviving this kind of behavior are not reassuring. And while there is opposition, this administration is unusually willing to label people who disagree with it as traitors. Looking back on Lyndon Johnson during Vietnam—I think few people are really conscious of this, and I'm maybe in a better position to comment on it than most—Johnson did not particularly do that kind of labeling. With a few exceptions, generally there was not a big McCarthyite-type attack on people who disagreed with him, especially in the establishment, as traitors and unpatriotic. There was some, but not like today. Now "traitor" is being used promiscuously as a term for anybody who disagrees with the administration in any way. It's not only Ann Coulter, with her book *Treason*, throwing that word around. It's used so much that the sting is less, I find, for me. I hated being called a traitor, which did happen quite a bit because I put out the Pentagon Papers. You never get used to it. I thought of myself as very patriotic and I didn't like that. I just find now that it's used so broadly by the Ann Coulters, by the right, by the administration, by people like Ashcroft, that it's become somewhat meaningless. In any case, not being called a traitor by Rumsfeld or

Ashcroft is almost like not being on Nixon's enemy list. You feel, "What's wrong with me? Don't I deserve that?"

This administration's willingness to sling that term at senators is very, very unusual, and the senators don't want it. I totally sympathize with their dislike of hearing that they're not patriotic. But I will also say that I, along with the people who inspired me and worked with me in the anti-war movement, had accepted that we would be called names, even those names, and it didn't stop us. And senators, most of them, unfortunately, are acting in ways where I think they're overestimating the risk of being thrown out of office for speaking up. Many of them live in safe districts, but they don't want to hear that charge. They don't want to face it in primaries. They don't want to hear it at all, and they'll submit to the president, rather than to have to deal with that charge.

JE: You've described yourself as a cold warrior, but you say in one piece recently that you are also a "just warrior." I think the distinction you make there is very important given what you were just saying. The warrior myth and ethos are incredibly important politically right now. Bush is positioning himself precisely as not only a warrior, but as a warrior for American justice.

Many people in the military are aware of the restraints of just-war doctrine, and to be aware of that means to be aware that there are two strands of that. One is the question of whether the war is justified in its larger cause, and the other is the means by which this war is conducted. The essential core of that is the ban on the indiscriminate destruction, or the deliberate destruction and targeting, of non-combatants. That's extended by some of the Hague regulations, quite specifically, to targeting civilian "infrastructure," the things that benefit or support the health of a civilian population, like water supplies, electricity, sewage, things that to attack might cause epidemics, for example. The US deliberately targeted that infrastructure in the first Gulf War and again this time and, for that matter, in Serbia. Those were clear violations of international law, for which people could be tried at the Hague. In fact, if the US accepted jurisdiction at the International Criminal Court, a number of our presidents, Bush senior and others, along with people like Wesley Clark probably, as commander during the attacks on Serbia, a number of them would almost certainly be up for trial as war criminals, for having violated laws of war while at the same time violating this moral core of destroying non-combatants, civilians. Beyond that, of course, there's the great loss of civilian life directly from our bombs, and from our methods of attack in general.

So the just means of war, the law in war, is violated very much by the way we've attacked. That was true in Vietnam as well, especially by our air attacks. What's coming out rather recently is how widely we violated laws of war even on the ground. I was not too aware of that when I was in Vietnam in '65–'67. I was very aware of the bombing, and I did everything I could to oppose the bombing, both of North Vietnam and in South Vietnam, in recommendations and studies. I wasn't too aware of the My Lai-type massacre which, when it came out in '68, seemed to be quite an aberration. We're learning now, right now, that a year before My Lai there was also a tighter recon group that was devastating the countryside, killing civilians indiscriminately. It was what Robert Lifton calls an atrocity-producing or atrocity-generating situation. And that's what we have in Iraq right now. The attacks on our troops there are clearly inspiring a kind of trigger-happiness and a readiness for revenge in our troops, and I think it will result in the same kind of things we saw in Vietnam.

JE: You wrote in a recent piece that this administration has within it more domestic enemies of the Bill of Rights and the Constitution than in any we've seen before. Coming from you, especially, that would strike some as a frightening claim.

That's what I was saying earlier. I think that they not only want to repeal and revoke virtually all of the progressive reforms of the New Deal and since, to really bring back an essentially unregulated, non-unionized country, but in the same way I think they want openly to see the president given the power that he was delegated by Congress, giving him virtually an open and undated blank check that simply yields to him the kind of power that other presidents would have liked to have had, but didn't dare to ask for. On the whole he's been given across-the-board license to use military force as he sees fit. They clearly are trying to repeal that aspect of our Constitution that gives Congress that authority, something the founders wrote in order to limit our going to war, to make it harder to go to war, to put that in the hands of hundreds of people instead of one man. They saw the alternative as the attribute of monarchy they most wanted to avoid. And this administration clearly now is making a bid, after 9/11, to be regarded as an elected monarch, to wipe that out of the Constitution.

Likewise, with regard to other restraints on executive power, I don't think they take seriously any merits or advantages of the Bill of Rights, unless it's the right to bear arms. The right to free speech, free assembly, I don't think they respect that at all. I'm also not sure this administration would allow itself to be voted out of office very easily.

JE: What do you mean by that?

This is just speculation, just a sense of who we're dealing with, and I think we're dealing with very dangerous men to democracy. What I mean is that if polls indicate that they have a very close election coming at them, or are even likely to be defeated because of the economy or because of lack of success in Iraq, I believe that would markedly raise the probability of a terrorist attack in this country. And it wouldn't have to be entirely a US-engineered charade, as the anthrax scare seems to have been. We don't have proof that that was encouraged at any high level, but there's every reason to think that it was done at a middle level of the US government, someone who has been covered up, essentially, since then. They have lots of stores of anthrax and, if need be, anthrax could get into the mails again. Or it could be something else, in effect opening the door to an atrocity of some sort, a major crime, that would bring public support to the side of the strong man who used the boldest rhetoric in dealing with it, the person who painted in the most black and white terms, evoked a crusade against evil.

People in this administration who are probably very secular in their own views, like Karl Rove perhaps, do feel that the religious right, the fundamentalists, the dispensationalists are essential to the constituency of George W. Bush. They feel that his father made a mistake by not complying with their cultural attitudes as much as he should have. I think that's another element in this current situation that makes it very dangerous, because their views do not only support greater Israel—they have an alliance with Likud on this subject—but they also ready them to make threats of nuclear war and to see fundamental advantages in Armageddon.

JE: How do you respond to those who say it's an exaggeration to suggest that the stakes are markedly different in this election?

I believed the stakes in the last election were huge in the nuclear area, even though I didn't foresee that Bush's interventionist policy would be anything quite as bad as it has been. As a matter of fact, once again I was fooled by George W. Bush. I heard him arguing with Gore in the debate on the question of humanitarian intervention and nation building and I thought, "Gee, he sounds better than Gore on this issue." Even so, I thought the stakes were enormous because I did foresee that he would carry out the Republican platform of rescinding our anti-ballistic missile agreement, as has happened; that he would put the nails in the coffin of the Comprehensive Test Ban Treaty; that he would move toward the testing of nuclear weapons, which I'm sure he is doing at this point; and that he'd be more ready to use nuclear weapons, which has become increasingly clear.

So I thought the stakes were vast already, and that made me very, very critical of the Green Party, of Nader's strategy toward the end of the campaign of competing in swing states. I thought the arguments for that were ludicrously outweighed by the arguments against bringing Bush in. And I believe that for Ralph Nader to say four years ago that there was no difference between these two parties and these two candidates was a lie. I did not believe that Ralph Nader could believe such a stupid statement. I think he's still saying it, essentially, and I think he's still lying. I say that with great regret because I have admired Ralph Nader for a long time, and I still do admire everything I admired him for before that campaign. It tells me that under the pressures of the campaign, even a man with the integrity and intelligence of Nader can be led to say untrue things of great danger.

I see the next campaign in the same terms. Yes, we will not solve any problems, in a fundamental way, by getting a Democratic administration in. Most of these problems will remain, and I don't think Democrats will be very quick to get out of Iraq, to let go of that oil and that strategic position, to be charged from the right wing with appeasement. We'll have all those problems with a Democrat in the White House, but we would face much, much less danger, far less imminent danger and crisis than if Bush gets another four years. Another four years of Bush and his subordinates means a police state that goes far beyond anything that a Democrat, or even another Republican, if we had that choice, would be likely to institute even in the face of a terrorist attack. The likelihood of carrying out this imperial policy and reordering the Middle East, in the face of the obvious resistance we're seeing, would be almost inevitable under Bush, and much less likely under almost any rival. And this is no romantic attitude for the Democratic Party. I would even say that it would be great to have Bush's father back, relatively speaking. We really are facing an unusually bad threat. One can, on the one hand, say that both these parties are much more similar than they claim or should be, dangerously so, no question about that—but to say that there's no difference is just blatantly false and very dangerous.

JE: Finally, given your experience with the Pentagon Papers, what's your reaction to the leaking of counterterror intelligence operative Valerie Plame's name by someone inside the White House?

Well, you were asking earlier about whether I felt any similarity between the current situation and the past, and the Joseph Wilson case came to mind. Wilson, a former ambassador, actually used his authority to say that what the president said in his State of the Union message was unfounded and wrong. And this created a threat to the White House that I think is very similar to what the Nixon White House saw in the threat I posed in putting out truth about their earlier policies. I think the Bush administration's reaction is almost identical. An operation was clearly set up in the White House to discredit Wilson and to punish him in ways that would keep others from imitating him. That reflected their own awareness that their policy depends on deception and secrecy, like every imperial policy in history. Even dictatorships have always taken great efforts to disguise what they're doing and why they're doing it to their own people and the world community. Hitler pretended that he had been attacked by Polish border guards when he went into Poland. But in democracies, all the more, these policies are vulnerable to truth. Truth is very inconvenient for them, and they really want to stamp it out. Therefore, in the White House, somebody, we don't know who exactly yet, leaked the name of Wilson's wife and her role as a clandestine operative doing something that actually needs doing, tracking the proliferation of weapons of mass destruction. Her job does require secrecy, and they gave up a process that actually does serve American security in order to punish Wilson by ending her career, even at the cost of the lives of her assets. In doing so, they broke a domestic law called the Intelligence Identity Protection Act.

As a result, this has the potential for bringing down a number of dangerous members of this administration, including Karl Rove and Scooter Libby, Cheney's chief of staff. And when you say Libby, you're pointing directly to Cheney. This is being investigated by Ashcroft, so we can't count on anything coming out of it, but it may be that it actually will come out, that they will be found out, in which case Cheney will almost surely be subject to indictment, to impeachment.

That doesn't mean the Republicans will impeach him. They won't. But it could keep them busy when it comes to planning new aggressions. They'll have to defend themselves in court. In short, I'm saying that the White House has its own plumbers operation and is breaking laws just as clearly as the White House plumbers broke laws when they went into my former psychoanalyst's office to get information to blackmail me with. That actually brought down a large part of that administration, and that could happen again. That's a hopeful note.

Amherst, Massachusetts
November 11, 2003

Stan Goff served as a soldier in Army Special Operations (Delta Force, Rangers, and Special Forces) during the invasions of Vietnam, Grenada, Haiti, and on the training grounds of the Colombian and Peruvian armed forces. He taught Military Science at the US Military Academy at West Point, conducted classified missions in El Salvador and Guatemala, and was deployed with the ill-fated Task Force Ranger (of Black Hawk Down fame) to Mogadishu. He is the author of *Hideous Dream* (Soft Skull, 2000) and *Full Spectrum Disorder: The Military in the New American Century* (Soft Skull, 2004). He is also an organizer of Bring Them Home Now, a movement of hundreds of relatives of US troops in Iraq who say their family members in uniform are being made to fight an illegal and immoral war.

JE: We're trying to clarify what seems to be driving the Bush administration's war policy. Is this about empire in your view? Is it more of a neoconservative push? Is there a difference?

I think that Democrats would have eventually attempted to put boots on the ground in Iran and Iraq. I think they would have. But I also think they would have gone about it in a different way. The larger picture is being driven by the fact that we're about to hit peak oil worldwide, and there's this emerging global competition between the US and China. There is ongoing economic rivalries between the US and Europe, and so Southwest Asia becomes a geopolitical lynchpin in asserting US demands against these other economic blocks in the future. So I think it was fairly inevitable that either party was going to do this.

I think what created a problem for the Bush administration is that they were so driven by this core group of ideologues inside their administration who have a very unhealthy affinity for the objectives of Israel, which they see as our bulwark in the region—without understanding how that impacts on the collective psyche of the other people in the region, who feel humiliated and oppressed by the actions of the Israeli government. I'm not one of those people who say this is all about the US's relation to Israel. I think that's absurd. But I do think the confluence of that interest, and the perception of the confluence of that interest, have dangerously deluded Perle, Wolfowitz, and so forth.

But they also have a tendency to surround themselves with people who tell them what they want to hear, and that's what differentiates Bush II from Bush I. I think Bush I was someone who surrounded himself with people who really did have some geopolitical acumen and who were able to conduct realistic assessments. These were people who were sort of able to disentangle what they wanted to see from what they actually saw. That capacity is lacking in this administration. They went out and couldn't find anyone to tell them what they wanted to hear, and so they just kept ruling people out until they surrounded themselves with the people who were telling them what they wanted to hear, including Ahmed Chalabi, which is just remarkable to me. He's a con-artist. He's an embezzler. If he goes to Jordan today, he'll be imprisoned for 23 years of hard labor for bank fraud. I mean, he's a crook. And he conned Donald Rumsfeld, Paul Wolfowitz, and George W. Bush into believing that he had the big picture on Iraq. He convinced these people that there was going to be no resistance. He also convinced them that they were going to be received as liberators, and that is not what happened at all.

Chalabi convinced them, and others convinced them, that there really were weapons of mass destruction in Iraq, and that they were going to find them. Their experienced intelligence people told them otherwise. Their experienced military people in the Pentagon were telling Rumsfeld all along, "This is a bad idea." Strategically and tactically, it is a bad idea—for all the reasons that we're now seeing. But again, Rumsfeld had a way of marginalizing anybody who didn't agree with him and elevating anybody who did. There's a real sense of just overwhelming hubris in the inner circle of this administration, and I think that's partly what made things go bad more quickly than they would have gone otherwise.

JE: You've written quite a bit about public perception management in war, in this war in particular. Can't one make the case that it's necessary to manage perception during wartime? That it's necessary for the troops, to assure that people support the troops, especially given, as you've said, that a large segment of our population seems anesthetized by mass media and might not pay attention to the war if it weren't for this kind of "management."

Well, I think that's 90 percent right. That's exactly what it's for. It's to continue to maintain the support of the people or, if not the support, then at least the acquiescence of the people at home. But it is also to continue to blind people to the larger and deeper realities of the war. If you can keep people focused on the day-to-day stuff of the war, then you can continue to spit it out as a morality tale. And it's not a morality tale. There are GIs over there right now engaging in stuff like thrill kills. The same kind of sociopathic stuff that went on in Vietnam is going on over there right now, and it's going on with the knowledge of people in the chain of command. But it's being overlooked because it's expedient for it to be overlooked. So it's not all black and white.

The Americans are not the good guys in the eyes of the majority of Iraqis, and the only way that people can reconcile that at home is to somehow dehumanize the Iraqis. To think about the Iraqis as a mass, as people who are too stupid or too deviant to know what's good for them, when the fact of the matter is that Saddam Hussein was fairly unpopular throughout the country. Now the polls are showing that the majority of people in Iraq are saying that they were better off under Saddam Hussein, which objectively is true. In fact, before the first invasion and the US sanctions, Iraq was a very modern state. Now, I'm not going to sit here and be an apologist for Saddam Hussein. I don't think that's my role, but I think everyone has a responsibility to at least tell the truth. And there are two sides to the truth of this. The Ba'ath Party made some mistakes. The Ba'ath Party committed some crimes. The Ba'ath Party also had some tremendous accomplishments, and that's the complex reality that people don't want to get their heads around, because they are too interested in finding the good guys and the bad guys. But we're not dealing with good guys and bad guys; we're dealing with geopolitics. And that's why it's so difficult for people to reconcile what they're seeing now—"Something's wrong and I can't quite put my finger on it; we shouldn't be getting a steady stream of casualties." Somehow all of the pieces don't fit. So there's this sort of dissonance that people are experiencing, but they don't have any way to make sense of it, because they've been convinced that the world is divided between good and evil, and they don't understand the complexities that underlie geopolitics.

The objective of this war was never to get rid of Saddam Hussein. The objective was to occupy Iraq. But they had to have a bad guy. They had to have a symbol. They had to make this palatable, because they couldn't say we were going over there to gain control of a country that can potentially be a petroleum swing producer for the rest of the world. The reason that people are experiencing dissonance right now is because they don't understand that we are in a situation. We're seeing these uneven tactical victories. We lose one; they lose five. It is so reminiscent of Vietnam that it's chilling. But at the same time, nothing seems to improve over there because people don't understand. It is not a Manichean world of good and evil.

Military actions are political in their nature and the people of the United States don't understand that. At the end of the day, military actions don't have military objectives: they have political objectives. You don't measure military success by tactical outcomes. Military success is always measured by a political outcome. That's why I can categorically say that right now the United States has lost the war in Afghanistan and it has lost the war in Iraq, even though they are successfully occupying both. The political outcomes are not the desired outcomes of the people who are running the war, and they are not going to be. They are only getting worse.

In fact, most of their actions are now making matters worse because they don't have any way to relate to the contradiction between the military reality and the political reality, which is exactly what happened in Vietnam. Westmoreland saying, "Send me more people and I can win." He never got his head around the fact that all the Vietnamese had to do to win is endure. All the Iraqis have to do to win is endure. They don't have to win any tactical victories. They just have to stay a day longer. That's an inescapable fact, and it is one that I think they understand. I hear the spin: first it was Saddam loyalists, then it was terrorists, then it was Ba'athist remnants, and now it's supposedly foreign al-Qaeda. I haven't been in Iraq, but I think you can infer that the armed resistance to the US occupation in Iraq right now is more coherent than they're letting on. The reason that you can infer this is because there seems to be the ability to fairly seamlessly shift from hard targets to soft targets in a matter of less than 24 hours.

The other thing that is just now beginning to surface that's eventually going to be a real problem for the American military in Iraq is that they haven't solved the problem of Kurdistan. Turkey is a NATO ally, and it has no intention of seeing an independent Kurdistan grow up on its southern border. Here, you have an ally that's very nervous about what the US is doing with Kurds, who've never really tried to conceal the fact that they're looking for an independent Kurdistan, and who are now actively involved in increasingly hostile encounters with Turkmens and Arabs who are in what they consider Iraqi Kurdistan, which is also, by the way, one the richest oil patches in the country. It is an oil patch within sniffing distance of both Turkey and Iran. So the Europeans have big issues with the destabilization of the situation between the Turks and the Kurds, because Germany has a huge population of Turks and Kurds, and anytime something gets inflamed down there it turns into civil unrest and potential hostility between immigrant populations in their own countries.

So this is a situation that right now is not resolvable. Where does it go from here? James Gleick wrote a book called *Chaos Theory* and in it, he makes this really good point. You can come up with a mathematical equation that shows that it's absolutely possible to take a pencil and stand it on its point. You can write that equation, but you can't do it. Donald Rumsfeld has been writing equations to stand pencils on their points but he can't do it. That's the situation they've gotten themselves into in Iraq.

JE: You were talking about the potential for thrill kills in your piece, "Hold Onto Your Humanity." I'm wondering what you were trying to get across with that piece. I'm also wondering what kind of response you got to it. Did you get any responses, in particular, from troops on the ground?

Two of the hardest days I had this year were when I said goodbye to my son, and the day after the truck bomb went off on December 11 in Ramadi, which is where he is. It took two days before we heard anything from him, and we were on pins and needles throughout that wait. I'm in a real conflict about this war, and I don't think there is any reason to try to sugar coat that.

On the one hand, I don't wish anyone ill. I don't want to see American soldiers killed and wounded. My son is one of those American soldiers and I want all of them back. I want them all back exactly the way they left. On the other hand, I understand and respect the Iraqis' right to try and expel a foreign invader. If someone invaded the US, we would do exactly the same thing. So I understand that. They are contradictory realities, but that's the way life is.

Aside from the obvious concern that every parent or every spouse or every sister or brother has for a loved one that goes into a combat zone, the obvious fear that someone could be killed or maimed, I have additional fears. I have the fear that he's over there being exposed to unhealthy amounts of depleted uranium and other potentially problematic agents that we don't know about; that he's had that whole cocktail of immunizations that haven't been tested for their interactions and may very well be responsible for a fraction of the Gulf War Syndrome from the first invasion in 1991. And one of my biggest fears is that he'll come back as crazy as I was when I came back from Vietnam.

A lot of us went crazy in different ways. Some were worse than others. Some of us got better and some of us didn't. There's a very disproportionate number of people who are homeless, people who are drug addicted, people who are suicidal, men my age and a little older who were veterans of the Vietnam conflict. Disproportionate among those are the folks who were in line units and actually saw combat. If someone takes a life in the conduct of defending themselves I don't think we should blame them, but that doesn't make it any easier. It's not the sanitized thing that everyone sees on television or in films over and over again.

First of all, the bad guy's not a bad guy; he is just another person. It's not neat, it's not clean, and it's not cathartic. It's not something that you just walk away from—forget about the stress of being in an environment where that kind of contact is a possibility, especially in a conflict where you have difficulty discriminating among the people around you, among the indigenous population, between friend and foe. It creates a situation where you have a generalized suspicion of all people and that very quickly transforms itself into a very potent form of racism. You can go to Iraq right now and the vast majority of troops over there are already referring to all Iraqis as "ragheads" or "hajjis." That's part of the process of dealing with cognitive dissonance, because if there's a possibility that I'm going to be required to kill you, I can't see you as someone like me. I can't see you as someone who is worthy of my empathy or I might not be able to defend myself.

When I was going to Special Forces medical training, we had a fourteen-week lab. It was a goat lab and in fourteen weeks we went through about 400 heads of goats. We would have to anesthetize and wound these goats and then take them into surgery. Then they'd take the goats and shoot them and stab them and shock them. They were anesthetized, and we'd go in and do combat trauma management so we would become accustomed to working with live tissue. Inevitably, within the first week that we were there, people who had no opinion about goats at all learned to hate goats. They'd all start talking about, "Oh, they're stupid animals. They're nasty. They're this and they're that." We had to find a way to remove value from them, because of what we were obligated to do to them.

That's an inevitable consequence of a situation like this, particularly with an occupying army, because they don't have any justification. They're over there, but they're not all together sure why they're over there. They've been given some reasons for being over there, but a lot of them require higher levels of denial to maintain these rationalizations. Some people withdraw into themselves and take that stuff out on themselves later with drugs and alcohol and high-risk activities. Some people actually go and seek help and try to get better. They don't need to seek help inside the military community because the job of a military psychiatrist is to return you to duty; so if they go there, they're going to get a bunch of horseshit. And some people learn to like it. That's a little harder to describe. But when it happens it's really hard to reel those folks back in, because there is a certain kind of freedom associated with breaking the last taboos. And it can be euphoric. It can give people a real sense of power, and it happens to more individuals than people would like to believe.

It's not that hard to kill a human being. It's not. When you do, lightning doesn't strike you. Everything tends to just go on the way it was before, and nothing really dramatic seems to happen. If it happens a second time or a third time, some people, for reasons I can't explain, begin to develop a thirst for it. It's not a thirst for killing the enemy. It's a thirst for killing. I don't know how many helicopter pilots I've talked to who came back from Vietnam and said, "I just loved greezin' 'em." It was the biggest thrill of their life. It was just to find somebody where there were no witnesses and hose them down—way more common than most people realize. People in My Lai got caught, but that stuff was going on every single day somewhere. Maybe not on that scale, but it was going on all the time. And it wasn't going on because we were different.

I'm with Military Families Speak Out and Veterans for Peace, and the reason I wrote that piece was because military families were starting to write into our websites very concerned about changes they saw in their loved ones. They were changes that were red flags and suggested that this type of thing was starting to happen. They were starting to see an emotional distance creep into their communications with their loved ones, a hard edge developing in people that was some indication that there might be something a little bit sociopathic or psychotic going on. They were really concerned and rightly so. I wrote the piece to describe how that process happens to some people, why it happens, and how at the very bottom of it is the ability to redefine the people whose nation you occupy as somehow less than human. Because sometimes if people recognize what's happening to them, it's easier for them to deal with it, and it might be easier for them to find some way to prevent it from taking hold.

We got hundreds and hundreds of e-mails back: e-mails from people who had loved ones from other conflicts whom they'd seen this in, sometimes who'd committed suicide. I don't know how many e-mails I've gotten from people who've known folks who committed suicide. It's devastating. Or people whose loved ones disappeared into the street or into prisons or mental institutions. We got letters from family members who said, "This helps me understand what I think I see is going on and I'm sending it to my son," "I'm sending it to my husband."

And I got e-mails from people in theater that were 60 percent positive saying, "Yeah, this is real. I'm glad you wrote this. This is important." Of the other 40 percent, there were just a handful of them that were real flames. You know, "Traitor, coward…yada, yada, yada." A lot of them were trying to persuade me that I was wrong by saying, "Well, this is not Vietnam. This is different." As if it were somehow a phenomenon that was circumscribed solely within the boundaries of the Republic of Vietnam. So, it was interesting. You never know how much of an impact it has.

I re-sent it to my son after the truck bomb went off in Ramadi and he appreciated it. He appreciated it because there was a lot of tension. The truck bomb that went off in Ramadi was delivering a carpet for a general's office. That's why they allowed the truck inside the compound. And the bomb killed one and wounded fourteen. Three Iraqis were killed. And it was inside the compound. It was not outside the compound like the news said. A lot of these troops are detailed to escort Iraqis who do things like clean crappers, bring things in and out, and deliver supplies; that's their job, to escort them. That's what the kid who got killed was doing. He was someone who went over to Iraq with my son. And the first time we talked to my son we heard that anger, that edge. It was all about these "Fuckin' Iraqis." But after he had some time to calm down, and I sent that open letter to him, he said, "Yeah, you're right," and he appreciated it. We've heard from other military families, not just about that letter, but about how, in the heat of the moment, it's really easy to fall into that. It's important that you come out of the heat of the moment and regain your perspective.

JE: Norman Mailer wrote a piece recently talking about how this war has had special resonance with white working-class men. Do you see any connection between the way this war has been accepted in the mainstream and the thrill-kill phenomenon you're talking about? In other words, is the thrill of killing something that develops on the battlefield only, or is there some version of this here, in civilian life, some vicarious pleasure that men in particular are getting from televised war that they aren't getting from their more numbed-out lives?

I'm not sure exactly where to go. I'm not sure about where Norman Mailer is going with the masculinization of white working-class males, but there's definitely super-gendered stuff going on. I think there's a lot more to it than the fact that we watch a lot of sanitized, dramatized war on TV and the movies, and then we become so brutalized as a society that we can just accept that. I'm certain that's part of it. But I think there are some social scripts that are involved. I've noticed that cultural trends have a tendency to follow what's actually going on. In periods where the military becomes more and more central to the agenda of the state, there tends to be a tailing effect where there's more and more stuff that comes out of Hollywood that's very militaristic.

But I think militarism is a kind of ideology that has been fundamentally part of an American notion of masculinity for a long time now. I think that that's really an outgrowth of the post-World War II security state, which, not inconsequentially, was the first time that the United States actually maintained a standing army. It wasn't until after the Korean War that we started to maintain a large, standing army all the time. I don't want to generate any interservice rivalry there. I think the notion that people's ideas tend to follow their practices is true. And the military has been very central to the whole American project for the last few decades, and at points where that peaks, militarism tends to peak with it.

There's a constant renegotiation, redefinition, of American masculinity. And there are numerous masculinities. The epitome of that is always the military person—even though it's a caricature. It's a complete caricature. It's always portrayed in the mass media and entertainment as someone who's a rugged individualist in possession of all of these social skills who overcomes all adversity and obstacles. But in fact, military life is an institution. It very much tries to suppress individuality. Not individuality in terms of personality, but individualism; it encourages teamwork because it's very much about collectivity. It's one of the contradictions that a lot of people are going to see with the latest recruiting drives, because the recruiting drives tend to pander to what people want to see. They pander to these caricatures. Look at this "Army of One" campaign. I mean, what horseshit! An army of one? There are no armies of one! By definition there's no such thing as an army of one. You're never anything smaller than your fire team. You're always part of a group, and you always subordinate your interests for the common good of the group. It's a very cooperative thing internally. In fact, competition is ruthlessly driven out of everything except the office of personnel management system inside the military.

I have to wonder about the young recruits who go in with the idea of being in an army of one, thinking, "I'm going to get a skill, I'm going to be a special person, and everyone's going to look up to me." I wonder how they react once they get in there and find out what they're really doing is being submerged into the most thorough-going bureaucracy in the United States. How many people are going to be disappointed about that, in addition to the fact that the Iraq war is creating a retention and recruitment crisis?

JE: Turning to politics, how do you explain the male side of the gender gap that's developed since Nixon, the growing popularity of the Republican Party with men? Why have so many working-class white guys reached a point where they're voting Republican in greater numbers?

I don't think there's any one appeal of the Republicans. The Republicans have multiple constituencies. They've got sort of this libertarian group that's really interested in their fiscal conservatism and couldn't care less if people are snorting cocaine or having gay sex and all that stuff. They don't care. They only want to make sure you don't raise taxes on us. A huge chunk of the Republican Party's popular base is this millenarian Christianity. That can't be discounted. Without that there would be no Republican party. That kind of Christianity is closely associated with a lot of the evangelical religious groups of the South, and I think that's a relationship between the party and white working-class males in particular who have grown up since the Nixon "Southern Strategy" that specifically targeted its message around growing resentment against the political and social gains that were being made by African Americans and by women. And it was directed toward the South.

When, generation after generation, one's identity is completely tangled up in the polarity of male/female, masculine/feminine, and black/white, then that can be very irrationally threatening. I think it has created a backlash. In fact, people don't try to disaggregate the sex and race thing either. There's nothing that will inflame the political passions of many white males, both Southern and Northern, like seeing a black male with a white female. Now what's that about? We need to unpack that if we're going to really understand the appeal that demagogues in the Republican Party have. It's not a rational appeal, and that's why the notion that we can try to dissuade people from that appeal is not correct—because we haven't figured out what's at the bottom of it. In my opinion, it's a form of deep sexual panic, and this gender thing goes deep. There's nothing we're trained in more intensively from birth than our gender identity, and that training is preliterate; it is pre-everything. It's the first thing we understand about ourselves in terms of differentiating ourselves from other human beings: our gender. With regard to race, every campaign to roll back the social and political gains of black people in this country has been associated with propaganda campaigns that talk about protecting white womanhood—from the overthrow of Reconstruction to the implementation of Jim Crow, from the fight to keep blacks out of white units in the military to the Civil Rights Movement and the abolition of legal Jim Crow.

The appeal is still there today, even when talking about neighborhood schools initiatives. For a lot of people, it's not rational. It's about making sure white girls don't end with black boys. That's what it's about. How do I back that psychologically? I'm probably not qualified to do that. I've got my own ideas. But they're just based on my own experience being around white people all of my life, Southern white people. What's left of my family still lives in Arkansas, so it's not something I'm unfamiliar with. You want to get Billy-Bob mad? Send him a picture of a white woman with a black man. That's something that's political as hell.

JE: Given all this militaristic and macho bravado and the political edge to all of it, how do you see this election in terms of this president's ability to run on security?

You know, Bush is vulnerable on all the other stuff: the Bush administration is vulnerable on the war and it is vulnerable on homeland security. You can talk to any fire department or police department in the country right now, and they haven't done a damn thing on homeland security. They've done zilch; they've done nothing. They generate these orange alerts to frighten people, but in terms of what they've actually done to improve domestic security, they've done nothing. They've done less than nothing. In fact, they've gone out and systematically attacked corporate whistle blowers who are telling people that our facilities are not secure. The Bush administration has been the most ruthless administration in living memory in going after whistle blowers, and particularly whistle blowers that threaten corporate profits or threaten some federal agencies. If the Democrats go after them on homeland security, they'll eat them up.

JE: Finally, what's your take on the overall quality of political discourse in the wake of 9/11 and now during the war, especially as we head into the height of the campaign season?

There's a tendency to regard certain things as off-limits for some reason, out of some kind of a notion of decorum or respectability, which I don't get. Because behind all of those lies, they do some things that lack decorum that people don't even know about.

I for one don't think that we should censor photographs of people that are wounded or are dead. I think we should see them in living color every single night. They hide behind, "That would be insensitive." Well, of course it would be insensitive. We need to be sensitized to all the stuff that's really going on. There's this notion of respectability that also translates into what's on-limits and off-limits.

You have to look at what the counter-punch capacity is. There are a lot of people that should be asking what the Bush administration knew prior to 9/11, because the evidence is overwhelming that they had full knowledge that something was going on and they just didn't do a good job of stopping it. That's the reality. Now, that's not the same thing as saying that the Bush administration engineered it. There's some of that out there, too. But if you say that the Bush administration ignored its intelligence professionals and set up a situation where this could happen, that's off-limits. That's politically off-limits. Nobody will talk about that. And part of the reason they won't talk about it is because they can get counter-punched, which will put them in the same camp as the conspiracy nuts. There's this notion that there are some things that you don't go after.

I'm curious, just out of pure morbid curiosity, to see what happens after Super Tuesday, after the Democrats get done eating their own young. I'm real interested to see if the Democratic Party will stab their nominee in the back, which they've done in the past and they might do again. That's why I've got no respect for them. But if they get together, there's some heavy artillery they can release on the Bush administration. There's so much stuff that's not being discussed right now, and the cumulative weight of it all between March and November could be overwhelming, especially if things continue to go sour in Iraq.

I for one can't see how they can do anything else. A couple of manufactured stories at the right times, maybe the right orange alert, and the effective use of Diebold voting systems, and maybe they can pull it off again. I don't know. We'll see.

Raleigh, North Carolina
January 5, 2004

WILLIAM HARTUNG

William Hartung is an internationally recognized expert on the arms trade, the economics of military spending, and American foreign policy. He is director of the Project on the Control of the International Arms Trade at the World Policy Institute and is the author or co-author of numerous books and studies, including *And Weapons for All* (Harper Collins, 1994), *The Changing Dynamics of US Defense Policy and Budgeting in the Post-Cold War Era* (Greenwood Press, 1999) and *How Much Are You Making on the War, Daddy? A Quick and Dirty Guide to War Profiteering in the Bush Administration* (Nation Books, 2004).

JE: The Bush administration is amassing a massive campaign war chest to depict George W. Bush as a strong and steady leader in precarious times. What advice would you give American citizens about how to understand the rhetoric and imagery that's about to be unleashed on them?

Well, if I had a little window into the average American household, if I had five minutes on their TV screen at night, I would tell them how to decode the propaganda that we are going to see from President Bush about security. I would say to them: First, don't just look at the images—Bush landing on an aircraft carrier, Bush surrounding himself with our troops, Bush standing at the weapons factory. His public relations experts want him to look tough, they want him to look strong—in fact, even on Earth Day, the image they chose was him with an axe in his hand, clearing trails in the Adirondacks. This administration is so dripping with testosterone, that even to celebrate Earth Day this guy has to have a weapon in his hand. That tactic does work with people because it's *High Noon* all over again. In a recent survey of what movies presidents watch, *High Noon* was right up there. Of course, they didn't get the part of *High Noon* that was about standing up to McCarthyism, all they got was the part about using the gun.

I think they're hoping that people will just look at the image and feel that since 9/11 Bush has made defending us his sole focus. He's overthrown two governments, he's spent all this money, but he hasn't really done the things that really would make the most sense to protect us against terrorism. And that's when people would have to take the remote, turn off the TV, and read some independent news sources. With just a little bit of time—if people spent 15 minutes a day informing themselves instead of just accepting what they're handed—I think it would be clear that, first of all, we went into Iraq on the argument that Saddam Hussein was on the verge of getting nuclear weapons. We now know that justification is false. The Bush administration went into Iraq on the basis that Saddam Hussein had close links to al-Qaeda. We now know that that is not the case, and that the administration actually fabricated and falsified and exaggerated evidence to give that impression to the American people. I think one of the most shameful episodes came from one of the most decent men in the administration—Colin Powell, when he stood up at the United Nations and held up a vial of fake Anthrax while he was making the case against Saddam Hussein. He didn't say that Saddam Hussein was behind the Anthrax attacks, but that's what that picture said when they put it on the cover of *Newsweek*. People thought, "Iraq... Anthrax... Saddam Hussein... all part of the same thing."

In fact, close to 50 percent of Americans think that Saddam Hussein was behind the 9/11 attacks and that's because of the body language of the Bush administration, because of their allies on the right in the media and in foundations. What the Bush administration really saw after 9/11 was an opportunity to implement a goal that they'd had for a long time, which was to use the end of the cold war not as a reason to cut back US forces, but as a reason to say, "Hallelujah! We're the only superpower! If we really build up our military here, we can really push folks around, we can remake the globe in ways that we think are better for the United States and our interests." This attitude has a lot to do with making sure you have good friends in the oil-producing regions and making sure that you're not bound by treaties that keep you from using your power the way that you want to use it—that's the whole mantra of the neoconservative circle around President Bush.

JE: Can you talk about the influence of neoconservativism on this administration since 9/11? I'm wondering if you see the turn US foreign policy has taken, especially the decision to go to war in Iraq, as driven by the ideological, moral vision of the neocons, by a more realist foreign policy sensibility, or by American corporate interests? Maybe a mix of all three?

There's something different about this group around Bush. They are a special kind of Republican. They're against international institutions, they don't trust our allies, they prefer to use force over diplomacy, and, of course, they don't mind profiting from all of this while they're doing it. But even a guy like Richard Perle, whose hand's so deep into the cookie jar that he needs surgery to get it removed, is actually motivated more by ideology than by the money.

Their worldview really goes back to the Henry Jackson school of thought. Henry Jackson was a conservative Democrat in the '70s, a combination of pro-Israel and harshly anti-Soviet. He was the backbone in setting the stage for the Reagan revolution. A lot of guys who worked for Henry Jackson—like Richard Perle and Frank Gaffney, who runs the Center for Security Policy (the full-time cheerleading outfit for Star Wars and multi-tiered missile defense and so forth)—went from being moderate Democrats to conservative Democrats to Reaganites, and it had to do with their notion that you couldn't really do business with the Soviet Union. They believed that detente wasn't going to work; you had to be able to beat them militarily. In 1980, Keith Payne co-authored an article called "Victory is Possible" about how you could win a nuclear war. He said that in a war against the Soviets, maybe we'd lose 20 million people, but we could prevail. His argument was, "If you're gonna play the nuclear game, you've got to play to win."

That sentiment was rejected by Reagan himself in his second term, when he made these deals with Gorbachev. He made a statement in which he said a nuclear war can never be won and should never be fought, and that was partly his own beliefs coming around and it was partly his response to the peace movement that was taking on his policies. But the neoconservatives—their attitudes didn't change. Reagan changed with the times, he adjusted, he made deals with Gorbachev, he wanted to get rid of nuclear weapons, and he put Star Wars on the backburner. Guys like Frank Gaffney who were in Reagan's Pentagon were so outraged about this that they resigned. They went into these conservative think tanks, funded by Richard Mellon Scaife, the Coors family and, in Gaffney's case, also by weapons contractors like Lockheed Martin and so forth.

The neocons honed these "peace-through-strength," unilateral positions from the late '80s, through the Clinton era, culminating in the Project for the New American Century, which was founded in Clinton's second term. They wanted to return to the Ronald Reagan of the first term. This was the Ronald Reagan who joked around before his weekly radio address about nuclear war, saying "the bombing starts in five minutes"; this is the Ronald Reagan who said that the Soviet Union was an "evil empire" that could never be bargained with. They're still stuck in that moment in time. They never made the transition that Reagan made, and so they spent the '80s and '90s refining those unilateralist positions. Then in Herbert Walker Bush's administration, Wolfowitz and I. Lewis Libby, who was Cheney's deputy, and a number of the others actually drafted a national security strategy based on the idea that the United States should not only dominate our adversaries, but we should have so much military power that even our friends are afraid of us. This caused uproar when it was leaked and the Europeans got upset, and people like Colin Powell and George Herbert Walker Bush and, to some extent, even Cheney, said, This is kind of out there, guys. You've got to tone that down, because the end of cold war is not necessarily a green light for us to go ballistic in building up our military and pushing countries around, using the sword rather than diplomacy. But these guys never let go of that.

They refined these ideas in conservative think tanks, and they found a soul mate in George W. Bush, because he's more in tune with the Reagan of the first term than he is with his own father. In fact, when his advisers used to give him suggestions about things that he might do when he was campaigning, they said he always pushed them to go further. He didn't care about the ABM Treaty; he wanted missile defense. He asked them why we need an army, which seems to have an interesting reformist bent to it. But if you look at that statement in light of these fights between Rumsfeld and the army, it's clear they don't like the army because the army is grounded in some reality. They have to occupy countries; they have to deal with people face to face. Rumsfeld and the others want to do things at a distance; they want to have weapons in space; they want to bomb from 15,000 feet. They don't want to get down into the messy politics of these countries, which is why they're trying to run Iraq like some sort of privatized 51st state, and it's just not working.

JE: Some people have down-played the "neo" aspect of what the neoconservatives are doing and have argued that what we are seeing now is just an extreme example of "crony capitalism." How would you respond to that?

They're giving all these contracts to their buddies, like Halliburton and Bechtel and so forth, but they're not even delivering the goods. There's been articles recently saying that our troops don't even have enough water to drink. They get limited to a liter and a half a day because Halliburton can't handle the job. But they've got a no-bid contract with the army that was renewed. Dick Cheney (who went on to become

CEO at Halliburton) as secretary of defense under H. W. Bush, created this opportunity. He's the one who said, "Let's privatize the logistics of our overseas forces. Let's have private companies do essentially military planning for us. Let's have them maintain our vehicles, feed our troops, create the showers, build the bases..." He created that model of privatizing it, then, a few years later, he goes to work for the company that's benefiting from it, Halliburton. Halliburton then lost the contract while Cheney was CEO and regained it after Cheney was vice president. One of the reasons they got that contract back is because the folks in the Pentagon were saying, "Well, maybe this will sit well with the V.P.," and so forth. Even if he didn't intervene directly, the fact that it's the vice president's former company, the fact that he's still getting checks from them because his golden parachute was so huge, is very influential. They couldn't figure out how many different ways to slice and dice it, so on his financial disclosure form he says, "Well, actually I get somewhere between $180 thousand and a million dollars a year from Halliburton as part of my golden parachute I got when I left the company." His wife, Lynn, who's a neocon in her own right, spent seven years on the board of Lockheed Martin and is getting deferred compensation from the nation's largest military contractor. The Cheney family is essentially still on the payroll of the military industrial complex.

Similarly, George W. Bush's father gets 100 thousand dollars a pop to go give overseas speeches for the Carlyle group, which invests in military companies and is run by Frank Carlucci, Donald Rumsfeld's college roommate at Princeton.

These guys are thick as thieves, but I think it's not so much greed—they feel it's a sense of entitlement. They think they're the chosen ones who are supposed to be running the world. As part of that, since they believe in free markets and entrepreneurship and so forth, they feel that all of this money that keeps landing in their lap is just a nice by-product of the fact that they're better and better everyday in every way, fighting the good fight for humanity. They have huge blind spots and they don't understand that the stuff they're doing looks corrupt to almost everybody else in the world. The first contract for the rebuilding of Iraq was a no-bid, secret contract that went to the company that the vice president of the United States used to run, while neither our own allies, the British, who helped capture some of that territory, nor other American companies that could have done a better job, got to bid.

Perle and Woolsey and that whole gang around Rumsfeld are ideologues first. Even if you look at their business careers, most of their business connections are through a sort of crony capitalism. It's not because Dick Cheney was an excellent manager that they hired him at Halliburton. He went on a fishing trip with the head of the company and they said, Wow, everybody knows him in the Middle East, because he was the guy that helped win the Gulf War. He could open a lot of doors for us. But it wasn't because he was a fantastic manager. In fact, he almost bankrupted the company because he decided to buy Dresser Industries, which had all these unfunded liabilities related to asbestos. If he hadn't been busy pulling strings to get them government contracts, they might well have gone under—under his tenure.

Even Rumsfeld, who's got this kind of aura of having been this wonderful business executive, his first big job was handed to him by a guy named Ted Forstmann. Forstmann was a take-over specialist who help fund Empower America, one of the right-wing, neoconservative think tanks that Rumsfeld is on the board of, which, among other things, took out ads against Democratic senators in the '90s, questioning their patriotism for not supporting the full-bore Republican version of Star Wars. Forstmann took over this company, General Instrument, and installed Rumsfeld as the CEO. This is not Rumsfeld climbing the corporate ladder, this is not Rumsfeld showing his acumen as a businessman, this is Rumsfeld just having a buddy of his that he did political work with say, "Oh, here's a company to run." They run Washington the way Suharto used to run Indonesia. It's crony capitalism at its worst—and you can do that for a while, but eventually you're going to start hollowing out our economy. You're going to undermine people's faith in our democracy.

That's the point we're coming to now, where we can't just accept these guys based on the images they're projecting. We have to look very carefully at what it is they're doing. When Eisenhower warned about the military industrial complex, this is the kind of thing he was talking about, but he said we have to watch out for influence, whether sought or unsought, by the military industrial complex—by virtue of how large it is, it will inhabit space, accumulate power, and so forth. This is different. These guys are consciously using the military industrial complex as a tool to extend their own power, and I don't think even Eisenhower anticipated that anyone would be that bold and that brash. But Bush, he's doing his military industrial complex tour; after he landed on the carrier, he gave a speech the next day at United Defense in front of the big sign that said "United Defense." United Defense is owned by the Carlyle Group, which employs his father on retainer and James Baker, who is the one who helped him push through in the elections in Florida.

JE: How exactly does 9/11 fit into this?

The September 11 attacks gave them the political space to pursue their predetermined goals because, after September 11, people felt traumatized and they wanted to be defended; they weren't really in the mood to ask about the details. Bush came riding in saying, "I'm going to make this job one. I'm going into Afghanistan," where at least there was a link. The al-Qaeda training camps were there, and though it may not have been the smartest way to do it, there was a logic to it. But then they went on to Iraq—now they're talking about Iran and North Korea—and all of a sudden the issue of al-Qaeda has been pushed into the background. Although they have caught some of their people and disrupted al-Qaeda operations in Afghanistan, al-Qaeda is a network that operates in 60 countries, and operates pretty much off the grid. They launder money, they run illegal businesses, and they don't need a government to support them. Those guys that hit the Trade Center were twenty disciplined individuals spending a couple years of their lives and $200,000 to $500,000.

The problem with that kind of threat is that if people are that determined to do it, it's very difficult to stop. And overthrowing the government of Iraq or Afghanistan or Iran or North Korea has no bearing on whether this group can operate. In fact, it may make it easier for them because the United States posturing as the ugly American, brandishing the sword all over the world, pushing folks around, is almost a perfect recruiting poster for bin Laden and his guys. They can then say, "See? This is what the Americans are about. They're about using force. They're about trampling our dignity. And therefore, the only way to deal with them is through force—you've got to fight fire with fire."

If we had taken a more subtle strategy, which some of Bush's advisers suggested after September 11, our actions would have been more difficult to sell to the public because you wouldn't get the fireworks, the big images, the John Wayne thing. But a lot of things that work against this kind of terrorism are quiet, they're subtle, they're negotiations, they're agreements with governments to share information, they're intelligence and law enforcement cooperation. But those strategies don't make the kind of simple imagery that Bush is trying to ride to reelection. The most outrageous image for me, as somebody who lives in New York City, is the one he creates by having the Republican convention in our city. He's going to go to the Trade Center, lay the stone for the memorial, and he's going to politicize what should be sacred ground, the ground where those people died and where those heroes did what they did. He is going to exploit that emotion tied to the event to push his reelection and he is going to incorporate that image into his campaign. The Bush administration has realized that in American politics, images count for a lot. People may forget all the details, but the picture of him doing the Top Gun landing on the aircraft carrier will endure—and that's what they're hoping to do in New York City.

JE: Do you think any of the actions of the administration since 9/11 have made Americans safer and more secure?

The New York City Fire Department still doesn't have experts who can identify chemical weapons. Our bridges and tunnels do not have radiation detectors, so if somebody wanted to bring radioactive material in, it's dumb luck whether we catch them. They still haven't coordinated the watch lists among the various federal agencies to know who shouldn't be coming into the country, which is how some of the 9/11 hijackers made it in here in the first place. So, all the nuts and bolts, the boring stuff that doesn't involve blowing things up and having pictures for the evening news, is not being attended to.

In fact, there's a guy named Rand Beers who was a top official of Bush's National Security Council who resigned, saying, "You guys are fighting the wrong war here. You're over in Afghanistan, you're over in Iraq; you're not securing our homeland; you're not doing the nuts and bolts stuff that needs to be done. This whole Iraq adventure is just a sideshow that is distracting us from what we really need to do to protect ourselves." Not only did Beers resign, but two months later he came back as a top aide to John Kerry for president, which is almost unheard of for somebody who has a career in foreign service, a career government official like that. He not only resigned in that public way, but then said, "I'm going to figure out who's the most likely person to get you guys out of here, and I'm going to help them make that happen."

The people who really know what it takes to secure the country are very upset with Bush's approach, with all his grandstanding and all his posturing, and a lot of the professional intelligence community is upset about his administration distorting intelligence. The army is virtually at war with Rumsfeld and Wolfowitz over their miscalculations about what it would take to secure Iraq after getting rid of Saddam Hussein's regime. The Army turned out to be right. General Shinseki was right that they were going to need a couple hundred thousand troops. They ridiculed him. They tried to speed up his retirement. They said he was wildly off the mark, but who was saying that? Paul Wolfowitz. Paul Wolfowitz has never fired a shot in anger. He has never commanded troops. Eric Shinseki was in charge of our troops in the Balkans. He knew what peacekeeping was about, but these guys who claimed to be protecting our security are not taking the advice of the professionals. The professional intelligence community, the professional foreign service, the professional military are all being shoved aside by these neoconservatives, most of whom are chicken hawks who, when they got the chance to serve their country, ducked it; they got student deferments; they got their fathers to pull strings. Now, they're sending other people's kids over there to Iraq and it's open season on US troops over there. Every nutcase in the world who's got a beef with the United States knows where to go—just slip into Iraq, do a suicide bombing or take a shot at somebody.

They've got us bogged down in the wrong places, and they're making the threat to our troops and to our country greater. And when people like Wolfowitz and Perle and Rumsfeld distort intelligence and tinker with the process by which the president is supposed to get objective information about the threats to our country, that's actionable. These guys should be brought up on charges. There should be an investigation about whether these guys should be allowed to serve our country anymore, because it's criminal to send our troops to war based on falsified intelligence, based on puffed-up, exaggerated details. In the United Kingdom, where they have a system where the prime minister can't hide, Tony Blair's job is on the line for exactly those same kinds of things. Here in America, George Bush lands on an aircraft carrier, he does a ceremony at the Trade Center, and all is supposed to be forgiven.

JE: Every presidential election, it seems, inevitably gets talked about as "historic," as carrying unprecedented importance. This time around we're hearing that again, but it feels a bit more credible, a bit more in tune with history. For you, what are the stakes in the 2004 election?

What it really comes down to is: are the American voters going to sit still for this? Are we going to treat our democracy like some sort of spectator sport, like watching the Super Bowl? Or are we going to ask a little more of ourselves this time? Are we going to explore their claims? Are we going to look at the details of what this administration has actually done? Because I think they're out of line, not only with what a Democrat would do, but also with the traditions of their party. They're killing arms control treatises, like the Anti-Ballistic Missile Treaty, which was negotiated by that great radical, Richard Nixon. So, this is not just a Republican take-over; this is a very specific wing of the Republican Party—it's neoconservative, it's unilateralist, it doesn't believe in the rule of law, and it doesn't believe you have to tell the public the truth.

Just look at the number of people in this administration who are alumni of the Iran Contra Affair: John Poindexter at the Pentagon, who recently got ousted for some ridiculous scheme about having a future's market for terrorism run by the Department of Defense; their guy for Latin America, Otto Reich, who was serving until the Congress refused to confirm him, but they kept him around—he was the propaganda arm of Iran Contra. Elliot Abrams is now an envoy for Middle East peace and that's an outrage. Abrams was involved in trading arms to Iran to swap for hostages and aided and abetted a government that they claimed was helping terrorist regimes. Yet these guys are worried about whether some professor at a teach-in says something that they think is insufficiently patriotic. These are the guys who are unpatriotic. These are the guys who are undermining our democracy. And they're not teaching in school somewhere; they're running the country. They have their hands on the steering wheel.

If the public understood what a serious moment this is, that it's not just "they all do it," that it's not just another administration, I think people would rise up in outrage and they would throw these guys out by such a huge margin they wouldn't even begin to know how to steal enough votes to keep themselves in power. But I fear that this will not be the case. I fear that it's going to be a close election and that these images are going to mean a lot. Think of past elections, think of Michael Dukakis, for example, and you see him riding around in the tank looking like Snoopy. You remember the Willy Horton ad against him. You don't think of substantive things because our elections rarely turn on substantive issues anymore. This is one that needs to be decided on the substance. Our country faces real threats and these guys are not going after the right threats. They are pursuing a preexisting agenda under the guise of fighting terrorism, an agenda that is going to bankrupt our country, that is going to put our troops at risk, and that is going to make the terrorist threat to us grow over time, instead of diminish.

JE: In your view, what is the invasion of Iraq really about?

A lot of people have asked, "If Iraq wasn't about fighting terrorism, what was it about?" Some people have said it's about oil and that's not quite right. It's about power. It gives them power in several ways. Right now they control the tap on Iraqi oil. Not only will there be monetary benefits, more importantly, there will be global power benefits. If they have their thumb on that Middle East oil tap, they can use it also to leverage the Saudis, to get them a little more into line, a little less misbehaving with their folks funding terrorists and so forth. If they've got control of that Middle East region in the geopolitical sense, they also have much more leverage over our European allies, over allies in Asia, and it's a way of short-circuiting the fact that their overall policy for the economy is a mess.

In one sense, they're using Iraq as a little cash machine to fund their re-election, to give contracts to their friends, to bail out the US economy from the various miscues of their own economic policies. They want to remake the map of the world and they want compliant governments that are going to be run the way they want to see them run. One of the reasons they're not working with the UN in Iraq is that people like Wolfowitz and others in this administration have said that they don't want the UN in there, or the French and the Germans, because God forbid Iraq starts having German labor practices—unions and things like that. They view Iraq as a little laboratory for trying out their ideas about privatization, about free markets, their notion of democracy, which is a very diminished notion of democracy, much like they employed here when they seized the election in Florida—they didn't care whether the votes got counted. They want people in power that they can control; they don't want just any old person from Iraq who happens to be a democrat running that new government.

It's the power to use military and energy resources to reshape the globe in the way they think it should be shaped that motivates them. If you see the pictures of Rumsfeld and Wolfowitz looking at the map of the world in the situation room, joking around, you can tell this is what they live for. It's not just the money: it's the power, and you can't have the power unless you control the US military machine, which is why they went from these very high-paying jobs in industry back into this administration. They think this is their last chance to put their stamp on the world and they are intent on doing it, and unless we stop them, they will.

Manchester, New Hampshire
August 29, 2003

CHALMERS JOHNSON

Chalmers Johnson is president of the Japan Policy Research Institute and professor emeritus at the University of California, San Diego. He is the author of twelve books, including *Blowback: The Costs and Consequences of American Empire* (Henry Holt, 2000) and *The Sorrows of Empire: Militarism, Secrecy, and the End of the Republic* (Metropolitan Books, 2004).

SJ: In March of 2000 you released a book entitled Blowback *that became a big seller after 9/11. What is blowback?*

Blowback is a term the CIA invented. It's a bit of jargon. Blowback means not just unintended consequences of foreign policy actions, but the unintended consequences of covert activities that have been kept secret from the American public. So blowback simply means retaliation. And when retaliation hits from the people who were on the receiving end of our covert actions, the American public has no way to put it in context.

SJ: How does 9/11 fit into this?

9/11 was almost the classic example of blowback. That is, it is almost surely the most important use of political terrorism in the history of international relations. But the terrorism here was carried out by people who were our former "assets," as the CIA puts it—former agents of ours, people whom we lavishly supported in the '80s in Afghanistan to serve our interests against the Soviet Union. Once the Soviet Union, in 1989, withdrew from Afghanistan, we abandoned them. The country fell into a disastrous civil war that was ultimately won by the fundamentalist-motivated Taliban, who instituted a repressive, religiously sanctioned regime in Afghanistan. The people who thought they were our allies, including most prominently Osama bin Laden, the son of a very wealthy Saudi Arabian family, a man who joined the CIA and the Pakistanis in recruiting militants from around the world to fight against the Russians.

Bin Laden was disgusted by the fact that the Americans simply walked away and abandoned the country that they had helped to devastate. I mean Kabul in the early '90s looked like Hiroshima, it had been so badly decimated. He was also disgusted by the fact that after 1991 we based troops for the first time in Saudi Arabia, allegedly to defend the House of Saud, the royal house of Saudi Arabia. This was insulting and aggravating to many patriotic Saudis because these Americans were infidels being introduced into a country whose government is charged with defending the two most sacred sites in Islam, Mecca and Medina. For the United States it was a stupid thing to do. Even if military force could have influenced in any way the stability of the extremely authoritarian and dictatorial government of Saudi Arabia, such force should not have been based in Saudi Arabia. It should have been put aboard aircraft carriers or something like that, which would have been every bit as effective as putting 20,000 American troops at Prince Sultan airbase. This then led Osama bin Laden to become an enemy of the United States.

In fact, 9/11 was late in the day. He had already attacked our embassies in East Africa, American troops elsewhere, and the *USS Cole*. The World Trade Center had also already been attacked once. This was not, as the president put it, an attack on our values or an attack on America as Americans. It was an attack on our foreign policy by people who felt deeply aggrieved by it. They turned to an almost classic example of terrorism—what the Department of Defense calls asymmetric warfare—an attack on innocent bystanders in order to draw attention to the crimes of the invulnerable. This also made clear that "innocent bystanders" only refers to workers in the World Trade Center. They were not innocent bystanders in the Pentagon. That was the right target for these people, and they went to it in a ruthless manner. But it was blowback, pure and simple.

The interesting thing to me is when, on the morning of September 11, 2001, I was called by my publisher to say that blowback big-time just hit, neither of us instantaneously turned to Arabic or Islamic terrorism. We thought that it could be Chileans, Argentinians, Indonesians, Okinawans, any number of people around the world who have deep and quite legitimate grievances against the United States. In those days, just after 9/11, I thought that probably one of the most tragic scenes I had ever seen on American television was American women standing in lower Manhattan holding up photographs of what they feared were their dead husbands, brothers, children, lovers, asking for information. As I stared at these pictures, I said, Of course. I've seen this somewhere before, haven't I? These are the women of Argentina and Chile, holding up pictures and inventing a new phrase in Spanish, "*los desaparecidos*," "the disappeared," because they didn't dare say what they knew full well—that with the support of the American government, these people had simply been seized and executed, usually tortured first.

We knew that 9/11 was blowback, but we refused to say so. Rather than ever asking questions, like the most obvious forensic questions: What were the motives of these Saudi Arabian suicidal terrorists? We instead began to say that this was a clash of civilizations, that medieval Islam was attacking us because of envy for our lifestyle, or something of this sort. This was clearly a way of diverting attention from the fact that arguably, some very high-ranking officials of the American government bore at least partial responsibility for the deaths of close to 3,000 of their fellow citizens that day. That is, the line of descent from these particular terrorists goes back directly into Middle Eastern politics, the politics of oil, the overthrow of the Shah in 1979, and in the same year the invasion by the Soviet Union of Afghanistan. Our determination, as we put it at the time, was to give the Soviet Union its Vietnam by recruiting young militants around the world, in a sort of modern version of the Abraham Lincoln brigade to fight against the Soviet Union. None of this was brought out.

The people surrounding the president were the authors of these policies. They should have come forward and talked about it, discussed it, identified it. They didn't do so. They remained silent. And that, to my way of thinking, is as great a crime against the Constitution as some of the others that have followed.

SJ: It's interesting that the further we get from 9/11, the more the attack on the Pentagon seems to disappear from public view, lost in the media coverage. Why might that be?

Clearly it's part of the propaganda waged against terrorism to argue that they are attacking what they, and everyone else would agree, are innocent bystanders. It's at least arguable whether office workers sitting above the 75th floor were legitimate military targets in an international struggle. There is no argument about the Pentagon. It's *the* place. It has troops in 130 countries around the world. It's the place that runs 725 military bases in other people's countries. Therefore the attack on the Pentagon is something that the neoconservatives who have been managing our foreign policy since 9/11 would obviously not have drawn attention to. It would be the same way if there had been an attack on the Central Intelligence Agency. These are the two tremendous sources of power in our government.

The Pentagon is not a Department of Defense. It is an alternative seat of government on the south bank of the Potomac River. Forty percent of its budget is totally secret. All of the budgets of the intelligence agencies are secret and in violation of perhaps one of the most famous lines in the Constitution: "The public shall know how its money is being spent." That's what turns the country into a democracy, rather than a kingdom or a monarchy or something of that sort. It hasn't been honored in this country since World War II. The Manhattan project was totally secret, buried in the defense budget. No one ever got the full details of it and that's been the case since the mid-1940s. But there is no doubt that the people managing our government today (with the mindset of imperialists) would like to avoid discussing the attack on the Pentagon. Because if you focus on it, then you start thinking why the Pentagon? Why our military? What are they doing that would cause people to hate us? And to ask the question is virtually to answer it.

SJ: Your latest book is called The Sorrows of Empire. *For many Americans "empire" is a very abstract term. Could you elaborate on why you believe America is an empire?*

Classically, of course, empire simply means the acquisition, the domination, the military preponderance over foreign countries to bring them in some ways into your orbit, into your world. There are lots of different forms of imperialism, from colonialism to the satellite. The latter is a country whose foreign policy completely revolves around an imperial power, such as the famous satellites of the Soviet Union in East Europe and the American satellites today—places like Japan and South Korea, which cannot make a decision without getting the approval of Washington.

But the modern form of empire is manifest above all in the case of the United States, which likes to call itself a superpower. In this modern empire the equivalent of the colony is the military base. We have 703 of them in other peoples' countries. They stretch from Greenland to Australia, from Japan to Iceland. They are on every continent on Earth, except for Antarctica. In addition to that, we have some thirteen super-carriers that form carrier task forces that dominate the waters of the world. We can go anywhere with them. There's nothing that can stand up to them. And this empire has its own geography of closed-off areas, the base in which we often try to recreate American life abroad. There are

234 military golf courses around the world to keep the troops happy, and we supply airplanes to fly the admirals and generals to play golf or to go to the armed forces ski resort at Garmesh in the Bavarian Alps.

Not everything duplicates America abroad. A very large proportion of the armed forces today are female, but you can't get an abortion in the military hospital abroad. Last year there were some 14,000 sexual assaults on women in the armed forces. If you find yourself pregnant in Iraq right now, you have no choice but to go onto the market, so to speak, and try to negotiate an abortion in Baghdad, which I doubt is easy or pleasant. This reflects, of course, the religious fundamentalists that govern our country because, of course, you could get an abortion if you were in the United States.

It's a complex world that no one fully appreciates. Take on old British base that we run today, Diego Garcia in the Indian Ocean, from which we flew all three of our main strategic weapons, the B-52, the B-2, the B-1 for the attack on Iraq. We have no problems on Diego Garcia, because when we acquired it from the English, we deported every single indigenous person to the Seychelle Islands where they sit today in poverty. Okinawa is another classic case. It is the poorest, most southern of the Japanese islands. It's an island smaller than Kawai in the Hawaiian Islands, and there are 38 American military bases on it. The choicest 20 percent of this island is occupied by massive military installations, including our largest military base in East Asia, which was built for thermonuclear war. The modern empire today is not the old empire of colonies. It's not the empire of neo-colonialism (except in the case of Latin America), but is instead the empire of huge military reservations. In Britain they're all disguised as Royal Air Force bases. It also includes Germany, Italy, a series of bases ringing the Persian Gulf, four being built in Iraq as we talk, two new bases in Uzbekistan, in Kyrgyzstan in Central Asia. That's the empire today.

SJ: But isn't it a dangerous world? Don't we need to protect ourselves?

It's a dangerous world, no question about that, but the empire is not a response to that. What are the functions of this empire? What is it there for? There are about five things that it does, none of which, it seems to me, in any way makes the American public safer.

One is military preponderance over the rest of the world, to simply ensure that no rival begins to develop power that could, in any way, challenge the United States. This was stated by Paul Wolfowitz when he was in the Department of Defense back in 1992 and it is now official policy—that we will stop other countries from creating power that could be used against us in the future, or could create a balance of power, and this extends to outer space.

Second, of course, oil. The control of petroleum resources is a fundamental aspect of international relations. The irony of all this is we could totally free ourselves from dependence on oil from the Persian Gulf by technological means of conservation that are available right now. If you simply would produce a fuel-efficient automotive industry in America, you could end our dependence on foreign oil. Instead, we are profligate in our use of fossil fuels. The Chevrolet Suburban weighs three tons and gets about ten miles a gallon. It doubled its sales after 9/11. The symbol of the United States after 9/11 became, here in Southern California, someone speeding down the freeway in a very heavy SUV with an American flag attached to his radio antenna.

A third purpose of the empire is to conduct espionage on everybody. We can listen to any e-mail, any fax, any telephone call anywhere on earth. We even have submarines for penetrating and tapping fiber optic cables, the only form of communications that doesn't send off a bouncing ray that can be picked up by satellites and things of this sort.

The fourth function of the empire is to serve the interests of the military industrial complex. We are, by order of magnitude, the largest suppliers of munitions anywhere on Earth. Most Americans are not aware of how terribly important the Pentagon is to our national economic life. Arms are not normally—certainly not in the most important amounts—sold by the manufacturers. They're sold through the Pentagon itself, where some 10,000 people work on foreign military sales. It's supplying weapons of all sorts to people around the world. A huge business has developed to support this—about a half-million American soldiers, spies, teachers, contractors.

The fifth function is to make life pleasant for people who exist today in our volunteer armed forces. When I was in the Navy, in the Korean War, conscription was in effect. A young man in America had to make a decision. Were you going to go in the Army, were you going to go in the Navy? What were you going to do? You had to do something. It was an obligation of citizenship to serve in the armed forces. It is not today. It has not been since 1973. People who serve in the armed forces are volunteers. They are not a citizen army as much as the Pentagon would like to have you pretend they are. People join the armed forces today largely to escape one or another dead-end of our society. Minorities such as African Americans are more widely represented in the armed forces than they are in the work force at large.

The broader function of empire is simply imperialism. It's this kind of ideology that has grown up in the wake of the cold war, propounded quite openly by what we are calling neoconservatives in America, which identifies the United States as a colossus athwart the world, a new Rome, beyond good and evil. We no longer need friends. We don't need international law. Like the old Roman phrase, "It doesn't matter whether they love us or not, so long as they fear us." That's very much the ideology that's at work today.

SJ: What stake do ordinary Americans have in the empire. Does it do them harm? Do they benefit from it?

I've tried to lay out in my new book, *The Sorrows of Empire*, the costs of empire. They can be grouped in four general areas. One is perpetual warfare: one war after another after another. We become a warfare state. The system is set up to go to war. We're going to find wars. We've already had two major wars, Iraq and Afghanistan, just since the turn of the century.

The second great cost of an empire is the weakening of civil liberties. Right now as we talk the fourth and sixth amendments to the Constitution are dead letters. We have given the President the power to incarcerate an American citizen in violation of habeas corpus, not read the charges to him, not allow him to defend himself, not give him an attorney, not have the evidence against him presented to him. That's the Sixth Amendment. Gone. The Fourth Amendment, freedom in your own property, in your own home, from government surveillance—thanks to the Patriot Act, that has been largely suspended. The FBI and the CIA can now do clandestine espionage on your personal activities, for example, the Internet sites you visit, and no judge can stop them. These are serious developments. They're far enough advanced in my belief to say that I doubt very much that the Constitution of 1787 actually still prevails today. Hannah Arendt, the famous political philosopher, noted that tyranny can always prevail over others, but its cost is the transformation of its own society. Militarism and imperialism go together. They have an unbelievably corrosive effect on republican liberty, on the balance of power, on the separation of power. It leads to the Imperial Presidency, to the trappings of empire, to the expansion of the Pentagon into any number of areas that it was never intended to be in.

We have today a Northern Command, located in Colorado, allegedly to defend the country against an external attack. We have never created such a command before, even during World War II, because we feared that it could become a focus for a military takeover. General Ed Eberhardt, the current commander of the Northern Command, has said that we might have to interfere with laws like the Posse Comitatus Act, enacted after the Civil War to prevent the military from interfering in civil elections and things of that sort. General Eberhardt said that the circumstances might develop in which we would have to abolish that. And I thought as he said it, "You don't realize, General, that the Posse Comitatus Act is there to defend us from you." That's why it was originally enacted, and today it's under continuous assault by the President, by his associates, by the Department of Justice.

The third great cost of empire is a tendency toward official lying, toward propaganda on the part of our political leaders, the refusal to be candid with the people, and the growth enormously of official secrecy. The best example is the speech given to the UN council on February 5, 2003 by Secretary of State Colin Powell, telling us of the tremendous threat posed by Saddam Hussein and Iraq. We now know in detail that virtually everything Colin Powell said was a lie, and he knew it was a lie, and the people like George Tenet, the director of the Central Intelligence Agency, who was sitting behind him, above all, knew that it was disinformation. That now becomes common, and it's a terrible cost to the republic.

There was also the President's 2003 State of the Union address. I have to admit that as a professor of international relations I simply find it unimaginable that in the most authoritative speech the President gives every year, the State of the Union, a speech given to a Joint Session of Congress and broadcast all over the world, you could have the president put in intelligence known to be false by our hyper-secret, very expensive intelligence agencies. The president and his advisors put in this intelligence stating that Saddam Hussein had tried to acquire raw uranium from a source in Africa when we knew that that was not true. It was a piece of fake intelligence. It is quite literally unbelievable that the President could make such a statement, that his advisors could have allowed him to make such a statement. I would have to say today that it would be an extremely naive person who would take any statement of the federal government at face value, who would not attempt to verify it through their own personal sources, sources they trust, and find other ways to confirm what the government is saying.

The fourth cost is bankruptcy, imperial overstretch. The current defense appropriation bill signed by the President in November of 2003 allocates $401 billion for the military. That does not include any of the $150 billion for Iraq. Let me offer a comparison to show the folly of this. Britain, on the eve of World War I, had trade surpluses running to maybe 7 percent of GDP. It was a rich country. It could afford a mistake and still get over it. The US is running trade deficits that amount to maybe 5 percent of GDP. And if the world starts deciding that the dollar is not nearly as attractive a place to keep their savings as maybe the Euro, then the American house of cards starts to crumble almost at once. The financial basis for that happening is there. As Herb Stein, a former chairman of the Council of Economic Advisors, once said, "Things that can't go on forever don't." What we're talking about right now is that the rigged American economy can't go on forever, and it's not rocket science to say so. Perpetual war, the loss of civil liberties, the lack of trust in government because they don't tell the truth, these are outrageous and unpleasant political developments, but they don't necessarily spell the end of the United States. Financial bankruptcy does. It brings it down.

SJ: There's been a lot of focus on the neoconservatives within the Bush administration. They obviously didn't invent American empire, but they have been described as radical enthusiasts for it. Do you think "radical" is a good way to describe them and their foreign policy?

I think they are extremely radical, and I think they have hijacked American foreign policy. General Zinni of the marine corps called them "chicken hawks," war-lovers who have no experience of barracks life or of war, who are abstract enthusiasts of empire, who have concluded that we are a good empire and that what the world needs is an empire. They compare us to Rome, knowing almost nothing about Roman history and what happened to the Roman Republic, which was at one time very much a model for our own Constitution. It fell apart on the same things that are pressuring our society today, imperialism and militarism. But the neoconservatives, at the very end of the first Bush administration in 1992, had already begun to make a classic, catastrophic error that could ultimately cost the Americans their country. They concluded that the collapse of the Soviet Union meant that we had won the cold war, that in some way or another we were now utterly the dominant power.

The truth of the matter is that both of us were in the process of losing the cold war. It was a losing proposition that had largely been over since the '70s as far as any threat of a Soviet–American military exchange goes. We reacted to the end of the cold war not by demobilizing, as we did at the end of World War II, and returning to civilian pursuits. We instead did everything in our power to prop up cold war structures in East Asia, in Latin America, and to try to find a substitute for the Soviet Union that would justify the huge cold war apparatus and keep it in being. Many theorists began almost at once to supply something that the Department of Defense and the military-industrial complex wanted: a new rationale for our military apparatus. They began to say that the new policy for the US must be to maintain preponderance over the rest of the world and that there should be no sources of power, hostile or allied, that could ever challenge us in any military manner. When this was first enunciated in 1992 by Paul Wolfowitz, a classic chicken hawk if there ever was one, it was largely derided at the time.

One of the interesting things to me is that these neocons all existed in the first Bush administration, but they were kept carefully under control. They worked for the government, but they were kept under control by Brent Scowcroft, who was President George H. W. Bush's national security advisor—not exactly a genius but a prudent old cold warrior. The thing that's different is that after the appointment of George Bush in 2000, and then the crisis of 9/11, they've come forward. They have no restraints on them.

While they were out of power during the Clinton administration, they created something called the Project for the New American Century, in which they propagandized their ideas. They also began to have in their ranks a strong element representing the Likud Party in Israel, or at least that element of Israeli politics associated with Arial Sharon, a famous Israeli general. They began to worry about places like Iraq and Iran, which Israel had identified as potential threats and rivals to its power in the Middle East. They had elaborate ideas about transforming the Middle East into what they said would be a democratic renaissance. It just seems almost insane on the surface of it that people who know almost nothing about these societies, know nothing about their history and how they were created, know almost nothing about the antagonism throughout the Middle East over the Palestinian–Israeli conflict for so many years, that they should imagine such things.

They were biding their time until 9/11 became precisely what they had said they needed a year earlier, a "new Pearl Harbor" that they could use to implement their program, something that could mobilize the public to the danger they're in, would allow them to exploit it. Within almost days after 9/11, Rice had convened the entire National Security Council with the question, "How can we utilize this event in order to transform American foreign policy?" Within hours of 9/11, Secretary of Defense Rumsfeld was talking about the need for a war against Iraq, without any evidence that Iraq had participated at all in 9/11. It was implausible on the surface of it. Osama bin Laden is rather obviously motivated by a deep commitment to the fundamentals of Islam, whereas Saddam Hussein and the Ba'ath Party are radically secularist. But these neocons literally hijacked American foreign policy. They wanted to go to Iraq first, but we now have evidence from inside the administration that they were warned off because the public wouldn't see the connection with Iraq. So they chose Afghanistan.

The Pentagon has propagandized what they call a stupendous military victory in Afghanistan. The truth of the matter is that the US went back in and bribed the warlords that had been defeated in the Afghan civil war to reopen it. They had been defeated by the Taliban and we offered them air support. This was not a particularly brilliant or edifying military strategy at all. It very quickly overthrew the Taliban but it also very quickly recreated in Afghanistan the kinds of pre-Taliban conditions that had given rise to fundamentalist mujahadeen terrorist activities. We see today that Afghanistan is once again the world's largest supplier of opium, and the attempt to write a new Afghan constitution appears to have collapsed in Kabul because of the ethnic realities of the country.

But then their real mission always was Iraq. And as we know, they began, catastrophically, to invent excuses for a war with Iraq: that it possessed weapons of mass destruction that were a major threat to our lives, to the lives of our allies in Britain and in Israel, and that Saddam Hussein had in some ways had some relationship with the Saudi Arabian terrorists that actually carried out the suicidal missions of 9/11. None of this proves to be true. It has been among the most embarrassing things for the governments of Britain and the US that have ever occurred. However, we know from public opinion polls that the public still believes that Saddam Hussein was in some ways responsible for the terrorist assaults on the US. Since, as a matter of fact, there is not one iota of evidence for that assertion, they must believe it only because that's what the President and his aides have repeatedly said. It's also been hammered home through a failed media that has simply parroted what the administration put out.

The neocons are in some trouble today. They did say that they believed our troops would be welcomed with open arms, that Iraq would be fabulously wealthy because it is the second largest source of petroleum reserves on earth, and we could easily step in and take over and profit from them. None of these things has proven true. An Iraqi freedom fighter, an Iraqi nationalist (just like a Vietnamese nationalist in the '60s), will resent foreign invaders in his country who are dominating his life, who are humiliating him in front of his family, who are barging into his house brandishing weapons in front of his children—that man until the end of time wants to kill Americans and is going to keep trying to do it. It is an unmitigated disaster to have gotten into this, and it is largely the result of allowing policy to be made by naïve, ill-informed people who were allowed to capture our government, and by a president who is ill-suited for the job in terms of training and background, who was not elected to office but was appointed by the Supreme Court, and therefore had dubious authority from the outset. This combined with a National Security advisor, Rice, who herself seems in over her head. She is an authority on a country that no longer exists, the former Soviet Union, who does not seem able to perform the role of National Security Advisor effectively, to coordinate a very diverse government and to have original and intelligent strategic thoughts of her own.

SJ: Given these failures, what, then, is the most effective way to fight terrorism?

The first thing is not to react exactly as the terrorists want you to react. There's no question that Osama bin Laden and al-Qaeda could not have imagined that they would succeed so wildly beyond their dreams. George Bush has played to the hilt the role of sucker, of being drawn in, responding improperly and unintelligently, to the attacks of 9/11—perhaps exploiting it for short-term political advantage to himself, to provide the legitimacy that he did not get from the Supreme Court in the first months of 2001. But the attacks on Afghanistan and Iraq have legitimated and generated throughout the world unbelievable support for Osama bin Laden. Americans don't seem to understand that Osama bin Laden is not the same thing as Saddam Hussein. Saddam Hussein has genuine enemies inside Iraq, people who suffered under his rule and had ample reason to want to see him gone and to seek revenge against the Ba'ath Party. Osama bin Laden didn't rule anybody, and there's nobody in the Arab world who feels that Osama bin Laden has betrayed them. My wife and I spent a good deal of time traveling in Indonesia. I guarantee you that anywhere on Java today you can find boys wearing tee shirts with pictures of Osama bin Laden, saying "Islamic Hero."

The primary technique of terrorism is to try to elicit a damaging overreaction, usually meaning the militarization of the affair, leading to the loss of life by innocent bystanders. When we do it we call it "collateral damage." But it means all those people killed by our high-tech bombing in Afghanistan or by the occupation forces in Iraq have got brothers and fathers and uncles, and those people are determined to gain revenge, gain respect for their families. We who lost the Vietnam War should have understood that most of those fighting against us were not communists. They were defenders of their country against what they saw as easily identifiable foreign invaders. And we lost it. We lost it badly because they were prepared never to give up. We now have the people who created this disaster, like Robert McNamara, acknowledging that. It is a bad testimony to the United States and our sense of history in this society that we who lost the Vietnam War could have so quickly forgotten what it meant.

SJ: How do we get out of this situation?

The crisis that we face today is essentially a Constitutional one. James Madison, the primary author of our Constitution, said that the most important clause in the Constitution is the one that gives the elected representatives, the people, the right to declare war. He then went on to say that it is a power that never should be given to a single individual. No person can assume that responsibility. In October 2002, our Congress gave up the power to declare war to the president. He can do it when he wants to, on his own decision, using nuclear weapons if he chooses. And we gave that power to him without even a debate. I believe that means the Constitution was betrayed. The president does not actually sign, or take an oath, to defend the people of the United States. He takes an oath to defend the Constitution. That's what he didn't do. He instead betrayed the Constitution. It is a Constitutional issue, and the candidate that runs against him should raise that issue directly, emphasize the rights of the people in the country, in the Constitution, and republican liberty. That's what the election needs to be fought about. If it's not, then we probably have to assume the United States is starting to tread the same path as the former Soviet Union and that it will soon, because of these pressures, start to unravel.

San Diego, California
January 2, 2004

JACKSON KATZ

Jackson Katz is recognized as one of America's leading anti-violence activists. In 1993, he founded the Mentors in Violence Prevention (MVP) Program at Northeastern University's Center for the Study of Sport in Society, and since 1996 has been directing the first worldwide gender violence prevention program in the history of the United States Marine Corps—the first such program in the United States military. From 2000 to 2003 he served as a member of the US Secretary of Defense's Task Force on Domestic Violence in the military. He is the creator of award-winning educational videos for college and high school students, including *Tough Guise: Violence, Media, and the Crisis in Masculinity*.

JE: There's been a lot of talk over the years about the gender gap in American politics, but most of the attention has been given to female voting patterns. What's your take on the male side of the gender gap—the fact that Republicans have been winning larger and larger numbers of white working-class, blue-collar voters?

It's clear that the Republicans have successfully attracted the votes of blue-collar, white men throughout the country, especially in the south but all throughout the country over the last generation—men who have voted against their immediate economic self-interest. So then the question is, why? I think it's an extremely important phenomenon to look into. Obviously it would make a significant difference in virtually every election, and certainly in presidential elections, if the Democratic Party could figure out why blue-collar men are going against their own interests to vote for the Republican Party. If Democrats did something to bring them back, it would radically transform American electoral politics at virtually every level.

JE: What's your explanation for this trend? What are these men responding to with their vote?

I think one of the key factors driving blue-collar white male votes to the Republican Party has been race, clearly. The Republican Party has successfully framed their party's identification with white people versus the Democratic Party's identification with people of color, especially African-American people. But I think also the Republican Party has very successfully marketed themselves as the party not just of white people, but of white men in particular. They've been able to masculinize the image of the party, the candidates they run for office, and political discourse itself. The rhetoric around the candidates and around elections is such that the Republican Party is clearly gendered masculine. So I think a lot of white, working-class men respond to the imagery, respond to that appeal, and respond to the pressure that then mounts on blue-collar men to identify with the Republican Party if they want to be seen as real men. The corollary to that is that the Democratic Party in this discourse has been feminized—the image of the Democratic Party is that it's a woman's party. It's a party for men who are not masculine. And therefore, if you're a man, a white man in particular, and you're a blue-collar white man even more specifically, for you to identify with the Democratic Party means that you have to be able to resist all the pressure that tells you that's wimpy, that that's not masculine, that it's not respected.

JE: What do "masculine" and "feminine," in the sense you're using the terms here, actually mean? These are abstract terms. How does this actually play out in politics? How does it reveal itself in conversations you've had with regular guys?

Consistently, in the rhetoric and discourse surrounding the Republican Party versus Democratic Party, you'll hear over and over again that the Democrats are soft on crime, that they coddle criminals, that they're weak on communism, weak on terrorism, weak on defense. You can then contrast that with the discourse surrounding the Republican Party. Republicans are supposedly strong on defense, tough on crime, tough on communism during the cold war. And within this binary opposition of strong/weak, steady/unsteady, tough-talking/intellectual, hard-line conservative/bleeding-heart liberal—in each case, if you look at those binaries the Republicans come out as the strong party, the party of winners, the party of getting tough. In each case, the Democrats come out as the party of losers, the weak party, the party that's soft on crime, soft on terrorism etc. I think that translates into the mainstream discourse with men, and with women, in predictable ways.

JE: Isn't it true, though, when you look at how they govern and at the differences in their political philosophies, that Republicans are the tougher party, for better or worse?

No, I think it's an absurd construction. It's absurd on its face. But this is political rhetoric versus reality. I mean, if you ask the typical white working-class guy why he supports the Republicans, he'll often say, "Well, they're strong on defense. I trust him on national security issues." And if you ask, as I have many times, "Okay. What's the difference between the Republican strategies and budgets and priorities on national security and the approach of the Democrats in those areas?"—what you'll find is that a lot of these people don't even have an answer for you because they don't know. I think that part of what they're doing is responding to the rhetoric. They're responding to the image. They're responding to the discourse rather than to their own thoughtful examination of the issues. For example, on military spending issues, while policy wonks might understand the difference between one missile system and another, or this budgetary increase in contrast with another, the average person doesn't know any of that. The average person, including the average voter, is often just voting based on perceptions. You can often hear in everyday political discourse with guys that their perceptions are based on flimsy evidence, on images, on rhetoric, on peer pressure, not on a thoughtful examination of the issues.

JE: In this culture we've had a tradition of thinking that women are the emotional ones, that men are more cool and rational and women more subject to the heart and the passions. You'd think that women, then, would vote more emotionally than men. But in fact, and this relates to what you're talking about here, we know from extensive polling that women—more than men—seem to vote based on a candidate's position on issues of import to them. The irony in what you're suggesting is that men are the ones who are voting emotionally.

That's right. One of the great ironies is that while the traditional conception is that men are logical and women are more emotional, when it comes to a whole set of political issues you could literally make the exact opposite case. You can make the case that women as a sex class tend to be more rational, more logical in their decisions about who to support, based on a candidate's positions on health care, on education, on day-to-day issues that affect families and people generally. Men are more likely to be swayed by emotional appeals to toughness, to national strength, to defense and security, and the economy in a very general sense, as opposed to more specifically what it is about the economy that leads you to support one candidate or the other. So it reverses the stereotypical construction that women are more emotional and men are more rational.

JE: The neoconservative intellectual Robert Kagan, in his recent book Paradise and Power, *actually writes that the US is from Mars and Europe is from Venus. His point is that Europeans, like the French, can sit around in cafés and look down at America as an unsophisticated, bullying, cowboy country, but that it's American might and strength that actually enables them to be safe enough over there to engage in their little intellectual critiques of the US. This seems to be at the heart of the neoconservative philosophy that's come center stage in this administration—that post 9/11, strength and force are key, that the world's a dangerous place and it's naïve to think that being nice will solve our security problems. What do you make of this?*

One of the ways that the neocons have gotten political support for their aggressive military adventurism is the idea that there are bad men out there, and that the only way we're going to stop those bad men from hurting us is with good men using greater force. That's a fairly persuasive argument if you don't know the issues. No one's arguing, no one I know would ever make the argument, that we don't need to use force in self-defense against terrorism or against any form of aggressive violence. The question is not whether we need to use force, or whether we need to defend ourselves. The question is how and why. The fundamental question is how we're going to go about doing that, not whether or not we need to defend ourselves. So I would reject categorically the idea that if you oppose the Bush agenda, or the right-wing, or neocon militarism, that somehow that means you're saying, "Come get us. We're just going to be defenseless." That's ludicrous. No one would make that argument. There are more subtle and sophisticated ways of approaching terrorism than just brute force and expansion of our military and imperial domain.

JE: Shadia Drury, a scholar who's written extensively on the philosophical roots of American neoconservatism, told me recently in an interview that neoconservative philosophy and ideology are obsessed with virility. She talked about how there's this sense of looming catastrophe and perpetual danger that runs throughout their work, and that their core belief is that this danger calls for an aggressive, virile approach to politics and policy. In your mind, does this mark neoconservatism, especially as it's been realized in Bush's foreign policy, as more defensive or offensive in nature?

One thing that's clearly going on in our political discourse is that unilateralism has been gendered masculine, while multilateralism has been gendered feminine, so that Bush and the neocons, in their unilateralist approach, have positioned themselves as men of action. They're taking action, whereas multilateralists are just sitting around talking while the terrorists are terrorizing. This, by the way, is one of the significant tropes in Hollywood westerns. We have the townspeople being menaced by this evil man, and they're ineffectual in responding. They're talking, going to church, praying, and none of it's working. The only thing that works is when John Wayne rides into town, or Clint Eastwood rides into town—he doesn't say much, but you know he's packing heat. All of a sudden he takes action and the townspeople are saved. What I think is also really interesting is that Dick Cheney is from Wyoming and is clearly invested in a certain notion of masculinity that's straight out of Hollywood Westerns. Even though he's an intellectual, he gives off this aura that talk is cheap, that action is what defines a man. That's very persuasive, visually, dramatically, and cinematically. A related point is when Bush is criticized as being a cowboy by, say, European media or others even in this country. And while that's usually meant in a derisive, ridiculing way, that's actually what strengthens his support among white working-class men because the cowboy invokes incredibly powerful imagery, positive imagery, in the American psyche. It's imagery based in some reality, but is mostly based in mythology from the cinematic and novelistic construction of the cowboy and the frontier, from the masculine myth of the rugged individualist. I think that's a part of George Bush's appeal. But while Dick Cheney is authentically from Wyoming, George Bush is from the Northeast. He has an elite prep school and Ivy League education. But he's constantly trying to emphasize how much of a Texan he is and how cowboy-like he is. You see, in magazine layout after magazine layout, George Bush in cowboy hats and boots, clearing brush on his ranch. There's no question that that's part of the constructed image of George Bush as a masculine man. This has enormous resonance, especially with blue-collar white men, not just in the South, but all over the country.

JE: What about perceptions of the UN in this context?

The UN is a multilateral organization, by definition. People have to talk. It's a messy process. It's international democracy at work, and it's been gendered feminine, or less than fully masculine. The real way to solve these problems is not to have conversations about it, and not to go through the sloppy process of democracy, but actually just to take action because the United States has the power, both the economic as well as the military power. We can do it, and the thinking of the neocons is that we have to do it, because if we don't do it, no one else will. What's not interrogated is what action needs to be taken. The assumption is that it's obvious everybody knows what needs to be done. You need to invade these countries, you need to increase the military budget, you need to increase the domestic surveillance of dissent in the United States, and the only one who has the guts to do it is George Bush, the neocons, and the Republican Party. The Democrats don't have the guts to do it, even if they know it's the right thing. It's a fairly persuasive argument, if you've never heard the alternative, if you've never heard that there are a number of different ways of approaching this problem that don't involve these tactics—tactics which, of course, produce their own backlash. One of the things that a lot of people don't understand is that while sometimes military aggression, like interpersonal violence, can seem like it's coming out of an offensive impulse to dominate, it's often the case that violence is used defensively based on fear. In other words, you strike out because you're afraid of getting struck. This is related to what George Gerbner calls "mean world syndrome." His basic point is that when people are exposed to massive doses of media violence, especially boys, they are more likely to see violence as the necessary response to real world situations because they perceive the world to be even more violent than it really is. So if they think that the person across from them might strike them or shoot them, they are then more likely to shoot first, pre-emptively or defensively, because they're afraid it's going to happen to them first if they don't. I think you could generalize and say that that's true in the world in real terms. That is, the projection of power is not just a projection of power. It's also defensive, even though it might look offensive. And it is on one level offensive. But it's also based in fear. I also think—and this is by no means an original insight—that when people are fearful, they're more likely to support policies and candidates that address that fear. They're more likely to vote against their own economic self-interest if they believe that their personal safety is at risk. I think that's clearly the strategy of the Republican Party coming into the 2004 elections. It amounts to this: There are bad guys out there, they're trying to kill us, trying to hurt us, and we have strong men on our side who are willing to take action, even when it's not popular.

You're safer with us, even if you don't like what's happening in the economy, if you don't like the fact that you don't have a job, if you don't like the fact that there are all kinds of problems at home. At least you're safe. And with those other guys, meaning the Democratic Party in this case, all bets are off. You're taking risks, because they don't have what it takes to respond to this challenge.

JE: When you look at the gender gap, and see that women are less likely to support Republicans than men are, does what you're saying imply that American women are less afraid than American men?

There is a gender gap, there's no question about it. The Republican Party has been more successful at attracting white male votes than they have at attracting white female votes around these appeals. There's no question about that. But there are a significant number of women who have bought into this worldview as well, so it's unfair to say that it's just men and women. But in most national elections since 1980, there has been a notable gender gap. It's really important to look at that. But when people have looked at the gender gap over the last 20 years or so, they've focused on the women's side of it. Analysis has focused primarily on why women are supporting Democratic candidates more. The questions have been centered on the concerns women bring to the political discourse and their voting choice. That's an important discussion, to say the least, but what's been much less studied, which is incredible, is how men's gendered identities and lives have shaped how we think politically and how we vote. I think part of the confusion here is that when people hear the word "gender," they think it means women. And so "gender in politics" to a lot of people means "women in politics," and what gets missed is the dominant group, which is, of course, men. So I think it's really important to look at the men's side of the gender gap, at how men are responding based on our gendered identities, rather than just looking at how women do so.

JE: And given that, since 9/11, the gender gap has largely held, are you suggesting that men are more afraid than women of terrorism?

I wouldn't say that men are more afraid. I would say that a lot of men have an attitude that we know what's better for women than they know, because we understand men better than they do. In other words, some men believe that it's nice to talk about health care, employment, education, childcare issues. Those are interesting and important, but not really as important as our physical safety in terms of being defended against the terrorists. And we men understand the intent of these terrorists, and a lot of women just don't get it. And, the thinking goes, we need to privilege our understanding of the dangers of the world because we know men better than women do. That's part of it, this very patronizing, patriarchal attitude. Again, there is something to be said for needing to be defended against violent assault. I would never in a million years argue that we don't have to defend ourselves against violence. That's absurd. I would never stand for any political program that didn't respond aggressively to threats to the safety and security of civilians and innocent people, whether in the United States or all around the world. But that's not the argument that thoughtful critics of Bush make—that we need to just lay back and be vulnerable. But that's the way it's constructed. The way it's constructed in the popular discourse is that you have two alternatives: one is to aggressively go after these people, these men, these bad men, these violent men, and the other is to lay back and let them just wreak havoc on us and kill us with impunity. When people are faced with that choice, of course they're going to say, "Let's defend ourselves!" But that's a false set of choices. It's a ridiculous reduction of reality. So I think what needs to happen is we need to have a more thoughtful national discourse about the alternatives to the neocon worldview, the alternatives to the Bush administration's response to terrorism. The Democratic Party so far has been ineffectual at trying to do this on a national level, ineffective in trying to articulate a point of view that people can grasp, one that successfully argues against the current policy and the current administration.

JE: Can you talk more specifically about the gender gap in light of this election's hot new demographic—the so-called "NASCAR dad" voter?

Again, you have this sound-bite culture in political discourse where "soccer mom" last election stood in for middle-class suburban mothers driving their kids to school with concerns about family-related issues and daycare and health care and education issues. This time around we have the "NASCAR dad," a stand-in for blue-collar men, especially Southern white men, who resonate with a set of issues and a certain kind of political rhetoric about strength, about patriotism, about guns. The Republican Party has very successfully presented themselves as the party that responds to the NASCAR dad segment of the population. Again, the term is just political shorthand for white working-class voters, especially in the South.

JE: Why do white working class men seem to need this image? Why does it appeal to them, in your view?

If you look at a strict economic analysis, the real wages, the real earning power of blue-collar men and blue-collar workers in general has declined over the past 30 years—even with the rising stock market and the high tech boom and all these other macro economic factors. One thing that's been consistent is that the earning power of blue-collar workers has declined steadily. So what do you hold onto if you're supposed to be a provider for your family and respected in your job? You're on the economic margins. You're not making as much money. Your earning power isn't as much as your parents' earning power. You can't even afford a house. In some cases, you're struggling to get your kids in school, to pay for school, much less a lot of the other amenities and material things that you see on TV that everybody else supposedly has. What is your identity as a man? I mean, obviously one thing you can hang your hat on is your ideology of manhood. You're a man, you take care of your family, that's an important piece—and by extension you support policies and a political party that takes care of the country, that protects the country, and I think a lot of men will vote against their immediate economic self-interest for a set of policies based on how they resonate with this notion of manhood. I mean, look at some of the key issues that are remarked upon as cultural issues, not these strict economic issues. You have gun control, abortion, patriotism. In the south, it's the Confederate flag. That's all about identifications with and symbolical images of manhood. Look at guns, for example. Look at the discourse around guns. To me it's obvious that there's more going on here than a concern with the Second Amendment on the part of the voting population who cares passionately about guns. It's much more than a concern with an abstraction like the Second Amendment. It's an emotional connection, it's masculine conditioning and socialization, and it's boys' relationships with their fathers growing up and learning how to shoot. It's much more about their identification as men than it is their identification with an abstract principle like a Constitutional amendment.

JE: You've talked about the importance of language in political discourse and communication. Can you talk about George W. Bush's notorious language gaffes, about how this works to create a certain image for him? Also, can you say something about how his anti-intellectual reputation and image may or may not work to lend cover to the deeply intellectual, philosophical roots of the neoconservatives who have actually crafted his policies?

One of the things that George W. Bush has been able to do more successfully than his father, George H. W. Bush, is to distance himself from his aristocratic lineage. The Bush family is prototypically aristocratic: Northeast, old money, Yankee blue-bloods. But that doesn't play well with white working-class voters, in the South or the Midwest, or anywhere really. So what George W. Bush has been able to do is frame himself and present himself as kind of a folksy guy you can have a beer with. This contrasts sharply with his father, whose image was definitely more that of a distanced elite. So I think the fact that George W. Bush is so inarticulate actually works in his favor, because it makes him more like just regular guys. In other words, there's an anti-intellectualism that runs deep in American culture, and it certainly runs even deeper among men, working-class men even more specifically. This anti-intellectualism carries within it a distrust of people who are smart, who are educated, who are articulate, because they're easily framed as elitist. They think you're fools. They think you're trash, if you will. And the Republican Party has been able to say successfully to working-class white male voters, "We respect you, whereas the Democrats have contempt for you. They're elitists and they have contempt for you." By having people like George W. Bush, Ronald Reagan, candidates like that as the sort of spokespeople for the Republican Party, the white working-class voters lose sight of the fact that the blue-blood, Brooks Brothers bankers in New York are supporting this party. The elite of the elite are supporting the Republican Party. But this spokesperson, the candidate, they can relate to on a personal level. That's where the conversation has to go—that this is all about image. This is not about a thoughtful understanding of the issues. This is about construction of presidential masculinity and the image of same. And it's incredible how little this is even discussed, because we know, for example, for at least the last quarter of a century, the primary expenditure in political campaigns on the national level is television advertising. In other words, when you talk about Bush amassing a war chest for the campaign, the hundreds and millions of dollars that he's raising, the vast majority of that money is going to TV advertising. The question then becomes: what is the image being constructed in this TV advertising that is so effective? You would think that people would look at this even more carefully, but the discourse around TV ads in academia and elsewhere over the last several election cycles hasn't really delved into the gendered aspects of it. They'll talk about the claims, whether the claims are accurate or not, whether they're based on evidence or based in some kind of persuasive rhetoric—but there is virtually no thoughtful discussion about how the candidates are being constructed as products that people are essentially purchasing. The gendered aspects of that candidate construction is what I'm concerned with here, and I think the Republican Party gets this—even if they couldn't articulate it in the words that I'm using. Mike Deaver got it, Lee Atwater got it, Karl Rove got it and gets it, and a whole bunch of other Republican strategists get it. They understand that if you market Republican candidates as masculine candidates, then blue-collar, white male voters will respond positively to your candidacy. It's not about the issues per se, it's about the way the candidate's image and the framing of the issues help to create a package that is persuasive. The gender aspect of it is central.

JE: Can you talk about what's behind the kind of political advertising and image-making you're talking about? One way to look at it is by looking at what's in it. Another way is to look at what's behind it and who's behind it.

What frustrates me and what frustrates a lot of people is how the neoconservative intellectual elite has been able to use white working-class men to support their imperial ambitions, the expansion of the military budget, etc. I don't think they respect these men on a fundamental level. If they did, they wouldn't support a politics that helps to reduce their earning power, cuts childcare and education, and so many different areas that these working-class men need in their lives to support their families and themselves. This is something that really offends me, and a lot of other people: How many of these men who are the neocon intellectuals avoided military service when they had the chance, or when they were of draft age? They avoided it, but yet they're willing to send blue-collar men, white, working-class men, and men of color from the poor and working classes off to kill and die for their imperial ambitions. But they're sitting in their tony offices in

Washington and New York writing these papers and publishing these articles and making this high theory while the blue collar guys are the ones who are actually on the ground, doing the hard work and in fact getting killed for it.

JE: But can't the case be made, despite all of that, that Bush is a strong leader?

Bush is often talked about as being a strong leader, and one of the reasons why his political constituencies support him is because they see him as a person who takes action, who takes charge, who's a leader, whether you agree with him or disagree with him. There's some truth to that. I wouldn't say that's completely fallacious. I think that he has led in a certain sense. He has moved, for example, from actually losing the popular vote to establishing some radical right-wing positions and has done that successfully. You could say that he has led the Republican Party to the right, moved an already right-wing party further to the right, and so in a sense has successfully demonstrated some leadership. But you could also make the case that by misrepresenting the threat posed by Saddam Hussein, by hyping the evidence of WMD, you could make the case that he backed down from telling the truth about the real reasons for invading Iraq, regardless of what they are. Why didn't he use his persuasive powers and presidential platform to level with the American people and say: this is exactly what's going on, instead of manufacturing evidence and instead of misusing CIA intelligence and such.

JE: The famous slogan of the Clinton campaign in '92 was "It's the economy, stupid." If you were advising Kerry and Edwards right now, what sign would you want to hang in his war room?

In 2004, the Democrats need to hang up a sign that says, "It's the masculinity, stupid." The Republicans are going to try to feminize the Democratic party and the candidates. They're going to try and run the campaign by attacking the masculinity of the Democratic candidate. They succeeded it 1988, when Michael Dukakis was the Democratic nominee and looked goofy in a tank. They tried it with Clinton with the draft-dodger stuff, but they failed. It's virtually guaranteed that this time around, again, one of the key strategies will be to present George Bush as the tough masculine leader versus this wimpy Democrat. Some of the terms are already out there. One place to look for the rhetoric that the Republican Party is using in this regard is talk radio. Listen, for example, to Rush Limbaugh, how Rush Limbaugh frames the candidates. He calls John Kerry, "Looks-French Kerry." It's an attempt to feminize him, an attempt to identify him with those soft, pacifist French. Or look at what he calls John Edwards: the "Breck Girl." This time around, if the Democrats are going to be successful, they have to figure out a way to turn that around.

Northampton, Massachusetts
November 26, 2003

MICHAEL KLARE

Michael Klare is Five College Professor of Peace and World Security Studies at Hampshire College and has written widely on US defense policy, the arms trade, and world security affairs. He is the author of many books, including *Rogue States and Nuclear Outlaws* (Hill and Wang, 1995), *Resource Wars: The New Landscape of Global Conflict* (Metropolitan, 2001), and *Blood and Oil: The Dangers and Consequences of America's Growing Petroleum Dependency* (part of the American Empire Project of Metropolitan, 2004).

SJ: First, just a general question: What role have struggles over resources played in international relations? How central have they been and how central are they now?

Resources have always been central. Since the beginning of recorded human history, resources have played a critical role in international relations as the earliest states fought over control of waterways and arable land. Imperialism was driven by the pursuit of resources. We wouldn't have had the European colonization of the Western hemisphere, of North and South America, if it weren't for the drive to gain control of, really to steal the resources of, the Western hemisphere. That's what brought Europeans here in the first place and drove European colonialism right up to World War I. World War I was a conflict that was triggered to a considerable extent by the competition between the European powers for control of overseas resources. During the cold war that got a little bit overshadowed to some degree by ideology—ideology is the driving force of world politics—but even during the cold war, you'll find that many of the crucial events were really driven by struggle over the control of key resources, particularly in the Middle East. The Truman Doctrine, the Eisenhower Doctrine, the Nixon Doctrine, and the Carter Doctrine are really all, to some degree or another, about protection of the oil of Saudi Arabia and the Persian Gulf, so that this has been an important part of international relations and conflict between states for a very long time. Now what I argue is that we are in a qualitatively new period where the struggle over resources is intensifying because of economic globalization. There are more actors out there trying to gain control over what remains of the world's resources and we are using these at such a frantic pace that we're beginning to reach the limits. We are beginning to approach scarcity of many crucial materials, so the competition for what is left intensifies. And the risk of violence over resources intensifies.

SJ: In terms of the Iraq war, how central was oil?

Oil was absolutely central to the Iraq conflict, but this should be seen in a historical context. The US concern over Iraq goes way back. It goes back to 1990 when Iraq invaded Kuwait and posed a threat to Saudi Arabia. At that time George H. W. Bush said that the Iraqi presence in Kuwait posed a threat to the oil of Saudi Arabia and the oil of Saudi Arabia is absolutely essential to the United States, to US security. Therefore we had to use military force to protect Saudi Arabia and then to drive the Iraqis out of Kuwait, and that was the first Persian Gulf War of 1991. That war was followed by the containment of Iraq. Rather than go all the way on that first encounter to Baghdad, as some advocated, the first President Bush and then Bill Clinton said that we will instead contain Iraq, we will surround Iraq, we'll bomb its facilities whenever necessary to try to keep Saddam Hussein in a cage and leave it at that.

Then the new President Bush came along and it was clear from the very beginning that he felt that the strategy of containment was inadequate. It was a failure; it demonstrated weakness on America's part. More importantly, it also precluded the United States from going into Iraq and developing Iraq's oil, which this president had determined was absolutely essential down the road for America's oil requirements. So it was very clear that at the beginning, President Bush and his advisors were determined to continue where the war had been left off in February 1991, and move on to Baghdad as had been talked about at the time.

SJ: Why did the Bush administration want to move beyond containment? What's behind the new policy?

I think we all have to remember that when George Bush entered the White House in February 2001 his top priority was not terrorism or national security, as it has become since then. The top priority in the White House was energy. The very first thing he did was to create a national energy policy working group headed by Vice President Cheney to address the nation's energy security. This was brought about because there was an energy crisis at the time. There were blackouts in California. There were oil shortages around the United States, and more importantly, just a year earlier the United States had passed the 50 percent-mark of dependence on petroleum for the first time. This was deeply distressing to American policymakers—it meant that from that point on, as America continues to consume more petroleum than it produces, it will become ever more dependent on imported petroleum.

This issue more than any other preoccupied the president and his cabinet in their first few months in office. Vice President Cheney conducted a study and produced a report, the National Energy Policy (NEP) report on May 17, 2001, which was a blueprint for the nation in terms of its energy, and much of this is known. He called for drilling in the Arctic National Wildlife refuge and a lot of subsidies to domestic oil and coal and nuclear and electricity producers to ramp up domestic energy production. The part that is not well known about the NEP is that the plan also calls for a substantial increase in US involvement, political and otherwise, in foreign areas that the US is becoming increasingly dependent upon. The plan calls for increased oil procurement from the Persian Gulf, from the Caspian Sea, from Africa, and from Latin America. Because those areas were assumed to pose resistance of one sort or another to American involvement in their oil either for nationalistic, political, or historical reasons, or the fact that many of those areas harbor anti-American sentiments, it was understood that the US would have to play a much more aggressive, assertive role in gaining access to the rest of the world's oil. This was the backdrop for September 11, 2001.

During the entire summer of that year, right up to September 11, President Bush was campaigning for implementation of the NEP. That was what was in the forefront of his mind, and I think you can see the invasion of Iraq as a consequence of this, as well as many other things. The aggressive US intervention, insertion into the Caspian Sea basin, with bases being set up in Uzbekistan, Kurdistan, Tajikistan, American troops being sent to Georgia, talk of building up a naval presence in the Persian Gulf area. All of this shows how the pursuit of energy became intertwined with the strategy of anti-terrorism. Those two policies have become one and the same under Bush; from now on, you will not be able to separate them. Wherever the US is interested in oil, there is an anti-terrorist component to that. We see that in Columbia, for example, where the US intervention was originally about drugs, but now the thrust is protecting the oil pipelines, and with a much more visible presence of American forces. Same thing in the former Soviet republic of Georgia and in other parts of the world; there's talk about building bases in Africa. All of this, on one hand described as part of an anti-terrorist strategy, but underlying it is a blueprint, a Cheney blueprint, for increasing American's access to and control over the rest of the world's oil.

SJ: So the war on terror is being used as a kind of camouflage?

In my view, the strategy of anti-terrorism, the war on terrorism, has a certain identity of its own, but it was imposed on top of an early, geopolitical framework of resource strategy, of resource predation. So one became inserted on top of the other, in a way that you can't separate them anymore. It's true that in some of the areas where the US is interested in oil, there is also a threat of terrorism, like in Central Asia, and in the Caucacus, there are terrorist groups that could be said to pose a real danger, but the US also has geopolitical interests there, so you really can't separate the two. The war on terror is being used as a vehicle to get the financing and the resources and the manpower to vastly increase America's military presence in these areas of geopolitical interest to the United States, like Columbia, Africa, and Central Asia. So there is an intertwining of the two policies. One way you see this interconnection between anti-terrorism and oil is the increasing focus on the protection of pipelines, maybe not something that Americans think about so much, but more and more oil is coming from inaccessible places, and it has to flow through pipelines. Pipelines are natural targets for saboteurs and terrorists, and so more and more, American military policy is going to be focused on the protection of these very vulnerable facilities. We see that in Iraq. The pipelines have become a major target for the anti-American resistance; hence more and more American military effort is going into protecting the far-flung Iraqi pipelines. We're involved in protecting the pipelines in Columbia, in Georgia, in other parts of the world. I think you'll see how anti-terrorism and the protection of oil have coalesced into one single activity.

SJ: Could you just explain what is different about the Bush Doctrine, especially as compared with the Carter Doctrine?

I think there are two features of the Bush Doctrine that are distinctive and dramatic. One of them is the infatuation with the use of military force, of the effectiveness of military force as a tool. Prior leaders—including the President's father, George Bush I, Bill Clinton, and other recent American presidents, ever since Vietnam—have been very reluctant to use military force because of the risk of it producing a counter-action of American forces being trapped in quagmires around the world, and the fact that the public is reluctant to experience casualties. In any case, for a combination of reasons, there has been real reluctance to use military force. The Bush people feel very differently. They feel that the use of military force is a useful instrument of power, that it has to be exercised periodically or other people won't respect us, won't be fearful of us, which is their intention—to make other people fearful of us. That's dramatically different. They don't hide this. They're very explicit in the national security strategy of the US and in other speeches. They say that the use of military force is a necessary component of American policy that must be exercised periodically for it to remain effective. So that's very different. For example, I think that the invasion of Iraq was partly about Iraq, specifically what happens inside Iraq. But it was just as much intended as a signal to Iran, to China, to Russia, to other countries in the region, to Saudi Arabia, that the United States will use military force when its officials deem it necessary. Therefore, you had better manage your relations with Washington in a way that satisfies American objectives. And this policy implies that force will be used on a recurring basis—has to be used on a recurring basis—so that the efficacy of the threat remains strong. And I really do think that if there's another Bush administration, we should expect that occasions will arise in which the use of force will be likely—can't say when or where or for sure—but that this project of retaining the efficacy of the use of military force will be a feature of the second Bush administration.

The other aspect of the Bush Doctrine that strikes me is the global scale of it, the sense that America must be the dominant world power. In the past, we've had regional policies—a European NATO policy, an Asia Pacific policy, a Middle East policy. Now we have a policy of global intervention and domination. I think that's the essence of the Bush Doctrine; the US has to be prepared to overcome adversaries anywhere in the world that they might arise. There are no safe havens, no safe areas. We must be able to operate everywhere. Again, this is explicit in the national security doctrine of the US and you see it now in the plans to revamp the disposition of American military forces, the deployments with the acquisition of new bases in Central Asia, Africa, in Southeast Asia. They're making American forces have the capacity to operate anywhere in the world, without being tied down as they were in the cold war period, when we had a large military infrastructure in Europe and NATO and another one in Japan. This is now seen as a hindrance to the exercise of America's global power. It ties us down. So instead, we're going to have less elaborate bases, but they're going to be like a checkerboard everywhere, so the Pentagon can move its forces overnight to anywhere in the world where the higher authorities think they may be needed. This too is very dramatic a departure from the past.

SJ: The term "empire" has been used a lot to describe this new constellation of forces. Do you think it's appropriate to call this a new American empire?

I don't think that it's an accurate term, perhaps because of my study of history. I think empires of the past have had an explicit project of exercising control—down to the last item—over what happens in the places that came under colonial rule, to readjust their institutions, to impose language and culture and all of that. I don't think that these people have the same project in mind. They're much more interested in overall domination, of playing the world policeman, of using force when they see it necessary. Behind that, really, I think there is a strategy of predation, that the world has to be made safe for the procurement of resources that are needed by the United States, especially oil, wherever they are. As long as the local potentates cooperate in that project, we're really not interested in how they manage their local affairs, or imposing our culture on them. That could happen; it might not happen. But we want access to their resources, and access for our corporations to do business there. In that sense, you could call it an imperial project. But it's not like the British and French empires of the past.

SJ: Do you think that a second Bush term will make the world more secure, will make Americans safer from a terrorist threat?

History tells us a lot about this; after all, Rome operated under much the same fashion for a very long time. And there's no doubt that being able to threaten the use of military force will intimidate some people from doing things that they might otherwise have done. So you might say that it will have some effect. But at the same time, it's going to produce hostility and resentment from a lot of people who don't like this heavy-handed behavior, and what it's going to lead to is the search for vulnerabilities in the United States, for what the military calls "asymmetrical advantages." For ways of getting back at the United States through unconventional means. I fear that this heavy use of military force will inspire others to look for ways to get behind our defenses and to cause havoc in one way or another, and that could be very dangerous. So over the long term, it could be counter-productive. Yes, in the short term it may show a certain amount of self-restraint on possible adversaries, assuming there are any, and Iran would be an example. I think Iran is not going to do anything with Syria that's going to provoke the United States, because they're fearful that what happened to Iraq will happen to them. But at the same time, I think others in other parts of the world will be seeking ways to get around America's strengths in unconventional means, and that could be far more dangerous in the end.

SJ: Some people have argued that it's really Dick Cheney who is pulling the strings in the Bush administration. Is he a neoconservative or is he more of an old-fashioned oil man?

My sense, first of all, is that Dick Cheney is the most important policymaker in the Bush administration, other than the president himself, that it's Cheney who makes the crucial decisions on big economic and foreign policy issues. We have to recall that he was the secretary of defense during the first Bush administration. He was the architect of the first Persian Gulf War. At the time, he made it very clear that he followed a geopolitical model of US security affairs, that geopolitics was prime. He was the one who determined that the United States had to intervene in the first Gulf War because of the threat of oil supplies. It was he who pushed that.

I think the Cheney energy report that came out in 2001 also reflects his obsession with conventional, classical geopolitics. Of the Earth, the sea lanes, the crucial sources of supply in a way. This is different than the neoconservative agenda in some respects. I think he's less interested in ideology and politics, more with power and control and wealth.

Now, I guess you could say that the Bush administration really is an alliance between this more traditional, power-seeking, geopolitical perspective, and the ideological interests of the neoconservatives. They have shared interests in some places, like in Iraq, where the two came together. Both saw an advantage in invading Iraq. But I don't think they're always going to align. For example, in Asia, I think you see a different path being taken. I think the neoconservatives are much more ideological and zealous about Taiwan and going after North Korea, but I think this would be detrimental to America's long term economic interests. Therefore, that kind of extremism, of adventurism, has been ruled out in Asia, and I think that shows the influence of Cheney in this administration.

SJ: What are the specifics of the Bush/Cheney energy policy?

Bear in mind, when Dick Cheney sat down in February 2001 to study America's future energy policy and to devise an energy blueprint for the US in the 21st century, it was clear that the nation was at a crossroads. We understood that if we continued to go down the same path, we were going to become increasingly dependent on Saudi Arabia, the Persian Gulf, and the Caspian, and so on, and that this would lead to increasing military adventures. But people were saying at the time: there is another path of developing alternative sources of energy, of diminishing our dependence on petroleum, of improving fuel efficiency, of vehicles, of developing hydrogen as an alternative source. This was not new. This was on the table. And Dick Cheney and his allies in the administration clearly and consciously chose to go down the route of more imported oil, more petroleum, more of the conventional energy strategy that we've pursued.

Now, here's where the influence of the big oil companies comes into play, because we know, from the records, that commission—it's called the National Energy Policy Development Group, the NEPDG—we know from the records of that group that all of the advice they solicited was from Big Energy, especially the Enron corporation, more than any other. These companies were also major donors to the Republican campaign in 2000. Of course, Cheney and Bush and others were themselves inclined to support that point of view, and they understood that a radical shift towards an alternative energy system would be costly to Big Energy—they would have to make huge investments in environmentally safe technology; they would lose some of their profits. So Cheney and his allies made a conscious choice to proceed down the path of petroleum addiction, of imported oil dependency. That's what's so striking about this administration and its commitment to preserving the existing energy infrastructure. It's not for lack of an alternative, or lack of information and ideas about what has to be done. Everybody knows what has to be done. We have to move swiftly away from dependence on petroleum as our major source of energy and natural gas, and rapidly begin to develop the alternatives that will be absolutely essential in another ten to twenty years, when oil and natural gas become more scarce and the environmental consequences of relying on these carbon-based fuels become so threatening, so perilous, that we must make this shift.

What they've done, and this is one of their biggest crimes, is to push way into the future the transition that must be made, that we all know must be made. We pushed it ten, twenty, thirty years into the future, when the costs of doing so will be colossally greater than they are now, and the pain of making this transition will be so much greater. A second Bush administration will dig us deeper into the grave of this old energy system, make it harder to move forward, when it's clear that this is something we must do rapidly and soon.

SJ: So there really is difference this time between the Democrats and the Republicans?

Let me put it this way: we don't know what a Democratic alternative to Bush might favor, so I can't speak to what they would do. What I could say is that a Bush administration is going to continue the policies we've already seen, and, in my mind, they will all make us all much less safe than we are now. They'll do so in two respects. First of all, by increasing our dependency on oil from volatile, dangerous areas like Saudi Arabia, Central Asia, the Caspian region, and Africa. They're absolutely committed to that. Pursuit of the oil of those countries is going to stir up hostility, resentment, and terrorism against the United States. So, that's for sure: they'll make us less safe in that respect. Secondly, it seems clear that they're determined to pursue a strategy of unilateralism in international affairs, the unilateral use of force, giving up on international institutions, and our allies. This is absolutely catastrophic for the United States. They could pretend that we live in a world where only what we do matters, but anybody who understands the international economy, the international environment, the political and social forces underway in the world, economic globalization, clearly understands that the United States cannot solve the problems facing us alone. We must have the cooperation and the support of other countries in the world to solve the big problems we're going to face. By behaving in a unilateralist fashion, we're alienating our allies, we're pushing them away, we're making enemies. We're undermining the international institutions that we will need to support, to preserve, to protect our vital interests, in a vastly more complex and threatening world, a world in which terrorism is just one part of the problem, but where economic malaise and migrations and environmental decline and international crime are all part of a larger framework of dangers. We cannot deal with these dangers alone. We must have the help of other countries, and the Bush strategy is weakening our security by pushing them away.

Northampton, Massachusetts
January 12, 2004

LT. COL. KAREN KWIATKOWSKI

Karen Kwiatkowski is recently retired from active duty in the United States Air Force as a Lieutenant Colonel. Her final assignment was as a political-military affairs officer in the Office of the Secretary of Defense, Under Secretary for Policy, in the Sub-Saharan Africa and Near East South Asia (NESA) Policy directorates. During Lt. Col. Kwiatkowski's time at NESA, she worked the North Africa desk, in the sister office to the Office of Special Plans, and witnessed first-hand the way the rationales for the war in Iraq were constructed inside the Pentagon. She is the author of two books on African issues, *African Crisis Response Initiative: Past, Present, and Future* (US Army Peacekeeping Institute, 2000) and *Expeditionary Air Operations in Africa: Challenges and Solutions* (Air University Press, 2001), teaches with the University of Maryland University College and American Public University System, and is an adjunct faculty in Political Science at James Madison University. She is a regular contributor to LewRockwell.com, and has had articles about her work with the Department of Defense published recently in the *American Conservative*.

JE: What did you see at the Pentagon that first started to concern you?

When I moved to the Near East South Asia directorate in May 2002, I became exposed for the very first time in my life to the politics that were happening in the Pentagon. My boss was Bill Luti. Above him, of course, was Doug Feith. My eyes were opened to what was going on in Middle Eastern policy. When I was in sub-Saharan African Affairs, we never saw Mr. Feith and we never received taskings from Mr. Feith. There was no involvement whatsoever of Mr. Feith, and there was no involvement of Dick Cheney in sub-Saharan African affairs. But all that was noticeably different when I moved over to Near East South Asia.

I was just amazed at what I saw. When I researched what was happening, I found that the population of that office of political-minded people, political appointees, was far beyond the usual concentration of political appointees that you would find in the office of the secretary of defense. There was very much a concentration of political appointees in general, and specifically a concentration of political appointees of what I would call—and what most people would recognize as—a neoconservative political persuasion with regard to foreign policy. These were people in the Pentagon with a foreign policy agenda, and they were concentrated in this office, noticeably so.

They had been elsewhere as well, but this office was making policy to support what I call a propaganda campaign to convince the American people that we needed to invade Iraq. This had been going on before I joined them. In May of 2002 I wasn't paying attention to it, but it had been going on before that. In fact it's well known now that Iraq was brought up on the afternoon of 9/11. They were saying, "How can we, the Pentagon and secretary of defense, use this to go into Iraq?" But I was unaware of that until I began to see it firsthand.

JE: Why do you call what was happening in the Near East and South Asia office "propaganda"?

Propaganda is a harsh word. It is something that governments do. I was not unfamiliar with the idea of putting a popular spin or putting a positive spin on information. But what I saw in the Near East South Asia office—particularly with Bill Luti and eventually when the Office of Special Plans was formed under Abram Shulsky—what I saw was a very focused program of developing propaganda. That propaganda was aimed to convince people within the Pentagon and others at the State Department, people at the NSC, and the American people, that Iraq was somehow complicit in the attack of 9/11. Of course we now know it's not true, but that was one of the messages that was being developed.

Another message was that Iraq was a major weapons of mass destruction threat, not just to its neighbors, not just to the region, but to the United States of America. Working as a policy analyst, a political military officer, which I had been doing for years, and even before that, I had lots of exposure to intelligence. Even when I was in sub-Saharan Africa, we still got global intelligence, which would include Iraq. In 1991, we had invaded Iraq, so Iraq is obviously something that we had intelligence on, continuously, for the last decade. What I saw was not the use of this intelligence as information, as analyzed recommendations or supporting fact, but the use of this intelligence to provide bits and pieces of a propaganda story.

JE: Can you explain what the Office of Special Plans was and the importance of the "talking points" memos they produced?

When in August of 2002 the Office of Special Plans physically relocated out from where we were and moved up into different spaces under Abe Shulsky, one of the major products they provided to us as a sister office was a set of "talking points" that we action officers, political military officers, would utilize when we prepared any kind of policy paper, or any kind of information that we would be presenting to our higher ups, to visitors, to guests, or to anyone like that. These talking points were drawn from intelligence. I had seen the intelligence at least up to the secret level, and these talking points were never classified higher than secret. You could find bits and pieces of fact throughout, but they were framed, articulated, and crafted to convince someone of things that weren't true: 9/11, al-Qaeda being related to Saddam Hussein—the very things that a year later President Bush himself denies and feigns surprise about. Well, I worked in a place where they concentrated on preparing this story line, selling it to everyone that they could possibly sell it to, and insuring that it was used.

It was mandated that we take these talking points and include them in their entirety to every paper that we gave to our higher ups to prepare them to talk to people outside the Pentagon. It was very interesting in that we in the Pentagon, uniformed people and professional civilians, were being propagandized as well as the American people. I think that's really what caused me to look around and find out what was going on. Twenty years in the military working for government taught me that of course the government puts a positive spin on what it does, and that it tries to deny guilt until the very last minute. I understand that. I've been a party to that. That's propagandizing other people outside of government: the taxpayer, the customer, the media, etc. But I had never seen where that kind of propaganda was actually aimed inside of the Pentagon. And here it was. It was aimed at everyone outside of the small circle of political activists in the Pentagon.

JE: What were the origins of this propaganda campaign?

I needed to know more, and I studied these folks and their backgrounds. I had read all I could about Richard Perle. At the time I was in the Pentagon, he was the chairman of the Defense Policy Board; he's no longer the chairman, but he's still a strong member. I read all I could about Doug Feith, formally of Feith & Zell, whose only overseas client was the country of Israel. I looked at these things and asked, "What do I know about these people and their agendas?" Their agendas were wide open; they were out there. Richard Perle had published a co-written document in 1996 called "A Clean Break: A New Strategy for Securing the Realm." It was a document that's still out on the Internet, a document that he and others—some of whom are people that I also knew in the Pentagon and some of whom had received political appointments over at the State Department—had written as part of former Israeli Prime Minister Benjamin Netanyahu's campaign strategy. The document helped look at what kind of long-term security strategies would be adopted and would be suitable for Benjamin Netanyahu to proclaim as he ran in this campaign in 1996. If you read it you will see that it calls for regime change in Iraq. This was 1996!

But fine, that's for Netanyahu. What does that have to do with us? Well, it wouldn't have anything to do with us, except all of the same people who were preparing these strategies, developing them, researching them, discussing them and trying to play them out in an academic environment—an intellectualized environment—are suddenly transplanted to the Pentagon. They were no longer in an academic and intellectualized environment; they were in an empowered environment, and the things that they were doing seemed to track back to things that they had advocated in previous times as academics.

Information about this neoconservative agenda was out there, the planning had been done long before the Bush administration had come in. In one way that explains why the administration was so successful in convincing the American people, and so successful in populating the power center within the Pentagon, within the State Department, within the NSC to a lesser extent, and certainly within the vice president's office. There is a network that had been in place during the Clinton administration, and these same people worked on documents.

The Project for the New American Century (PNAC) is another organization with plenty of stuff written out there. They have a website. It's out in the open. Dick Cheney and Donald Rumsfeld, and a number of neoconservative intellectuals, were involved in developing PNAC. It was formed as a think tank and it developed a strategy for increasing and projecting American power. If you look at the signatories to the various products that PNAC put out, the names are Cheney, Rumsfeld, Wolfowitz, and all these guys.

So when they came in with Bush in 2000, they came in as a network of people who had worked together. That's not necessarily unusual, in that they were the party on the outs, and of course they associated with each other during the out years. In that sense there's nothing crazy or dangerous about this—except that the agenda that they had was an agenda to take us to war, and it relied on lies. It relied on stories that had to be woven and created and told and sold to the American people.

JE: How did the propaganda that was being produced in the Pentagon relate to what the White House was doing?

During the same time frame that I was looking at these "talking points," I was also listening to speeches by President Bush, in Cincinnati for example, or speeches by Dick Cheney. As I'm listening to them on the radio, I'm also reading them on the page, and I'm seeing the same words. That's huge political control. If you can keep everybody on the same page, that's great. But the things they were saying weren't true. They were false. They were lies, creative storytelling. What was coming out of the president's mouth and vice president's mouth were the same things that were being given to us to put into our senior civilian leadership's mouths. It was not based on intelligence that we saw. It was based on a very selective reading of the intelligence and a creative packaging to convey these two big points that the president and vice president and the whole neoconservative community used to justify this pre-emptive war on Iraq: that Saddam Hussein has WMD that are going to hit us soon, and that he's planning and working actively with terrorists and probably did 9/11.

Of course we deny that now, but certainly that was the message that was put forth to the American people and put forth internally to all of the untrusted people in the Pentagon, which is basically what you were if you weren't a political appointee. The Joint Staff is full of generals and admirals and their military staffs and professional civilians; there are not as many political appointees in the Joint Staff as there are in the Office of the Secretary of Defense, and the joint staff was not a trusted entity. They couldn't be trusted to say the right thing, so they were propagandized along with us.

JE: In your view, what was the ideological vision that was driving this propaganda push? And do you feel it colored their own view of how an invasion of Iraq would play out?

The neoconservatives have a political agenda with regard to foreign policy that they had been working on and writing about for years and years. It was their post-cold war vision for American power. They didn't call it empire, but they described how they felt America should proceed in the international community. Those folks were put in place long before 9/11, so certain changes were happening long before 9/11. When 9/11 happened, George Bush was activated. We needed to go do something and his neoconservative advisors were already in place and telling him what to do. That's why Iraq was brought up as early as September 12 or maybe the afternoon of the 11th.

They wanted to know how we could use this to take steps in Iraq to unseat this guy we don't like anymore. We used to like Saddam—we put him in place and supported him for many years—but now we don't like him; neoconservatives felt he needed to go. 2002 rolls around and the propaganda begins. George Bush compromises himself by lying to the American people, Dick Cheney compromises himself by lying to the American people, and we go into this war.

The Pentagon's policy shop did an extremely poor job of planning for the aftermath of the war, because people like General Zinni and any number of folks working in the Joint Staff and in other departments who suggested that it was not going to be a cakewalk were seen as the enemy. People who suggested we may have problems with nationalism, problems with this army, problems if we don't collect these folks as prisoners and they are out there, problems if the Ba'ath party is able to reorganize—all these suggestions of possibilities based on past experience like Somalia—these folks in pre-war planning were seen as the enemy in the pre-war propaganda phase. If you suggested that it wasn't going to be a cake walk, you've just made a problem for President Bush's pre-emptive war plan, because his pre-emptive war plan is not only that there's this huge risk—WMD and terrorism—but also that we can do this on the cheap. That was part of selling the whole thing to the American people.

Anyone who suggested it might not be cheap was contravening the propaganda, so they weren't listened to and they weren't given any breathing space. Of course Zinni was right, all these folks were right, and so in 2003 Bush starts looking around going, "What's happening? I thought you guys said it was going to be flowers and candy." By his own admission George Bush reads very little, by his own admission he travels overseas very little. He is not a foreign policy expert; he's a domestic political practitioner. I think Bush in some ways was surprised. Bush has no military experience. You don't learn a lot from going AWOL in the National Guard in Texas, and I think he was truly a little bit surprised that his advisors—many of them neoconservative advisors who were very happy to see this thing go forward—were wrong.

JE: Do you think that that the fact that very few, if any, of the neocons served in the military is relevant to what is happening now in Iraq?

It makes a difference, because there are a lot of things that you gain serving in the military. There are a lot of things about it that aren't good—it's very bureaucratic, for example—but in the military we practice things, we write articles about what we're going to practice, and we do exercises. It's like a football game where you have a plan. You practice it, you go out and play, after the game you go back into the locker room, and if you lost, the coach yells at you. If the quarterback fumbled some passes, he gets yelled at. It doesn't matter if he's the captain and it doesn't matter if he's the best guy on the team; if he screwed up, he gets yelled at. The military is like sports, in that you have to be able to take the heat for the good of the team; you look at what you did wrong, and you try to do it better next time.

In the military we have lessons learned, we practice, and we have what we call "hot washes." There's something that you gain from that that. None of the folks in our government today who are making these decisions understand this, and so what happens is they personalize their performance; it becomes part of their identity and their value as a person. So they're very reluctant to hear criticism. They're very reluctant to accept the fact that they screwed up. In Iraq, US government planners screwed up. Did the military do fine? CENTCOM did great, and in fact pulled some things out of the fire for these policy planners, who had done a very poor job of preparing for what it might look like the day after, or the week after. Soldiers know how to do this, and they did fine. The part that was a failure was the agenda, which is a false agenda.

American imperialism has no place in our tradition. We've been imperialistic in the past, but it has always been an aberration for this country. Pursuit of American empire—particularly a military empire, which is what the neoconservatives embrace and see as destiny—is not part of the American tradition, so there's mistake number one. Trying to do something that the American people don't really want to do, that's one mistake. If you had a hot wash after the game, you could discuss this and you could do so in a way that doesn't denigrate or reduce us as people. To the people who advocated this we could just say, "Look, you made a mistake, and we're not going to do that next time," but these people don't have that experience.

We call them "chicken hawks" because none of them served in the military—they didn't wear a uniform, and they all had other things to do. None of their children served in the military either, so this is a double chicken-hawk whammy here, because George Bush's daughters don't wear a uniform. It's funny that he says, "You know my daughters are the same age as Jessica Lynch." Yes, but there's a big difference: Jessica Lynch wore a uniform and did what you guys told her to do.

I really think it's not just lack of military experience, that it's also lack of sports experience. If you look at George Bush and Dick Cheney—Rumsfeld's a wrestler, but that's an individual sport—team sports is what they're missing. In team sports people are allowed to make mistakes; they're allowed to be criticized in the group and come back the next day knowing that, yes, you're a good player but you really screwed up badly, and they can take that kind of criticism.

There's a book that was written back in the early '90's, a book on management for women, called *Hard Ball for Women,* and throughout the book, it used the team sports analogies, as a way for women in management to understand how the game is played in business. To understand how men, stereotypical men, would proceed with decision-making, how they would move forward and act. One of the things the book pointed out is that in the '70s, '80s, and early '90s, women had far less opportunity to play team sports than they do today. So women in business during this period were at somewhat of a disadvantage with most men, in that they never really had the formative experience of being part of a team and being criticized when you screw up. These men who are neocons—notice that there are very few women neocons—fall into that same category of women statistically who have never played team sports experience, and they're very, very sensitive to any kind of criticism. They have yet—Wolfowitz to this day, Doug Feith in particular, Bill Luti of course, and Dick Cheney, who is in total denial—they have yet to admit that there were even the slightest mistakes. Richard Perle, another one who's never played a team sport, do you know what is his reaction to criticism is? "Well, you don't know enough. You're not smart like me and therefore you don't understand what we were doing. It was really right; it was just implemented poorly"—always pushing the excuses out.

The fact of the matter is that every mistake that has been made dates back to the pre-emptive war doctrine, which is no doctrine at all and certainly will not be sustained post-George Bush. This doctrine was certainly a mistake, and it's historically unjustified. There's just no foundation for it. Another mistake was lying to the American people for the whole year of 2002, acting like we would win this war on a shoestring, creating all these false expectations about how we would be greeted by the Iraqi people, when now we see it getting uglier and uglier and deadlier and deadlier each day. All of these things constitute mistakes made by Dick Cheney, George Bush, Rumsfeld, Wolfowitz, Doug Feith, Bill Luti, Abe Shulsky, Richard Perle, the Defense Policy Board—and not a single one of them will even admit they were mistakes. I think they're afraid to admit it because where they come from with no military experience, no hot wash experience, and no team sport experience, if they admit it's a mistake they'll feel it as a crushing blow to their entire reputation and to who they are. And that's very scary for them.

JE: Based on your experience with these people, do you think the neocons actually believe their own rhetoric about spreading democracy in Iraq? Or do you think it's a front for something else?

Paul Bremer is working to shift power to some Iraqis that we like. He wants to make it look like we're shifting power to all Iraqis, but certainly we can't do that because if they had democracy in Iraq, it would be a democracy that most likely kicks our military bases out of there and kicks the military footprint out, which is partly why we went to war. There is a strategic military reason to occupy Iraq. We have four big bases in Iraq, we have numerous smaller bases, and these bases are intended to stay there. The new government of Iraq that Paul Bremer is working to deliver to them in some way is top-down centralization. Bremer would be a prized member of the Ba'ath Party. Centralized state control: "I tell you what to do. You do it." It doesn't allow for any feedback or any type of market operation. He fits perfectly with the Ba'ath Party agenda. He runs the state like most of the communist parties ran their states, which was very ineffective.

But what they're trying to do is to have an Iraq that is a friend to us, not an Iraq that is liberated—that's just totally bogus. We never intended to liberate the Iraqi people. We intended to liberate Iraq from Saddam and have a military footprint there. We'd been trying for a long time to lift our footprint, our military bases situation, from Saudi Arabia. We've done that now. We have Kuwait, we have the 5th Fleet in Bahrain, we have a nice base in Qatar, but it's a little too far south, and we have four bases in Iraq. Beautiful bases. We can hit Syria. We can hit Iran. We can keep tabs on Afghanistan. These are some of the things we can now do.

And the plan for an independent Iraq, if you can even use the word "independent," is that our bases will stay there. They we will be there as a security provider for whoever's leading that country, and we'll have a great interest in seeing who that is. That is not democracy and that is not liberation, but it is very much part of Richard Perle's 1996 strategy. It is very much part of the Project for the New American Century's vision. It was never about Saddam Hussein being bad because he gassed Kurds when he was our ally back in 1988. It wasn't about that. It was about us needing bases and needing a trusted, friendly country and capital in Baghdad. That's what we needed.

If you look at what was written by the neoconservatives prior to George Bush taking office, you see these things are all part of their plan. When they came to power again, they carried the plan out, without changing it, through subterfuge, through propaganda, and through political maneuvering. They did not do it honestly and they did it in a very expensive manner, in money and in blood, in treasure from this country, in the lives of our young men and the lives of Iraqis, costing us our reputation internationally. There were very many costs involved, but they succeeded in some ways.

JE: How does Afghanistan fit into this scenario?

There's another big aspect of what it is that we're pursuing in the Middle East, and that includes Afghanistan. And it is natural resource control, efforts to reduce risk in world flows and that kind of thing, and this has been on our agenda for decades; it's not necessarily new. Invading foreign countries and occupying them is a little bit new. In the old days, what we would do is put our guy in charge, like we put Saddam in charge. We'd help Saddam achieve power and he was our ally. That worked for a while, but the neoconservatives are a little bit more aggressive and a little bit more imperial in how they approach this. It is not just about politics, but it relates to strategy, and strategy and security relate to natural resources, especially for an energy consumer like our country.

In Afghanistan, it's really in some ways uglier. Osama bin Laden is credited with 9/11, and he was being helped by the Taliban, although it's actually reversed: he was helping the Taliban a little bit more than they were helping them. But there was kind of a symbiotic relationship between Osama's folks and the Taliban running Afghanistan. After 9/11, going into Afghanistan to hunt down Osama bin Laden, which is what we said we would do, was a very popular action. By most people, it was seen as a decisive move by George Bush; it had widespread popular support. Even people who oppose war with Iraq generally see some logic in going into Afghanistan.

But the interesting thing about Afghanistan, and this is again out there for anyone who cares about it, is that the plan to invade Afghanistan was in place long before 9/11. At least by June 2001, the plan to invade Afghanistan was ready to go; we were set to topple the Taliban and put our own guy in charge. Why?

In the past, we were actually allied with the Taliban in some ways; we worked with them when they kicked the Soviets out. Furthermore, the Taliban was a very conservative group—pro-Islam, traditional Islamic interpretation—but they were anti-communist. So in some ways we were on their side. But the Taliban needed to go because, since 1996 or 1997, they had been unable to provide security for a particular oil and gas pipeline project that was going to cut across the northeastern segment of Afghanistan and across into Pakistan and then branch off.

There were two parts. Pakistan was the outlet for the proposed pipeline. There was also another leg of the pipeline that would go into a town in India that happened to be the site of a huge Enron power plant. It was funded largely by the World Bank and partly by the government of India. It's non-operational now because part of the fuel that was going to produce this electricity never got there. And the pipeline project had been stymied largely due to security concerns in that part of Afghanistan. The Taliban had been in charge for six years and had had a very difficult time consolidating power.

They had a difficult time securing that part of the country, and because they could not make progress, the pipeline project's primary investor, Unocal, an American gas and oil company, had basically withdrawn. Several of the folks in George Bush's Afghanistan program and Middle East program used to work for Unocal. You'll know two of the names: Hamid Karzai, president of Afghanistan, used to be a Unocal consultant; also, Zalmay Khalilzad, who is currently US ambassador to Afghanistan, was the envoy there and is now a very significant guy in the current Bush administration. [Editor's note: And a founding member of the Project for the New American Century]. So we have two former Unocal folks acting as the US allies in place in Kabul, and guess what? One of the first things that Hamid Karzai did when he took over—when he was put in place with his American body guards at the time—was to call up the other countries in this trans-Afghanistan pipeline project and get it back on track.

Now, for a long time I had not seen a map of our bases. I had seen a map of the proposed pipeline going through the northeastern part of

Afghanistan, but for many months I had been looking for a good map of our bases. I found one not long ago. It's identical. If you map the proposed pipeline route across Afghanistan, and you look at our bases in Afghanistan—military bases, Special Forces, logistics troops and those kinds of things—they match perfectly. Our bases are there to solve a problem that the Taliban could not solve. The Taliban couldn't provide security in that part of Afghanistan. Now that's where our bases are. Around our bases we have some security. We're taking some mortar, fire, and there's some stuff that comes into our bases because we're targets, of course, but in general there's a radius around US military bases where you have some security.

So, what does that have to do with Osama bin Laden? It has nothing to do with Osama bin Laden. It has everything to do with the longer plan, in this case a strategy that I wouldn't necessarily call "neoconservative," but that fits in perfectly with the neoconservative ideology. It's an ideology that says that if you have military force, and you need something from a weaker country, then you need to deploy that force and take what you need, because your country's needs are paramount. It's the whole idea of unilateralism, of using force to achieve your aims.

JE: Can you say a bit more about the unilateralist bent of neoconservative thinking? Where, and why, do you see them differing from foreign policy realists in rejecting the value—or at least the pragmatic benefits—of international law?

International law doesn't matter to neoconservatives, in part because they haven't served in the military and in part because they are not internationalists. They don't recognize the idea of reciprocity. Reciprocity applies to free markets in trading. Reciprocity is a foundation of the global free market or any free market. Reciprocity is certain norms of behavior that allow you to be predictable to people, or to countries, or to organizations that don't know you very well. How can I know that when I give you five cents you're going to give me five cents worth of product? If I don't know you, if I haven't conducted business with you, I may not know. If I know that you and I both adhere to a certain standard, though, that says when a person gives you five cents, you give him five cents of product back, then I can operate with you. This is the foundation of free trade, a foundation of diplomacy, and a foundation of international relations.

Neoconservatives discount internationalism, in part because they fail to understand the market. They are not economists. Find me an economist who is a neoconservative. Most of the neoconservatives pay very little attention to the structures of market relations. They don't understand them. So because they're not sensitive to the market, they discount internationalism; they discount the idea of reciprocity.

In terms of security and behavior, because they haven't served in the military, they discount the idea of having norms of war. They discount the idea of a just war. A just war becomes whatever they say it is. That's what they prefer, having never been POWs and never likely to be POWs. The Geneva Conventions were an attempt to prevent the barbarism that occurred in Europe with the Great War and World War II. Your POWs are not tortured and my POWs are not tortured. Well, this administration is very ignorant of what internationalism is; they see it only as a negative, and they see it as letting the UN tell you what to do when certainly that has nothing to do with it. They don't understand reciprocity. They've never served in the military or run their own business in the sense of being sensitive to the marketplace. Because they are ignorant of these things, they discount reciprocity's value and it's going to be very costly to us.

JE: How do you think the Iraq occupation is going to play out in the 2004 Presidential election?

Unlike George Bush, Dick Cheney, Richard Perle, Wolfowitz, and Rumsfeld, most Americans have a child, or a cousin, or a brother, or a spouse, or somebody in their community who is serving in the military. Those folks are going to come back from Iraq. They're going to start telling their stories. And we're going to be touched by this. So it'll be an election year where foreign policy cannot be shuttled off to the side.

George Bush has a lot of incentive to get Iraq off the front pages, if he can do that at all. He wants to show us success, to be able to check that square, to be able to say that we liberated the Iraqi people. He wants to say that we've done these things and have brought the soldiers home. That's what the American people want. They want the soldiers to come home. They want everything to be nice again. He will move in that direction this year, and he's already started to do it.

This fall Karl Rove is guiding Bush's campaign. You already see rifts and anxieties among the neoconservative foreign policy group, who, while they have their bases, also have other agendas in the region.

Certainly regime change in Syria was on the list. Democratic reform, if need be through outside force, was something they wanted for Iran. If you read Richard Perle's writings and those of the Project for the New American Century, they will tell you it's not just about Baghdad. The road to Damascus leads through Baghdad; this is out of the neoconservative writing. They understand what it is that they're doing regionally. It's not liberation; it has to do with regime change. The neocons wanted to continue on, and they're being stifled, at least in this election year, because George Bush can't take those kinds of chances.

JE: Do you see George Bush as a traditional conservative? Is he a neocon? Where do you place him, and his Republican administration overall, within the context of American conservatism?

Most Americans, and particularly most Republicans who consider themselves part of the conservative party, do not believe that Bush embraces traditional conservative values. He will play that card though. His religious associations, his advocacy, his respect for God and those kinds of things are important, and they are part of traditional American values. This country's founding fathers for the most part not only believed in God, but were religious folks, and felt that that was an important, civilizing force. So George Bush will appeal to that and, in that sense, his religious appeal, to the Protestant side in any case, will be a traditional thing.

But he is not a traditional conservative, and most conservatives recognize this. Bush creates a huge rift in the Republican Party as it is today. In Congress and in the heartland, people see his excessive spending, his domestic activities, the huge number of mandates, his No Child Left Behind education bill, as very top-down. A centralizing, federalizing mandate for public education is contrary to the traditional American approach toward education. So there is already a huge questioning going on amongst conservatives themselves as to whether or not George Bush is a conservative. And if he's not, what is he and how did he get there?

Traditional conservative foreign policy tends toward, if not isolationism, then toward a truly defense-oriented foreign policy. Free trade, engagement of trade, have been a tradition for 400 years. Even before we were a country, when we were a colony, trading was where it was at. However, George Bush has problems with that as well, because he needs votes from all kinds of people and many people today in

America feel that their jobs are threatened as a result of too-free trade. So true conservatives, conservative intellectuals and thinkers will, and already have, articulated a great deal of concern about George Bush, in that he is not really part of it.

For many years now, for decades, both Republican and Democratic parties have gone to the center to achieve their votes. So, George Bush won't have a problem if he can rely on the conservatives not to vote Democratic. He will have a problem if the conservatives stay home. He needs their votes and he'll be walking a fine line throughout the campaign season. There are many conservatives in this country, and some of them are Democrats and Independents and many are Republicans and Libertarians; we have a whole large swath of people who consider themselves conservative and traditional Americans. Bush will need to woo them and he will need to encourage them and inspire them. The problem is that when he tries to inspire them through things like budget cuts for things that traditional conservatives feel are unnecessary or represent an unconstitutional role of the federal government—as he does those things, he may put his center at risk. So he's got a tough job.

JE: As a conservative yourself, how important is this presidential election to you?

To me it's very important, although I harbor no illusions that a Democratic administration would not continue with the Iraq process. I want the soldiers home now; that's what I believe is the correct thing to do. I don't believe a Democratic president will do this, but a Democratic president will change the major cabinet secretaries and remove many of these advisors who have basically been living in fantasyland and forcing the rest of us along with them. So I think it's very, very important. There's a whole sense of "Does your vote really matter?" It's hard to say. However, in the last election the Democrat candidate, Al Gore, received a great number of votes. The vote count was very close on the popular level, in fact he exceeded the popular vote count. The Electoral College vote was also very, very close. This is the whole drama of Florida. I think that tells people that their vote does count, and I think many people care. A lot of people who voted for George Bush—I hear from these people, they write to me, and they're conservatives or libertarians—they say, "You know, I voted for George Bush in 2000, and I will never vote for him again." Now, does that mean they'll go to a Democrat? No. But what it means is they won't vote for George Bush. George Bush has lost a vote. If George Bush loses a few votes from what he got last time, he will not be president again.

So I think it's interesting. You can talk about it philosophically: "Does your vote count?" I would say that your vote counts and your non-vote counts. If you're a Bush supporter who feels that George Bush is not being a traditionally conservative, fiscally conservative, and humble-foreign-policy-delivering president, then perhaps you should not vote for George Bush. Should you vote for an alternate candidate? Well, that's your call. But you certainly shouldn't give your vote to George Bush when George Bush is not the man who represents you. I could be wrong, but I do think that Karl Rove is extremely worried about the average American conservative in both the Democratic Party and the Republican Party, not to mention independent conservatives. Karl Rove is very concerned with getting that guy out to the polls. And there will be a huge amount of money spent lobbying to get those folks out. I think it's going to be a hard battle, because I think many people feel betrayed; many conservatives have been betrayed by George Bush and they will not be inclined to give him their vote. And that will put his opponent in office. It wouldn't be a vote of confidence in the opponent necessarily either.

What it means is that George Bush is not going to get those votes that he counted on the last time. I truly believe it's going to be a big problem. And I'm optimistic that he will not be reelected, but he's got a lot of money and he will spend it to make sure that conservatives like me go out to the polls and give George Bush a vote. He'll try.

Shenandoah Valley, Virginia
January 6, 2004

NORMAN MAILER

Norman Mailer published his first book, *The Naked and the Dead*, in 1948. *The Armies of the Night* won the National Book Award and the Pulitzer Prize in 1969, and Mailer received a second Pulitzer in 1980 for *The Executioner's Song*. His most recent work is *Why Are We at War?*

JE: You wrote recently that 9/11 did enormous damage to American morale, that it damaged us to the core. How do you see the influence of 9/11 on the American political and cultural landscape, not to mention the American psyche, as this election season and this war continue to unfold?

I would say that in my life there have been three events that have altered American history. First of all, there was Pearl Harbor, and then there was the assassination of Jack Kennedy, and then there was 9/11. And 9/11, I think, is almost as large a blow, and in a certain sense, psychologically speaking, it's a deeper blow than Pearl Harbor, because Pearl Harbor actually ended up galvanizing America for war. And what characterized World War II, in my memory of it, was that—while any war is immensely complex, of course—there was a central unity in America about that war. While there were people who opposed the war, they were essentially a true minority. Pearl Harbor was almost a plus for America in a funny way; I think if the Japanese had to do it over again, they would recognize that was not the way to do it.

9/11 is still a question, because 9/11 went very deep into the psychological core of American well-being. We'll never be the same after 9/11—because average Americans, in my opinion, never think of themselves as being hated in other countries. They consider that either the ruses of ugly foreign politicians, or else envy or jealously, but essentially the feeling is that we in America are okay. We're terrific. The country has had a feeling for a long time that it's blessed, and 9/11 created a seismic wave, if you will, of unrest, anxiety, and all the things in America, in the American psyche that were not nailed down, were now rattled loose. It created not only a terrible inner fright—a nightmarish quality was introduced into American life, and examples of that were the anthrax scares that followed, which were absurd looking back on them, but at the time everyone's in a panic. After all, everyone alive is guilty, more or less, to a degree, and what people began to feel is "I'm guilty," "I'm the one who's going to get injured in an attack."

So in my opinion, the Republican administration are very cold, savvy people, up to a point. They know America very well. George W. Bush knows the average American immensely well, because his intelligence is no greater than the average American's. And that's an asset as well as a liability. Stupidity is a strength because intelligent people finally become weak before stupid people, because they can't penetrate the stupidity. And George Bush is happily stupid that way. So he has a wonderful understanding, up to a point, of how Americans work. He knows that half the country, at least, psychologically speaking, has a structure that's like a button board. Just press the right button, and you'll get the appropriate response. He knows words like God, America, Freedom, Democracy, Compassion, Conservatism, and he uses those words.

I think instinctively he knew this was a golden opportunity. An extraordinary opportunity. 9/11 gave him the sanction to do things he couldn't have done before. Now whether that started with him or not, I don't pretend to know. But the people around him, for a long time, ever since the cold war ended with Russia, have been dying to make a big move into the world. Globalism, which a couple of years earlier, under Clinton, was an aspect of that, was a relatively peaceful, dubious aspect and much resisted for many good reasons, as well as reasons perhaps not so good.

I don't pretend to be any kind of authority on globalism, but what I do believe is that there are two kinds of love in this country for America. There are those who love America, as I would say I do, because of the freedom here. That freedom has given me the opportunity to do an enormous amount of work, given my essential laziness, and enabled me to say things that I couldn't say in every country. Now you pay for saying things, but you don't pay a terrible price. You don't pay such a price that it freezes your courage. So in that sense, I love America for what it offers, for its freedoms.

But there are people who love this country religiously. Their fundamental belief is that America is God-inspired, and that God wants us to make the whole world like America. Well, to me that's a horror. Because if you make the whole world like America, there won't be a decent spot left where you can think. It will all be high-rise buildings, super-highways, pollution, glut, overproduction, and the essential meaninglessness of making money for money's sake will take over the world to a huge degree. We are not equipped to present democracy to the rest of the world. We are too ignorant here, we're too stupid, we're too self-satisfied, we're too vain, and we have a dubious species of democracy as it is, because money talks much too much in our democracy. When you have a country where the richest people are making 500 times as much as the poorest wage earners, then as far as I'm concerned, you're back with the pharoahs. We have a set of religious beliefs here to the extent that we must support the wealthy, the rich, that the rich are in terrible trouble, that if we don't take care of the rich everything terrible will happen. My opinion is that the rich can always take care of themselves. That's why they're rich: they have a wonderful skill for making money. They don't need government help. They need to be impeded by the government. It will bring out the best in them and, at the same time, it will level the playing field a little bit.

So in that sense, going back to what I was saying just a little earlier, when you're that rich, to avoid guilt, you have to believe that America is God's will and that America should be put all over the world, should be explained to the rest of the world, should dominate the rest of the world. Behind the whole business with Iraq, as a terribly sour comedy abstracted down to its smallest motives, was the sense that Iraq had to be invaded because it was the first step in going toward American empire. Ever since the cold war ended, there were people who were fuming on the right, thinking this is the golden opportunity, now that Russia is out of the way, for America to take over the world, and we're not doing anything about it. Those damned liberals, those soft heads, are keeping us from doing what is our godly mission. So Bush and company found 9/11 an enormous springboard into trying to carry that out.

Now, I spoke about how intelligent—not intelligent, but how shrewd—Bush is in relation to the American people, and some of the worst elements of the American people—I mean he knows them well that way. He knows nothing about the world. And he is surrounded by people who play to that. Some of them knew a little more about what the difficulties might be in Iraq, but they went in blissfully, knowing they had a fabulous military machine, and they knew they'd win the war with nothing, with no great effort or no great price in terms of lives. They had absolutely no sense of the immense difficulties or what's involved in trying to bring democracy to a country that's been tyrannized for 30 years, and on top of that was never put together as a nation, but was put together by an act of will of the British and a few other powers after World War I. Given the fact that it was also a semi-poor country—it had wealth but it was not a thriving country—it was almost asking for a dictator. Because that's the formula for dictators, that you have a country that doesn't have enough money and has huge divisions, and the only way it can function is with a dictator, because if you have democracy you have civil war. So democracy is not for all countries. Democracy is an advanced state of being. Democracy is achieved by a certain sense of sacrifice in the people who create the democracy in the beginning. The people who created the American democracy were ready to die for their ideas and figured they well might. There's that famous remark by—was it Benjamin Franklin?—"We must hang together, gentlemen, or we will all hang separately."

The notion that democracy is a wonderful potion, that you can just walk into a country, conquer it, and inject it with democracy, is a profound fallacy. Democracy has to be earned. On top of that, to come to a country where for 30 years they've been under the hegemony and the dictatorship of this absolute tyrant, this monster, if you will, means that practically everyone in that country, at one point or another, went in for shameful compromises. To stay alive and to take care of your children, you had to pretend to things, you had to do things that curdled your stomach and scorched your soul. Why? To stay alive and protect the family. And in that sense they are all ridden with hideous bad conscience.

Now to go in there and conquer them from without, where they don't even get rid of the tyrant by themselves and at least have that liberation, which is crucial—it won't work. When a country has a tyrant, it's up to that country to get rid of that tyrant. The same rule applies to countries that applies to individuals: If there is something god-awful wrong with you, ultimately the cure has to come from within. The will to cure oneself has to be there. These countries that are dreadful are dreadful; but they have their own history, they have their own logic, they even have their own pride. If we think that democracy is the finest system on earth—and I think it is for countries that are well-to-do—those countries that are not democratic will find their way to democracy or they're going to remain dictatorial and awful. But it is not our function on earth as a country to solve every other country's problems, because, I will repeat: we are too stupid, too ignorant, too vain, too arrogant, and too untried. We don't even have the cynicism of the French, who know how difficult it is, or the odd, offbeat humor of the British, who also know how difficult it is. No, we go in, and we're so wonderful that we're going to take it over and make it marvelous. We're going to make it shine.

That's why we've gotten into huge difficulties there. I'm not speaking after the fact. I will take credit—you know, I'm an expert, which means I'm right about 50 percent of the time—and one time I happened to be right was about what was going to happen in Iraq. I knew it was going to be a disaster. But the disaster is precisely because real democracy in Iraq means one of two things—civil war or a Muslim theocracy. Now, we can't let that happen. Since we can't let that happen, and since we've also made this a wonderful gathering point for terrorists, we're going to have something go on there year after year after year if we refuse to leave. In the meantime, the $87 billion [spent on Iraq] would pay three and a half million people a salary of $25,000 a year. That's an incredible figure if you think about it, when you think about all the jobless here. Public works programs could give people jobs that they don't have now, and are not going to get.

But instead we're spending that money with the notion that we're going to start an empire drive. Because the only explanation for Iraq that makes sense to me is not that we're interested in bringing democracy to Iraq, or getting rid of a tyrant, but that this was the first step in controlling the Middle East. Once we could control the Middle East, we could control the rest of the world. We could come to a *modus vivendi* with China, where they'd be the Greeks to our Romans, because they're going to be much, much better at computers than we've ever dreamed of being. Right now people of Asiatic extraction in our universities tend to get far better marks in science and engineering and economics than we Americans do.

JE: Let's shift gears here and turn to one of the central claims you make in your New York Review of Books *piece, "The White Man Unburdened." You talk there about the war, and the drive to war, in relation to the American male, the American working-class male in particular. We've heard about the so-called NASCAR dad voting block throughout this election, and still we're seeing that Bush is maintaining political strength with men; he's continuing to benefit from the male side of the gender gap. I'm wondering what you think when you see Bush being positioned by Karl Rove as a tough-talking, straight-shooting guy.*

I wrote the piece first, and then noticed a demographic that a Democratic pollster was presenting that said, in effect, just that. That the white working-class male has moved over to George W. Bush. Well, that's for a variety of reasons. You can attribute Schwarzenegger's victory in California to the same thing. It was as if the more women he groped, the more men voted for him. Why? Because women's lib, with all of its achievements, also created a great many evils and ills, whether they like it or not. And one of them is that they downgraded the American male. The average American male no longer feels the happy, easy confidence he had, right or wrong, ten, twenty, certainly forty years ago. I remember when I was young, we just took it for granted that being a man was terrific, and women were wonderful; they were our support system. All of that has been altered. But in the course of being altered, we've also been vilified as men, told that we're no good. This is a rage to the American working-class male, and so they were happy that Schwarzenegger groped all these women. They were very happy about it. They thought: now all those feminists, they're just going to have to put up with it, and like it or lump it, we're going to have our guy in.

That has a parallel to George Bush's essential sense, his grasp, of the fact that he'll appeal to men as long as he's tough-talking and macho—which, by the way, is not a word I sneer at. It's an important word to me—but he abuses that word. It's one thing to have a sense of being macho; it's another to abuse it totally. Bush abuses it. For example, he posed with Arnold Schwarzenegger after his victory and said, "We both married well, we both have been accused of speaking English badly, and we both have big biceps." Well, what kind of ignorant, stupid, dull, low-level vanity is it for him to compare his biceps, whatever they are—and I couldn't care less because they can't be fabulous—to Schwarzenegger's, who spends his life on his biceps, for God's sake?

JE: Can you say more about why this sort of thing works with men?

Macho's a word that's been much abused. Women's liberation has taken ideological tanks and driven them through the concept. The average man, by now, is afraid to use the word. It's almost like speaking of excrement. It's that bad of a word. The fact is, and it's much misunderstood, that people who are truly macho live very dangerous, demanding lives that are never at ease because their machismo is always in question. In fact there's almost a mathematical human equation there, which is that to the degree that you're macho, the more certain it is that you're going to die an early death, because if you keep meeting every threat and imposition on your ego, sooner or later you're going to crash. I think implicit in most men is a feeling, a very basic—indeed, almost primitive—feeling, that without courage a man has nothing. The question is how much courage is needed, particularly in the modern world. So to make one's peace with machismo, to decide how macho you are, and how much you're not going to be macho, is crucial to manhood.

Now that's terribly abused by people who abuse machismo as a concept, and Bush does. He does not have the right to consider himself macho. He's never been tested physically. He avoided the war in Vietnam, avoided his National Guard training. He's never seen combat. He's never been a physical type. He was a cheerleader, if I recall correctly, at Yale. He was a fraternity type. He's the born fraternity president, with all the pluses and all the minuses of being fraternity president—the minuses being the smugness and shallowness of spirit that are absolutely required to function well in that position. So he's not qualified to speak of himself as macho, but he's shrewd enough to know that those working males out there are very angry, and that if he presents himself as macho—as he did of course with that ridiculous flight in the backseat of that fast plane to land on the carrier in full combat gear—if he presents himself that way, they'll buy it. They'll buy it because they need it.

Brooklyn, New York
October 29, 2003

ZIA MIAN

Zia Mian is a physicist and member of the research staff at Princeton University's Program on Science and Global Security. His work focuses on nuclear weapons and nuclear power issues, especially in South Asia. His publications include *Pakistan's Atomic Bomb and the Search for Security* (Gautam Publishers, Lahore, 1995), *Making Enemies, Creating Conflict: Pakistan's Crises of State and Society* (Marshal Press, Lahore, 1997), and *Armaments, Disarmament, and International Security*, (Oxford University Press, 2003). In addition to his research and writing, he is active with a number of civil society groups working in the area of nuclear disarmament and with the peace movement.

JE: Could you put the invasion of Iraq into its relevant historical context, especially regarding the realignments after the cold war?

This was the third time in the 20th century, so to speak, where the American elite and the American state has sought to find ways of capturing and crystallizing its power in the world. The first one was of course after World War I with Woodrow Wilson and his 16 Points and the League of Nations. The goal then was—as the European empires had been devastated during World War I and the United States had emerged as an economic and military power—to try and set a new international arrangement based upon its own notions of how the world should work. That didn't get very far, in part because of the Depression.

So after World War II what you see is that the United States emerges even stronger in comparison to the European powers and tries again. This time they tried to create the United Nations, the World Bank and the International Monetary Fund, and NATO, as a military alliance to consolidate and make permanent the American military presence in Europe. In short, you see them trying to take advantage of that moment of influence that they had after World War II to try to make sure that there would be no rivals.

After the collapse of the Soviet Union in 1990, people returned to that question, saying, what can we do, now that we are again unprecedented and unequaled in influence in the world. So this was the third time in the space of 100 years that people took themselves back to this question, "How can we remake the world the way that we would like it to be?" So what we're seeing now is an unfolding of that whole dynamic all over again, and people like Condoleezza Rice and others,

189

if you read what they have to say and pay attention, they draw explicit parallels to these previous experiences. So Condoleezza Rice has written about how she sees the world now as what it was like in 1946 and 1947—in other words, when the United States was the dominant economic power in the world and where it had used nuclear weapons on Hiroshima and Nagasaki and was the only country in the world with nuclear weapons. The goal was to intimidate the rest of the world to accept the new international order that the US was proposing.

The rise of the Soviet Union, and especially the testing of Soviet nuclear weapons in 1949, and then the cold war and the capacity the Soviets showed to be able to compete, at least for a while, in this kind of development of the instruments of mutual genocide, restrained both sides. Containment, which was the US strategy, was reciprocated: the US contained the Soviets, the Soviets contained the US. The absence of that containment has freed the US, at least as its policymakers see it, to try again now. Some of us think that the goal is really not just a question of consolidating power using existing institutions, but perhaps to actually reconstruct an entirely new set of institutions where the kinds of international fora (like the United Nations, etc.) may no longer actually be relevant at all to some of the people in power in the United States. We may be in for a period of fundamental restructuring of the world as we know it.

JE: But isn't the world in a dangerous and chaotic period of globalization-driven change right now and therefore in need of stabilizing?

It's a question of where you see it from. Because one of the things that the exercise of power does is that it cuts both ways. The US exercises power in the world to create stability, but people who are on the receiving end of that power see themselves being oppressed, and so they resist. As a consequence, this process of trying to pacify the world and get it to go along with what the United States wants actually creates the resistance the US is trying to quell. In that sense, the more you exercise power, the more resistance you create. US military planners and strategic thinkers recognize this, and one of them pointed out quite recently that in the case of Iraq sending in more troops isn't an answer—that just creates more targets. That recognizes a fundamental dynamic of this situation: that the more the US tries to impose itself on the world, the more places and the more kinds of people will feel the edge of US power and will say, "We're not putting up with it." So this is not the way that will actually get us out of the situation that we find ourselves in. It only makes things worse.

JE: In your own work you have written a lot about nuclear proliferation. How do the policies of the Bush administration affect the dynamics of proliferation?

Proliferation has emerged in the last fifteen years as a key concern of United States policymakers but, in my opinion, they miss a fundamental element of what's actually going on. That is the fact that they never start by asking the question that if a Third World country is trying to build nuclear weapons, what makes their leaders think that nuclear weapons are an answer to the problems they have? What makes elites in Third World countries like North Korea, like Iraq, like Iran, Pakistan, India, and so forth, why do they think that having nuclear weapons solves any problems? Because the United States taught them to think about nuclear weapons in particular ways. Once you accept that, then you realize that you are actually creating the problem yourself. When the United States insists that its 10,000 nuclear weapons are the cornerstone of its defense and its security, of course others are going to think, if this is the magic bullet that creates security for the most powerful state in the world, then we should also have a piece of this. We export our ways of thinking because the world is relatively transparent, after all, and we use domestic arguments to justify domestic decisions, but other people are listening also. Elites in Third World countries are paying attention to what the US is saying and doing, and unfortunately, in my opinion, drawing completely the wrong lessons, which is that if we are confronting a nuclear armed empire, the only way to resist is to have nuclear weapons ourselves. But, again, it comes back to the US being the author of a way of thinking and a way of behaving in the world that others emulate because they see that this is what power is, and this is how power is exercised in the world. When they do that, they just clone themselves by using the US as a model, so proliferation is actually driven by the US possession and justification of its own nuclear weapons.

Now the Bush administration in particular is wanting to have nuclear weapons for the next 100 years. It is putting in place programs for designing and manufacturing new kinds of nuclear weapons. The old production facilities for making nuclear weapons were built in the early years of the cold war and now they need to be replaced if the US is going to continue to develop and sustain a nuclear arsenal. The Bush administration is committed to this redevelopment and giving nuclear weapons a future, so they are building these things. So we will have not just, as some people hope, another American century, but another nuclear American century.

JE: How does 9/11 fit into this?

September 11 represents multiple things. The first, of course, is that it was a terrible and appalling act of violence. But when you understand where it comes from, it makes the whole situation more complicated. The first complication is, of course, that the use of massive violence against civilians as a way of putting pressure on governments was actually invented by the United States and Great Britain during World War II. They bombed cities in Germany and then cities in Japan to force governments to change, to concede defeat. Since then, this has become part of what military strategies are available to states. Now you're seeing the same strategic notions being made available, because of technology, to groups such as al-Qaeda that aren't states. So this use of massive violence to make governments change their minds about policies has become something that's open to larger numbers of people, to a larger number or groups—basically to anyone with a political agenda. So in a sense we are the authors, at one level, of 9/11 ourselves, because we introduced into the world a way of thinking about how things can be and should be done, justifying it in terms of "Oh, we're at war."

JE: What do you make of the way ordinary Americans have understood what's going on?

One of the things that people have been doing is trying to understand how Americans have thought about and understand, and misunderstand, what's been happening in the last year over the war with Iraq. Intensive polling has been used to try and understand where people are on this, and it's been discovered that 60 percent of Americans share one of three fundamental misconceptions about what's happened in the last year.

The first misconception is that the United States has clear evidence of Saddam Hussein's involvement in 9/11. The second misconception is that not only have we found weapons of mass destruction in Iraq already, but that Iraq used weapons of mass destruction against the

United States in the war. The third misconception is that the rest of the world actually supported the United States in the war against Iraq. The polling data suggests that 60 percent of Americans have one or another of these three misconceptions. And when you look to see who in particular has these, it turns out that people who watch Fox News are the largest group that has these misconceptions. It actually does correlate with where you get your sources of information.

Now this tells you something very important, because these misconceptions shape completely how people react to what's going on; none of these things are true and yet such large proportions of people believe them. So we have to ask why do they believe these things, why do they watch Fox, and why do they believe what they see on Fox? When people pursued this question a little bit further, one of the things they found is that it doesn't connect with political identity—it doesn't matter whether you're a Republican or a Democrat or an Independent. The major thing it correlates with is: "Do you support the president?" People who say they support the president regardless of their own party affiliation are much more likely to have these misconceptions. We seem to be in a situation where the notion of trust in authority and the president is suppressing people's critical judgments. They're not being skeptical about what they're being told. They're not asking, why is this true, why should I believe you? They're just seeing the president say this, and thinking, therefore, it must be so. One of the things that is critical in the next period is to reawaken critical sensibilities, to reintroduce skepticism, to reintroduce this question of whether power and national political leadership should be blindly followed.

Really, the key question that everybody must ask themselves now is, why should we believe what people in power are telling us? It's not just people on the left or intellectuals who are making this kind of argument. Even people who are from within the political and military leadership in the United States have become concerned. For example, General Anthony Zinni, who was the commander of US Central Command in the entire Middle East up until 2000, has expressed deep concern and skepticism about what happened after 9/11, with how people in the administration who had prior political agendas used 9/11 as a catalyst and an opportunity to carry out plans in the Middle East that they had harbored for a long time. He actually draws an explicit comparison with Vietnam—that the nation was deliberately misled into war as it had been during Vietnam. So when people like that start to express skepticism about the relationship between what government says and what government does, and you see those lies turning up in public opinion, then we really are in a grave democratic crisis. Because democracy requires skepticism about power, otherwise you can never even try to think about holding people accountable, because accountability only comes into play when you think that some of the things that power is doing may potentially be wrong. If you just trust them to do the right thing, you never consider the possibility that you need to hold them accountable for anything.

JE: Are you confident that the United States has the institutional structures in place to encourage the kind of democratic skepticism you talk about?

I think that what we've seen over the last few years is starting to take us to a rather scary place, because democracy itself is a relationship between people who organize themselves as a way of disciplining the institutions to whom they have granted power over themselves. But to be able to discipline institutions that have power, you have to have certain ways of actually being able to understand what they're doing. And that assumes that those institutions are honest, that they're not deliberately trying to deceive or distort or misrepresent. One of the things we've seen in the last year is the deliberate use of simple propaganda tools by the Bush administration to confuse and to organize public opinion in particular ways. The landing of the president on the aircraft carrier is a classic example of this kind of thing, where the president presents himself as the leader of the armed forces of the United States, as a hero, and that basically builds a sense that people should line up behind the troops and behind the president. That attempt to create a mass that has exactly the same view and exactly the same position starts to have a certain oppressive quality when it comes to dissent, to asking questions, because then you're not just challenging what the president is saying, you're challenging the US troops. You're challenging the state. The whole question of dissent becomes problematized this way when you try to organize people to all line up exactly in one place.

It's always important to remember that governments learn from previous governments about how to govern, and the Bush administration has lots of savvy people who looked at the Bush administration in the first Gulf War, who looked at the Clinton administration during the '90s, and said, "What lessons can we learn about how their use of the media worked and where their use of the media didn't work?"—so that we can not make the same mistakes and be more effective, as they would put it, in getting the message across. Institutions of power learn how to govern, how to rule more effectively, and so the notion that somehow there's a kind of stable relationship between people and government isn't, I think, a useful one. We have to learn how government learns so that we also learn and are always able to keep up with what they're trying to do with us. Otherwise it's a losing game, and eventually government will become more and more effective at managing public opinion, at manufacturing public opinion, at eliminating the kinds of public opinions that it doesn't want to see. The goal of government eventually is to be able to govern without dissent so that everybody buys into the message. There's a great importance to learning to critically view the media, learning to critically listen to what people in power are telling you. Because without that criticism and without constantly being reflective about what we know and what those in power are trying to do to us, we'll never be able to break out of a situation where we will be a managed public, rather than a contentious public. And contention is central to democracy.

JE: You've talked a lot about institutions, and I'm wondering how relevant that analysis would be to those Americans who say that they vote "the man" and not the party. The Bush campaign team is clearly going to position George Bush as the kind of tough, fearless man who's needed to guide us through frightening times. What would you say to people to clarify the institutional forces behind this very simplistic, but nevertheless compelling, persona?

This is an amazingly interesting question because I think that one of the things that we've actually seen is that the role of the leader in national politics has been transformed in the last several decades. But it's not just in the United States; it's actually taking place in democracies around the world. For example, Tony Blair has a relationship to politics and people in Britain that actually in deep ways resembles that of George Bush in the United States. It actually happens over and over and over again when you look at the domestic politics of democracies.

One of the things at work here is that in an age where mass media is available, institutions don't carry well. They're hard to explain, hard to capture, hard to represent. Leaders are much more telegenic; they're much more available to have all kinds of meanings piled onto them. When you look at institutions, people have much greater familiarity with institutions because people work in places. There's a famous saying in

America that I've actually quite liked: "It's the system." And the whole point, in one sense, of the management of democracy now has been to take attention away from "the system" and make it "the man." People have a sense of the system; people know that there are structures of power. But if you take attention away from the structures of power and just present the individual, people have a completely different set of ways of relating to them. In this way we're heading back, perversely, because of media, from democracy back to monarchy, where all kinds of values and relationships and questions of trust are embodied in the leader in the way that they used to be embodied in the king, who's a distant figure, and yet a human figure. He's larger than life, and yet somebody you can identify with. In one sense it is because mass media makes this possible now; the president can come on television and speak to the people and they see a face. They see a biography. They see somebody who is, at one level, like them a little bit, even though they have completely different trajectories and relationships to power. But it's a relationship that is starting to emerge across the world now, where the role of the media is actually distorting the practice of democracy by taking emphasis away from institutions and embodying it into individuals in ways that only kings were able to do in the past.

JE: The war in Iraq has been justified on the basis that it is bringing "democracy" to the people of Iraq. How would you respond to that?

The United States actually has no perceptible commitment to democracy. When you look at the history not just of the Bush administration but of the last 50 years, it's actually hard to find any American administration that has had a principled commitment to democracy. 2003 is the 50th anniversary of an historic event—the overthrow of the elected government of Iran by the CIA. The prime minister of Iran at that time, Muhammad Mossadeq, tried to nationalize the Iranian oil industry so that Iran and its people would benefit from the oil that was theirs and the CIA staged its first coup. An elected prime minister and government were overthrown and the US replaced him with the Shah of Iran, who was willing to do whatever the US said.

The following year, having achieved success in their first coup, they had one in Guatemala, because they learned they could do it and get away with it. That process has gone on and on. Most recently there's clear US involvement in the attempted coup in Venezuela against President Hugo Chavez. So nothing at that level has changed.

The first choice of the US is not to have to stage a coup, but to support people who've already taken power and who will do what the US wants. That's ideal because then you are not responsible at all. Pakistan is famous for this. The first coup in Pakistan was in the '50s and the US was happy to see it happen. The second coup was in the '70s and the US was happy to see it happen, because in both cases the Pakistani military that took charge was willing to be party to US strategic planning. The first was to fight the war, the cold war; the second was to fight the Soviets in Afghanistan. Now General Musharraf, who staged his coup in 1999, is willing to be an ally in the war against terrorism. So the fact that he overthrew an elected prime minister, violated the constitution, and has now declared himself president doesn't matter. The fact that Pakistan tested nuclear weapons doesn't matter. What matters is that he's willing to do what the US wants, which is basically to go chase al-Qaeda around. So in that sense, when you ask where the US commitment to democracy is, it's nowhere to be seen.

The most extreme example, of course, is Israel. The whole notion that Israel is a democracy and that the US supports it because it's a democracy is laughable. What the US is actually presiding over is a systematic, illegal, massive violation of international law and elementary notions of democracy. The occupation of Palestine is a clear example of fundamental, undemocratic, unjust practice, and yet the US says, "We should be even-handed." This is not a matter of even-handedness. Where does even-handedness come into it when somebody is breaking the law? You don't want a neutral mediator when somebody's breaking the law; you want somebody to stop the law being broken. But that's not a role the US is willing to embrace, because Israel serves other interests and that's the point at play here over and over again.

JE: You've talked about the American empire as being different from all other empires. Was this as true of the empire under Clinton as it has been under Bush? Are there significant differences between them, or do you see a more fundamental continuity?

There are important distinctions between the Clinton administration and the Bush administration, but these are recurring distinctions between administrations in US history, and actually between administrations in most countries, because states always have to have this tension between the balance of consent and coercion in the exercise of power and trying to get what you want in the world. So within administrations there are people who say use more force in the situation and we'll get what we want, and there will be those who say, look, there will be a price that the other side will be willing to accept, so offer them aid, give them something, and they will bargain with us. So this balance of getting somebody to collaborate, getting somebody to say yes, as opposed to making them say yes, is something that's always part of the political calculation and the political infighting within and between administrations. During the war against Iraq we've seen some people like Colin Powell and others in the State Department say, "Let's go to the United Nations." What they mean is that they want a certificate, a license to be able to fight the war. On the other hand, others within the administration say we don't need anybody to tell us what we can and can't do; let's just do it anyway. So it's a question of how to get what you want.

But neither side is willing to question whether what you want is right. Should you be able to want this? At one level this was the same between the Clinton administration and the Bush administration. One should never forget that it was the Clinton administration that presided over the sanctions against Iraq where hundreds of thousands of Iraqi children died. It's a different way of trying to get what you want. But this difference does matter, because I think at one level the Clinton administration would have been much more hard-pressed to get into the situation of war that we've seen, which actually involves over 100,000 American troops invading and occupying Iraq, American soldiers shooting Iraqi protesters on the streets of their own capital city. So the distinctions matter. But you have to keep those distinctions in mind within the larger context of the fact that the differences really are relatively narrow about how to get to where you want. Both Democrats and Republicans, both Clinton and Bush, wanted to see a way of bringing down the Saddam Hussein regime. It was President Clinton who passed the Iraq Liberation Act, authorizing $100 million a year to pay armed guerillas in Iraq to bring down the Iraqi administration of Saddam Hussein. So it's a question of means. They both share the goals, but some means are more intolerable than others.

The other thing that both Clinton and Bush shared, but where the distinctions are important, is the question of nuclear weapons. President Clinton was willing to sign the Comprehensive Test Ban Treaty banning nuclear weapons testing. He was willing to make concessions to the US nuclear weapons laboratories so that he would have their support in signing this treaty. So the US basically has given billions of dollars to the weapons labs so that they can keep doing research and development in nuclear weapons, but President Clinton signed the treaty saying that we wouldn't do any more nuclear tests. President Bush has a different perspective. He wants them to do research and testing, and then he wants to deploy new kinds of nuclear weapons. There's a real concern that a second Bush administration may actually withdraw from the nuclear test ban treaty and start nuclear testing again, so that a new generation of nuclear weapons can be added to the American arsenal. That's an important difference because the US has 10,000 nuclear weapons. The US has a posture and policy committed to the use of nuclear weapons, even against countries that don't have nuclear weapons.

One of the great concerns that many of us have is that as resistance to the American empire mounts in more and more countries, and tragically more and more countries think about nuclear weapons as their answer to a nuclear armed America, we do lay the basis then for more and more nuclear armed confrontations. And because we will not be in the kind of situation that we had in the cold war, where the US and the Soviets had tens of thousands of nuclear weapons mounted on intercontinental ballistic missiles able to devastate each other's country and the whole world, we'll end up with situations like we have in North Korea. North Korea may have a couple of nuclear weapons and a missile that can reach as far as Japan or perhaps into the Pacific Ocean, but it won't be a massive threat to the US homeland in the way that the Soviet Union was. That makes it possible for US military planners to think about using nuclear weapons in war. But once you start to go there, as has happened with previous technologies, others will see that they will have to find other ways of fighting back. We start to bring into play the use of nuclear weapons in all kinds of circumstances as part of the struggle over power and the struggle over empire. The basis is laid then for massive and widespread proliferation of nuclear weapons, the use of nuclear weapons, and then the use of nuclear weapons as a way of countering US power. That will have tragic consequences because potentially millions of people may die.

JE: Could you talk a little about the Project for the New American Century and what its central principles imply for the future of the American empire?
The American empire has a strange relationship to time, and it's different from other empires. Back in the early '40s, Henry Luce wrote

a famous essay called "The American Century," and in the '90s we had a "Project for the New American Century." Actually this is a strange notion—that America not only has no territorial bounds, but time itself belongs to America. It's an American Century. Don't the Chinese live at the same time as the Americans? What does it mean to live in an American Century, both to be an American in an American Century and not to be an American in an American Century? Now those who are responsible for this Project for the New American Century include people like Vice President Cheney and Paul Wolfowitz, and people who occupy very senior positions in the Bush administration, so it's important to ask where they want to go in the world. I think there are three things that are at work.

At one level, they are revolutionaries. They want to remake the world to suit themselves because they find the world untidy; it doesn't fit their notion of how things should be. When you look at the Middle East in particular, you can see why they think it's untidy, because many of the countries that are in the Middle East were carved out in the period between World War I and World War II by the British after the collapse of the Ottoman Empire. It's "untidy" because these governments, these people, don't do what they are supposed to do. They are basically unstable and they complicate questions about the price of oil and who controls it and where it should go, etc. So there is an element of wanting to just sort things out so that everything will work properly. That's an important part of what's driving this—it's a management solution. Because the world the neoconservatives have inherited isn't the kind that fits their notions of what efficiency should be.

The second part is that now that there is no rival or peer or competitor to the United States, they really want to put in place institutions and ideas that will make American power palatable for everybody. The first part of that is making people accept that American power is here to stay. Don't even think about resisting it, don't think about challenging it, because this is the best of all possible worlds and there will be a place for you in it. So just give in.

The third thing is actually not about what they want to do with other people and other places, but what they want to do with the United States. This is a generation of people, Wolfowitz, Cheney, Rumsfeld, and others like them, who think that the movements of the '60s—for example, against the Vietnam War, the rise of the women's movement, the rise of movements for the rights of people of color and the environment and so forth—have shaken the traditional structure of authority. People have started to question what the natural order of society should be. The neocons see this as a challenge because they believe that we should basically know who is in charge. So people need to be re-disciplined. This is something that all Americans are going to have to think about: Are all the advances that have been made in the last 30 or 40 years, which go back to fundamental notions of civil rights and democracy and identity, are we willing to let these old men take them away because it somehow doesn't fit their notion that you are supposed to be deferential to those who know better, to those who are in charge. So this Project for the New American Century involves not just remaking the world, but remaking America.

JE: Is there anything different about the American empire from previous empires that gives you some hope for the future?

The US is fundamentally different from all previous empires in a number of important ways. The first of those is that unlike previous empires, everybody in the United States is able to read and write and therefore they have access to information about what their empire is doing in the world. Even at the height of the British Empire, most people in Britain couldn't read or write. The second important thing is that during the previous empires, democratic institutions like trade unions, political parties, NGOs, community groups were struggling to emerge as new ideas within society. In the US today we have all of those, so this is the first empire that already has democratic institutions. So the combination of those two things—that everybody in the US now has the capacity to know what the US is doing in the world, and that we have institutions that will allow people here to shape and control what their government does on their behalf—is completely new. The question is, are we willing to exercise those two things that we have, so that this is different from previous empires. Because previous empires have always had tragic endings. The future of the American Empire will be determined fundamentally by what the American people choose to do with it.

Northampton, Massachusetts
October 13, 2003

MARK CRISPIN MILLER

Mark Crispin Miller is a professor of media studies at New York University, where he also directs the Project on Media Ownership. He is well known for his writings on all aspects of the media and for his activism on behalf of democratic media reform. His books include *Boxed In: The Culture of TV* (Northwestern University Press, 1988), *Seeing Through Movies* (Pantheon, 1990), *The Bush Dyslexicon* (Norton, 2001), and *Cruel and Unusual: Bush/Cheney's New World Order* (Norton, 2004).

JE: You talk in The Bush Dyslexicon *about Bush's "inexorable decline" politically prior to 9/11. Can you take us through that period, up to 9/11?*

Bush was never a terribly popular president. He was never even sufficiently popular as a candidate. Sometimes it's hard for us to bear in mind that he never enjoyed a popular mandate. He lost the popular vote by about a half a million and, like his father, despite all the superficial differences, he simply doesn't touch people's sweet spots. By and large, even with the Texas twang, the illiteracy, and the Texas shit-kicker routine, he's still somebody people don't trust; he's still somebody people identify with privilege.

They managed to have themselves installed despite the will of the electorate, but that soon caught up with them. Despite the manful efforts of the media not to give them a hard time, their economic policies, their environmental policies, their position on abortion, all these things that they had soft-pedaled during the campaign were now becoming clear. Even over the clamor of the business about the pardon of Mark Rich, which preoccupied the first six months of American media attention, people began to smell the coffee. By the end of the summer of 2001, Bush was "tanking," as we say; he was taking a nosedive. Not only did the press personally dislike him because of his high-handed treatment of them, but more importantly, the people of the United States just didn't trust him and the economy was in trouble. His handlers sent him off to Europe to try and make things better for him, but it only made things worse. He was jeered and protested all over Europe, in city after city, and this is stuff that you just couldn't spin away.

But suddenly, as if by magic, September 11 happened. Not only did it solve all of Gary Condit's problems—because, as you will remember, he was more in the news than Bush was because of his alleged murder of Chandra Levy—but Bush was at once the beneficiary of this disaster, for perfectly understandable reasons. In times of crisis, people naturally sink to their knees and become a little bit infantile. They want to be protected. The founders of this nation understood that temptation and continually had to argue against succumbing to the temptation to do something for the sake of safety and security. So it's an old, old problem and an old, old solution. This was a magic solution to Bush's immediate political problems because not only was the population eager for him to stand tall as a kind of national father figure, but the press was even more smitten by his apparent transformation from Bozo into Winston Churchill—his apparent transformation.

Now, he did appear to be somewhat different when he spoke a few days after the tragedy. Let's bear in mind that the day of the tragedy, Bush conducted himself poorly and it was, in fact, an ignominious moment, however the White House wanted to spin it. Even Republicans were complaining about the fact that Bush just lit out for the territories at the first sign of danger. Nobody knew where he was. It looked bad. They got past that by 9/13 and the turning point came when Bush had his very well-staged phone conversation with Mayor Giuliani and Governor Pataki, at which moment the mayor shared some of his charisma with the president by elaborately saluting his swift and brilliant response to the tragedy. He made up all this stuff about how Bush had been on the phone to him immediately. Giuliani was the man of the hour, and he had something like presidentiality at that moment and Bush badly needed it. So he not only got Giuliani's blessing through that phone call, but he also turned in this remarkable performance, without a script, in the Oval Office in front of the press. His eyes were glittering with tears as he talked about this terrible moment when the nation was going to have to dedicate itself to the war on terrorism. I think you could see, if you were looking at him fairly objectively, that he was speaking from the bottom of his heart. He was convinced of his divine plan.

The important point to make about it, without speculating about his religiosity, is that when he now spoke, he spoke with a noticeable degree of self-assurance. Even when he didn't have a script, from about 9/13 on, he was fairly convincing as a righteous leader bent on revenge. This was not, by any means, however, a transformation. There was no difference in Bush because Bush has always been able to speak relatively clearly and coherently when his subject is revenge, capital punishment, or war—those are subjects that matter to him. So when he talks about them, he's fairly convincing; his sentences are short and clear. It's when he tries to talk about democracy, or education, or peace, or especially compassion, that he makes his most hilarious mistakes. It's not stupidity; it's insincerity. Well, here he was, speaking on his favorite themes, striking the pose that he believes he was meant to strike and he has an audience that had been terrorized into submission and into admiration. There was no way he could really blow that moment. People didn't want him to blow that moment. So all at once, he became something like a God in the eyes of the public and, even more, in the eyes of the media. It took the public about a year to come down off that high and begin to see Bush as just a president again.

As of this taping, I actually don't think the media have really managed to get over it. We have to remember that they were craven toward Bush and Cheney in the first place. They were never critical of that campaign. They were completely uncritical of the administration during the pre-9/11 months. What the atrocity did was to make a bad situation much worse. So where there had been a little muted criticism and where criticism was just beginning to find expression, now there was nothing but adoration. Bush was hailed for his brilliance, for his masterful handling of the crisis, when in fact, despite his convincing shtick, his convincing demeanor, his handling of the crisis was disastrous from the beginning. That's my view.

On 9/11 he was saying they hit us because they thought we were soft, which is absurd. Nobody thinks we're soft. They hit us because they thought we would strike back. And he has consistently continued to give Islamists the gift of a violent response. Then the administration went on to do things that they had planned to do for a long, long time and pretended that it was all part of the war on terrorism. So, I mean, his actual response to the crisis was catastrophic, but this is a culture of TV, where the press really only cares about, and only responds to, televisual performance. At a moment where everybody wanted a "Big Daddy," Bush did well enough to allow the press to marvel at his aplomb, at his stature. And it became a sort of self-fulfilling prophecy.

JE: Can you talk more specifically about his appearance at Ground Zero, the moment he took the bullhorn?

Bush got a lot of credit, of course, for his appearance at Ground Zero—which, by the way, he referred to the next day as a construction site. On his visit to Ground Zero a few days after the catastrophe, he took the bullhorn and stood alongside some of the rescue workers and basically did the one thing he has always been undeniably good at, which is cheerleading. He was a cheerleader at Phillips Andover, actually, and very good at it. He basically cheer-led with these exhausted and angry and frightened rescue workers around him and an audience of shattered New Yorkers, and he promised, very gratifyingly, that those responsible were going to be hearing from us pretty soon. It was tough talk—typical of him—but it was another moment that struck people as exceptionally eloquent, when it was just adequate. But it served his purpose of incorporating the whole tragedy into his own political spectacle.

JE: What do you make of the Republican Convention coming here and all the New York mythology it's going to draw upon?

The decision to come to New York and hold their convention is obscene and I think this is a common response. I'm not being eccentric when I say this. Every New Yorker I've talked to has found it extremely disquieting that the White House would use 9/11 as the backdrop for their nomination convention, aside from the fact that it's going to make the likelihood of a terrorist attack in this city, a second terrorist attack—if there hasn't been another one by then—that much likelier. But this is nothing new, you see. The Bush team has always brazenly exploited this tragedy for political purposes in the most appalling way. The Republican's Congressional Campaign Committee, for example, was selling photographs of Bush on Air Force One on the fateful day, looking decisive and gesturing decisively, and selling these for 150 bucks a pop. They were using pictures of this guy taken on that day when all those people had died as a fundraising tool—and it was a day when he'd run away. But what are you going do?

JE: You've mentioned the word catastrophe a few times. I've noticed myself that the word comes up again and again in the writings of a lot of neocon intellectuals. What do you make of this concern—or maybe fascination— with looming catastrophe?

These people are awfully transparent. Bush, for example, is always giving himself away as he talks, as his father did when he was president. Simply to giggle at his gaffs is often to miss the significance of what he's saying. The same is true with the people around him. They have a tendency to use the word "catastrophe" suspiciously often. They love the thought of catastrophe. I'm talking now about the neocons. It's even more the case with the apocalyptic, Christian, evangelical element—people like Tom DeLay and John Ashcroft. I mean, they really think that the end times are here and they're going do everything they can to make the place ready for Jesus' return. There's an apocalyptic current running through the whole pack of them. It's partly based, I think, on something pathological, and to some extent it's based on political calculation.

One of the oldest tricks in the book used against democracy or republicanism has been to terrify people, has been to create a crisis and to provoke a war. At that moment, sad to say, people often cease to become capable of reason. They cease to become capable of self-government. They become infantile. They want to be taken care of. They'll do whatever papa says they must do for their safety and their peace. James Madison made this explicit in a beautiful essay of his that was written during the crisis over the Alien and Sedition Acts in 1799, when John Adams and the Federalists were basically trying to do to the country something like what Bush and Cheney are trying to do now. Back then, the threat was France, and now France is not a direct threat, but it is an enemy. Madison said, and I'm roughly paraphrasing, that the dangers from abroad, whether real, pretended, or imaginary, had ever been used to make shackles to be placed on freedom at home. Beautifully put. He understood it completely. He'd studied the history of Athens. He'd studied the history of Rome. At the time that Madison was writing this essay, he was one of many people observing what had happened in France through the French Revolution, which had ceased to be republican and turned into a kind of military dictatorship under Napoleon. Like Jefferson and Tom Paine, he understood that tremendous tension between a military order and a civilian republic. They're two entirely different things. They can't actually co-exist. That's why the framers were so keen on the Second Amendment. It wasn't because they wanted there to come a day when every citizen could have an Uzi in his coat. That wasn't it. They were keen on the Second Amendment because they distrusted a standing army, and Madison actually said that no country has ever remained free that has a standing army.

We read Madison today and there's a shock of recognition and a sense of tremendous gratitude that he was one of the people who founded this republic and that we still have his words to guide us. It's a different experience to read the bit from G.M. Gilbert's *Nuremberg Diary* where he talks to Goering and they're talking about the differences between dictatorships and democracies and Goering says,

"It's always very easy to terrorize people into submission." When Gilbert says, "Well, democracy's different because people have independent means of information and you can't control the message so much," Goering responds, "It doesn't matter what kind of government it is. It makes no difference whatsoever: Communist, Fascist, democratic. You just tell people that they're under attack and they'll do whatever they're told."

This administration has not studied Madison's approach to that problem—his was idealistic; he was a believer in democracy. He believed in reason. Rather, they're students of the Goering approach: opportunistic. How can we get people to do what we want? Their use of catastrophe is utterly continuous with their co-optation of the media, with their promiscuous gerrymandering, and with all the other things they've done to subvert the popular will. They don't believe in democracy, and this is not a stretch on my part to say this. They are opposed to democracy and are working vigorously against it, so 9/11 could be understood as something that they welcomed. We don't know that they were its orchestrators. That may not be the case. They may not be that competent. But it would be hard to argue that they didn't have foreknowledge. And it would be impossible to argue that they're not trying to hide the truth about it, because they've done nothing but impede the 9/11 Commission, after having resisted even setting one up. This is a gang that needs people to be afraid. It's a gang that really can't have any political success whatsoever in a state of tranquility and peace of mind.

JE: You've just talked a bit about Madison, and it's clear that a lot of those we're referring to as neoconservative—Wolfowitz, Perle, and so forth—have their own view of history. So beyond the Goering stuff, these guys do have a carefully crafted argument that they feel is based in history. Can you talk about their approach to history?

The people around Bush are clearly students of history, not just Perle and Wolfowitz, but Karl Rove is a voracious reader of history. So they're not an ignorant bunch by any means. But their reading of history, and pardon me for sounding a provocative note, but their reading of history is actually similar to Hitler's in one way, which is that it's entirely based on their own grandiosity. They have studied history not to learn its bitter lessons, and certainly not to figure out how to craft the most just and most free form of government. Rather, they have studied history to figure out how to make this empire last forever. So it isn't only that they want the US to be an imperial power, they want the US to outdo all previous empires, not in its longevity, but in its permanence, which, for all their work in college and all their wide reading, is an insane program. What does it have to do with the Constitution? What does it have to do with democracy? What does it have to do with the pursuit of happiness? Nothing. It's about power. It's about domination. It's about control of dwindling resources. So their study of history is forked by their own opportunism. They're not people who have read history detachedly, but rather as partisans on behalf of an unprecedented empire.

JE: In your view, is this just a continuation of the Republican Party of our grandfathers, maybe just a little more aggressive? Or, as some have suggested, are these true radicals, people on the fringes of the Republican Party?

People make the mistake of thinking that this administration is conservative; that this administration is a step or two beyond the Republican Party of old. This is what Democrats think: that they're dealing with a normal administration. This is what leftists think. They think that this is basically capitalism in action. Well, there's some truth to that. Obviously, desire for profits has a great deal to do with this war and the war on terrorism, but it isn't really capitalism per se that these things are serving; it's just themselves. It's crony capitalism. It's the kind of capitalism that will actually alienate investors and elites in other countries and part of the elite in this country.

The fact is that this administration is by no means conservative. It is not your grandfather's Republican Party. Your grandfather's Republican Party, to put the best face on it, was a party that believed in strictly limited federal government, the preservation of states' rights, individual accountability, and a refusal to meddle in the affairs of other nations. I mean, that's my understanding of conservatism. And once upon a time it also entailed a certain level of civility and public discourse. The Republicans prided themselves on this Burkean sort of decency and manners and so on, and it was the rabble of populism that engaged in rudeness and demagoguery. We've got a very different situation now. Very different.

This administration has expanded the police powers of the federal government to an unprecedented extent. This administration has a shadow government in place because of terrorism. This administration's vice president, who, for all intensive purposes, is the prime minister of this system, has the largest vice presidential staff in American history. This administration has, in effect, repealed key sections of the Bill of Rights. They've actually suspended habeas corpus in their Patriot Act. They have made indefinite detention possible. They have completely ignored the Geneva Accords. They act with impunity wherever they want to go. There's nothing conservative about that. Nothing. Far from refusing to meddle in the affairs of other countries, they have made endless war their *raison d'etre*. That's what they're for: to attack this country and attack that country. It goes beyond the Middle East. It goes beyond Zionist influences, which are certainly at work, because they actually have their eyes on China. They are people who want war forever. This makes them much more like fascist movements than like conservative movements. Individual accountability is meaningless with these people, because they have the fanatics' tendency to turn blind to the effect of their own actions on other people. They're good; other people are bad. It's sociopathic. That's the way they look at the world. They become indignant if anyone resists or objects to their depredations. This is not the democratic frame of mind by any stretch of the imagination—or a republican frame of mind. It doesn't partake of the political process as we know it.

These are not people who can tolerate or even perceive disagreement. They see that as an attack. If you diverge from them on one point, you're the enemy. This kind of us against them, this kind of Manichean attitude, this tendency to demonize the opposition—we've seen this before. We've seen it among the Nazis. We've seen it among the Stalinists. We see it in al-Qaeda. It's a fanatical approach to political life. There's a strong strain of Christian fanaticism in this particular case, but it ultimately doesn't matter what religious coat it wears. We're talking about something that is profoundly different from Christianity, as Jesus preached it, and completely alien to democracy as we have been struggling for more than 200 years to realize it.

JE: As you point out in your book, Bush ran for president in 2000 largely as the anti-Clinton. He called over and over again on the stump for restoring "honor and dignity" to the White House. If someone were to say to you right now, "I'm a Bush supporter. For all of his problems, at least he restored honor and dignity to the White House. At least he made good on that"—what would you say in response to that?

If somebody were to say to me, "At least Bush restored honor and dignity to the White House. You've got to give him that," first of all, it would take me a couple of minutes to recover from my astonishment. But that's not unusual for me. I have that experience all the time. I would try to point out to this person that that's true only if we understand honor and dignity to mean not engaging in oral sex in the Oval Office. There is no honor among these thieves. There is no dignity there. They have routinely and outrageously lied and have engaged in the most astonishing self-dealing and cronyism. It makes the Tea Pot Dome scandal look like nothing. Halliburton, Bechtel, you name it. They have consistently misrepresented what they're doing in a really Orwellian way and they have tried and tried, and largely succeeded, in stabbing their enemies, and sometimes their friends, in the back. They have made the US reviled all over the world. They have given endless fuel to fanatical movements that hate the United States. They have trampled on people's rights, foreigners and regular citizens, to an extent that no one could ever imagine possible. I don't see where honor and dignity come into that.

But it's important to note that they did succeed in establishing that as their image, and it has a great deal to do with the religiosity of Bush's supporters. It is a matter of fact, by and large, that extremely religious people have a very difficult time understanding the distinction between public and private morality. So that when people say Richard Nixon was a much better man than Bill Clinton, they're saying that only because Richard Nixon was asexual, whereas Clinton at least had this reputation for being extremely lubricious and always hitting on women. That was exaggerated, but the fact that Clinton had a manifest sort of eroticism was enough to make these people say he was a worse person than Nixon, although Nixon committed public crimes far graver than anything that Clinton ever committed. Clinton really didn't commit any public crimes. But this is a mentality that doesn't understand what public morality means. It has no meaning to them. They personalize everything and they always talk in terms of sinfulness. So efforts to subvert the Constitution, which is what Nixon did, and which is what the Iran-Contra players did, and it's what these people are doing, subversive activity that would actually undercut democratic government and disenfranchise people—I can't think of anything worse in a democracy—this doesn't strike them as undignified or dishonorable. As long as you can persuade them that you keep your pants zipped up at all times, they'll be content that you are a completely upright person. Let me add that we have no idea what kind of a sexual past Bush has. Any rational person is going to recognize the likelihood that, given his history, his sexual past is probably much gamier than Clinton's. I mean, he's never been a serious or focused person. He's always been very self-indulgent and he has this sense of license that rich people often tend to have. But it doesn't matter. The official truth, the truth we're allowed to accept, is that he and Laura have a wonderful marriage, he's never strayed, he doesn't drink anymore. Although there's really no evidence for any of that.

JE: Did you see the recent piece in the New Yorker *about Karl Rove? The one that talks about how Karl Rove first met Bush, how he looked at the tin of tobacco in his back pocket and immediately fell for him and his charisma? Can you talk about the differences you see between the kinds of things you were just saying about Bush's being a private school boy and the specific image of him that's been crafted by Rove and his other handlers?*

Bush's propagandists have been masterful at crafting a certain image for him, an image that is actually based, to some extent, on his weaknesses. For example, this is a guy who can't really talk coherently without a script on subjects that bore or offend him, like peace, you know, things like that. That was immediately received as a sign of illiteracy and ignorance. There's some truth to that. This guy is easily the least curious executive in American history. He has no intellectual curiosity at all and he can't retain the rules of grammar if he ventures into forbidden territory. Nevertheless, it's not stupidity and it's not simplicity, but the Bush administration is perfectly happy to have people make fun of his grammar, for example, because they can spin that—and they have spun it—as a sign of his folksiness; that he's not a snooty, stuck-up elitist type like Al Gore—Prince Albert—who grew up in a hotel. He's not a guy who was born in Connecticut and was a legacy admission to Phillips Andover and Yale. He's not a guy who has the Queen of England as a cousin. He's not a guy from a fabulously wealthy family—whose grandfather bankrolled the Nazis. None of that is that case. He's just Will Rogers. He's just a regular guy and when he messes up the language it proves he's just like you and me. That's quite brilliant; to make Bush out to be a kind of Jacksonian figure, a kind of natural leader from the wilds. The fact is, however, that Bush has always been precisely the kind of figure that he has always used to criticize the '60s. He's always talking about self-indulgence and how terrible the '60s were—all about if it felt good do it. Well, that's him. That's him in spades. I mean, it may be *Animal House* instead of Woodstock, but that's still Bush.

So it has taken some skill on the part of Karl Rove and the rest of them to turn his weaknesses into strengths, and they've done that on every possible score. His history of substance abuse has been reconfigured into a narrative of personal salvation, even though there is at least one piece of evidence on the public record that he didn't stop drinking in 1986. There's a wedding video from 1992 that's on thesmokinggun.com, where he's drinking and drunk and actually being rather funny off the top of his head. It's the frat boy side of him. But the fact is, he's not drinking lemonade and he doesn't seem sober. But this whole picture of Bush has been as if set in stone, and it's not because his propagandists are so skilled; it's because media is so craven. It is because they, on the one hand, not only bought, but helped to create, the image of Clinton as the worst of the counter-culture, the big liar and the draft-dodger. When in fact on every single count the Busheviks accused Clinton of, Bush is guilty. Bush was a draft dodger. Not only that, he was AWOL. In fact, he was a deserter, because if you're gone longer than thirty days, you're a deserter. They guy was actually a deserter in wartime. If it had been Clinton, they would have just crucified him on the White House lawn. Clinton joined the ROTC to get out of the draft. That's not draft dodging. They called Clinton a crook. Clinton was actually entirely clean as the governor of Arkansas; the Starr Commission proved that. Now, I had a lot of trouble with Clinton's policies. I wasn't a Clinton supporter. But I think it's significant that he was successfully defamed, and his agenda, such as it was, impeded, entirely on the bases of these propaganda lies about him personally and about his wife. What's really telling, I think, in ways that even they themselves don't understand, is that every charge they made against him really actually refers to them. This is indeed a feature of a certain kind of malicious propaganda in every system.

If you examine, for example, the Jew as imagined by the Nazis, it's everything the Germans participating in the movement most hated in themselves. If you take a look at the personal lives of a lot of the people who attacked Clinton for his poor family values, you see the William Bennett syndrome again and again: this guy was going off to Las Vegas to spend millions of dollars doing God-knows-what while he was preaching virtue; Rush Limbaugh talking tough about junkies and pill-heads while he himself is addicted to drugs. And over and over and over again.

It sounds like I'm engaging in a kind of ad hominem critique—but that's not it. There is a tendency behind most fanatical movements, if not all fanatical political and religious movements, to engage in this kind of compulsive, malignant projectivity. Al-Qaeda does it to the decadent West. The Stalinists did it to the West. Radical Christians do it to sinners, humanists, and so on. The "Other" is always a kind of walking bundle of all those traits that you most detest in yourself. You can call it the Roy Cohn syndrome, I suppose, or the J. Edgar Hoover syndrome. But that's one of the most remarkable things about this movement, and one of the things that I believe nails it as profoundly un-American and largely pathological.

JE: Let's turn to Iraq. Can you talk about media coverage in the run-up to war and more specifically the way Saddam came to replace bin Laden in media coverage?

The Bush White House has had a very easy time for an outfit that has so consistently failed to do what it has promised to do. I mean, they promised us they would find Osama bin Laden and they didn't, so they very obviously shifted their attention to Saddam Hussein and made the preposterous argument that Saddam Hussein might give weapons of mass destruction to Islamists. Of course the Islamists would use them first on him, but that fact was lost on these people. So 67 percent of the American people thenceforth believed that Iraq and 9/11 were somehow related. We were told the Anthrax terrorist would be caught; he never was. Then when it comes to the guy who leaked the story about Valerie Plame, the CIA agent, they say we're not going to find that person. That's because they know who that person is, so they're not going to give him up.

None of this could have happened, and I mean none of it—whether we're talking about the war, or the attack on the Bill of Rights, Saddam Hussein being used as a replacement for Osama bin Laden—if the media in this country had recognized its constitutional obligation to keep the people sufficiently informed so that they could engage in self-government. This is the reason why we have the First Amendment. If you read anything about it by any of the founders, and it's completely unambiguous, the purpose of the media is to help the American people keep an eye on their government; to keep them sufficiently informed for republican democracy. It wasn't because they thought they could foresee a day when there would be full-frontal nudity in rap videos and they wanted to protect that. They didn't care. They didn't know about shock tactics like that. They didn't protect the press because they knew some day Rupert Murdoch would need to make a lot of money. It had nothing to do with it. It has to do exclusively with the fact that the people must have access to the fullest possible information about what the government is doing, or that country can't be free. So, it has been really quite understandable that so many people in this country think that Iraq was behind 9/11 because no one here ever contradicted Bush when he said that. I mean, no one did. Some of us did online and in little magazines, but we don't count. The TV journalists, the *New York Times*, the *Washington Post*, and *USA Today* were extremely tactful when Bush would deliver these unbelievable whoppers.

In that way, because our media is so passive and has so grievously abdicated its constitutional responsibility, we're really no different from any other closed society where people believe preposterous things. It's no different from Serbia under Milosevic, where they believed they were under constant attack from Croatia and Bosnia. I mean, if you only hear one thing and no one contradicts it, and you're not a professional skeptic or an intellectual or media critic, why should you be expected to imagine that something else is the case? It's not the people's fault.

JE: Do you expect that to change during the 2004 election cycle? And what do you think we'll see as the Rove media strategy as the election unfolds?

If this team wants to get itself re-elected, it's going to need another catastrophe to do it. It might not be an overt explosive catastrophe like the attack on the World Trade Center and the Pentagon. It might be a much subtler civic catastrophe involving the use of crooked voting machines to get this guy in office. But there is so much growing popular anger over the deaths of soldiers in Iraq, there is so much rage among the soldiers themselves because their tours of duty have been indefinitely extended and they're in terribly dangerous straits. The economy is such a mess and on certain issues like the environment where the majority is clearly quite progressive, everybody's aware of what they're doing, despite the fact that the press kind of soft-pedals it. In order for them be re-elected they're going have to resort to some stratagem, because I don't even think the most incompetent Democrat could lose this race. Some have claimed that Gore was the most incompetent Democrat and he didn't lose that race. My belief is that

Bush would have taken the White House even if Ralph Nader had never been born, because they had no intention of not taking the White House and they have no intention of stepping down from power now that they've seized it.

The press has started to become quite courageous toward the White House, but they have a very, very, very low standard for themselves. They have, as far as I'm concerned, still failed to press the point about the outing of the CIA agent Valerie Plame. This is a stone felony. There's no question about it—this is a serious high crime that compromises the national security. This is a woman whose job was to covertly track weapons of mass destruction, and these guys outed her and revealed her identity, and yet the media isn't making this a story night after night. That's what it comes down to. If the press is responsible, it won't just do one big story and let something go. It will do story after story after story. It will stick with it. They did this with Monica Lewinsky, which is a matter of no importance whatsoever, but they're not doing it with a crime as explicit as this.

Now, it is possible, and even likely, that as Bush continues to become more unpopular with the population at large, that the press will become a little bit more vigorous. They'll certainly become more ironic and more disrespectful, because that's standard operating procedure, but whether they'll do more than simply goof on Bush's grammatical mistakes, whether they will say, "This is a crime. This is unconstitutional," I can't really say, because what has happened over the last two years has been a grotesque miscarriage of justice and an absolutely grotesque violation of democratic procedure. And the media were complicit in it, so it may finally take something as utopian as media reform and work like ours just to keep hammering away at this stuff before these stories get their proper coverage.

JE: Speaking of irony, what do you make of the image of Bush landing on the aircraft carrier? This is an image—in a reversal of what Atwater and Bush's father did to Dukakis in the tank—that is now destined to be used by Democrats against Bush. Can you talk about the evolution of that image, about how it was taken up and seen by the media then and how people may see the exact same image now?

Propaganda has strict limits because history will always alter its meaning. Now, in their cockiness, in their arrogance, the White House team staged this big event on the Abraham Lincoln with Bush dressed up like Tom Cruise and a big sign that said, "Mission Accomplished," when the war was really just beginning. The response of the press to this moment was shocking, because they were absolutely slavering with glee and delight at how butch Bush looked, even going so far as to hail the expressions of jubilation by the troops on board that ship, whose benefits had been cut. There was no sense of democratic responsibility by the press whatsoever. So it wasn't their doing that ever jeopardized that image, rather it was simply the passage of time, the loss of lives in Iraq, the slog, the quagmire. Now that footage is completely unusable except by Bush's enemies. And I think there's a lesson in there that might conceivably offer us a little bit of hope, which is that this kind of monstrous overreaching that these people engage in, and their attempt to spin their way out of anything, ultimately can't succeed, because reality and history are bigger than the efforts of any cabal, even in the absence of political opposition.

New York City
November 6, 2003

SCOTT RITTER

Scott Ritter is a ballistic missile technology expert who worked in military intelligence during a 12-year career in the US armed forces. He was a major in the US Marine Corps, and spent several months of the Gulf War serving under General Norman Schwarzkopf at Marine Central Command headquarters in Saudi Arabia. He also led the UN weapons inspection team in Iraq from 1991 to 1998. He is the author, with William Rivers Pitt, of *War on Iraq* (Context Books, 2002) and *Frontier Justice: Weapons of Mass Destruction and the Bushwhacking of America* (Context Books, 2003).

JE: You're one of the few people who were actually there in Iraq, on the ground, looking for weapons of mass destruction. What do people need to know about what you found there, and what it means in light of what's unfolded since 9/11?

The first thing is to emphasize that there were in fact weapons of mass destruction in Iraq. This is not a debate about whether these weapons ever existed. We know Iraq had massive quantities of these weapons. We know Iraq was responsible under the law set forth by the Security Council of the United Nations to get rid of these weapons. That's why weapons inspectors went to Iraq. We also know that early on the Iraqi government lied to the inspectors; they concealed these weapons and obstructed the work of the inspectors, creating a very difficult situation in terms of the inspectors accomplishing their task. It was a seven-year job, from 1991 to 1998.

To simplify it, we'll break it down into three epochs. The first one, from 1991 to 1993, is when the Iraqi government tried to conceal things from the inspectors. The first thing it tried to conceal was the actual hardware; they denied having any biological weapons program, denied having a nuclear weapons program, and declared only 50 percent of their chemical and ballistic missile capabilities. By 1993, through hard work and sound investigations, the inspectors were able to get their hands on this hardware. The Iraqis blew them up, either in front of the inspectors, or, like a drug dealer who gets caught by the cops, they flushed them down the toilet, trying to hide evidence that they ever had these weapons. But we found out that they flushed them down the toilet and were able to recover them, and the Iraqis took us to these places where they blew up their ammunitions unilaterally, without supervision.

From 1993 to 1995, the Iraqis were still concealing. This time they were concealing programs. It's not that they have the actual hardware in the means of manufacturing. We got rid of that. But they're holding on to the intellectual property: the documents, the blueprints, the diagrams, all of which could be used to rapidly reconstitute a weapons program. By 1995, again through the hard work of the inspectors, we were able to compel the Iraqis to admit to all their programs, including the totality of their biological weapons program and nuclear weapons program and all of their chemical weapons programs. Everything was admitted. In the aftermath of the defection of Hussein Kamal, the son-in-law of Saddam Hussein and the general who ran weapons programs in the '90s, the Iraqi government was compelled to release the secret archive that they had been hiding from the inspectors, millions of pages of documents, diagrams, blueprints, and some material.

One would think that the case was closed. But now we have to throw in something else, which is concealment. You see, we knew the Iraqis were hiding the stuff from us. First the Iraqis denied ever hiding anything from us and then they acknowledged that they hid it, but it was all the unilateral actions of individual scientists. We knew that especially from 1991 to 1993, the concealment was run by the security forces of the president of Iraq. It's important that we not just account for the weapons, but we make sure that the means by which Iraq hid these weapons and obstructed the inspectors was acknowledged by Iraq, declared to the inspectors, and then verified as being dismantled and not operating. How can you give them a clean bill of health if they have this effective concealment mechanism in place? Who says they're still not hiding anything? So we had to come to grips with concealment. The Iraqis deny that the presidential security forces were involved, which only heightens the suspicion of the inspectors. So, we move forward from 1996 not with a concern that there are weapons out there. We're not looking for weapons—we think we've accounted for almost everything. Now we're looking for evidence that Iraq has an ongoing program of concealment. We're focused on presidential security. The more that we focus on presidential security, the more paranoid the Iraqi government gets, so the more they obstruct us and more they conceal things from us. The more they conceal, the more we're convinced that what they're concealing relates to weapons of mass destruction, when in fact what they were concealing related to presidential security. And now you have to throw in one other factor. Everything I've talked about up until now is about disarmament—what the Security Council says needs to be done in Iraq.

Iraq is not allowed to obstruct the work of the inspectors. When they do so, Iraq is breaking the rules. But the rules also say the inspectors are only in Iraq to carry out disarmament.

Since 1991 it's been the policy of every presidential administration to remove Saddam Hussein from power. Regime removal has taken priority over disarmament. In fact, Security Council resolutions require disarmament. The weapons inspection process that implements the decision to disarm Iraq was seen by the United States as a means to facilitate regime removal, not to get rid of weapons of mass destruction. So the United States, in particular the Central Intelligence Agency, used the weapons inspection process to spy on Saddam Hussein and to go after Saddam's security apparatus. So the Iraqis had a legitimate right to be concerned by this probing action by the inspectors, because there were CIA representatives on the inspections teams who were gathering data that had nothing to do with disarmament and everything to do with regime removal. So the Iraqis, in standing up for their own sovereign rights of national security, would block certain inspections that got too close to the president. But in doing so, they only fed the concerns of the inspectors that they were blocking the inspectors because there were weapons.

So you've created this vicious cycle of events that led to confrontation after confrontation after confrontation. And many of these confrontations resulted in Security Council resolutions condemning the actions of the Iraqis and were cited by President Bush when he said that the Iraqis were in violation of a score or more of Security Council resolutions calling for them to disarm. But the point is that Iraq was disarmed as of 1995. We still had an accounting issue on certain aspects of the programs, but we now know in the aftermath of the Gulf War that there were no weapons in Iraq. There were no ongoing weapons programs. Those had been dismantled as of 1995. All of the Iraqi obstruction between 1996 and 1998 had nothing to do with weapons of mass destruction and everything to do with protecting themselves from a CIA that was actively using the weapons inspection process to spy on Saddam Hussein.

What the American people need to know is that this was never about weapons; this has always been about getting Saddam Hussein. Even in the most recent spin of this whole weapons issue, the Bush administration knew that there were no weapons of mass destruction in Iraq, and yet they continued to use the inspection process as a vehicle to achieve the ultimate goal of regime change.

JE: We keep hearing now, from members of the Bush administration and defenders of their policies, that even if there are no weapons of mass destruction, at least we've gotten rid of a brutal tyrant, the rape rooms, and the mass graves. What's your take on this rationale that's now being floated that it's all been worth it?

Well, that's basically the argument of the ends justifying the means. And when we're speaking of the United States of America and the concept of democratic representation, one of the more important aspects is the concept of informed consent of the people. If you're going to go to war, you lay out the reasons for the war, the justifications for the war, and then you subject it to debate, dialogue, and discussion amongst the elected representatives of the people and indeed the people themselves. Once the matter has been hashed out, through informed consent, the policymakers go forward.

This war was all about weapons of mass destruction; that's what the debate was. That's the case the President made. To now retroactively go back and say, well, no, it's because Saddam Hussein's a bad guy. That is a truism: Saddam Hussein is a bad guy; he's a brutal dictator. We knew about the rape rooms. It's not a surprise. Finding mass graves isn't a surprise in Iraq. We knew these graves existed. We knew who was going into these graves. We knew why they were going into these graves and when they were going in the graves in the late '80s and early '90s, and we did nothing to stop them. To now come back and say in revisionist fashion that this is why we went to war is wrong, because this was not the debate that was had in this country. This is not the case the president made to the American people. If you're willing to accept that it's okay to revise justifications for war, what you're saying is that democracy doesn't matter in America—that this nation, and the principles and values upon which it was built, simply are irrelevant, and that the president is a dictator who can do anything he or she wants to regardless of the will of the people. No, informed consent of the people is mandatory to operate in our name.

JE: You open your book by talking about patriotism and different varieties of patriotism. What's your take on the surge in patriotism following 9/11 and now during the war?

Patriotism is love of nation, but I think in today's television society we like to simplify things. So the simplified vision of love of nation, the ultimate expression of love of nation, has been portrayed in the figures of the soldiers, the sailors, the airmen, and the marines wearing the uniform of the United States, storming the beaches, and sacrificing far away from home, or police officers. In the post 9/11 time period, police officers and firefighters have now been lionized as patriots and indeed they are. The men and women who serve so proudly in the armed forces are true patriots and so are the police officers and firefighters, but that's not the only way you can love your nation. That's not the only expression of patriotism, and indeed, in the case of the military, it's a very narrow expression of patriotism, because when you join the military, you actually unplug from the Constitution, so to speak. The normal concept of law that governs how we interact as a people is done away with. The soldiers, the sailors, the airmen, the marines operate under the uniform code of military justice and they don't have the same rights and privileges that we as civilians have, because they're going to be called upon to do some pretty horrible things, such as storm a beach or take out a machine gun or nest on a hill, to kill and put their life on the line. They'll be ordered to get into a situation where they will face almost certain death. This is what they do and this is why we appreciate their service. But that is not the ultimate expression of patriotism. I can tell you as a former marine myself that when I would go off to do service in the name of my country, I hoped that the American people were behind me, that there was informed consent in United States about the tasks with which I was charged to carry out. The time for a constitutional debate on the rights and wrongs of what I was being asked to do isn't when I'm crossing the line of departure. It should have happened before I received the orders to cross the line of departure.

The true patriot, I believe, is also that citizen who has read the Constitution of the United States of America, and who understands how important that document is in terms of defining who we are and what we are as a people; it is the person who lives that Constitution, and who expresses him or herself verbally or in written form to their elected representatives. That's what patriotism is: investing yourself into the concept of citizenship and holding those whom you elect to higher office accountable for what they do in your name.

I found it odd in the build-up to the war that the media would portray your ideal patriot either as the service member away from home, or somebody on the street corner waving a flag and shouting, "We support the troops." I can train a monkey to wave a flag. That does not make the monkey patriotic. I can't train a monkey to read the

Constitution or live the Constitution. On the opposite end of that street was another group of Americans who also had the American flag and who said, "Support the troops, but bring them home." Those are patriots, too. We have to understand that the definition of patriotism cannot be hijacked by people with a specific ideological agenda. A patriot is somebody who loves their country and how they express that love can be by waving a flag and blindly supporting the president. But I would say that those people are limited patriots because they truly don't understand the concept of representative democracy. If you're simply going to nod yes when the president says something, you're not much of a citizen in my book. Then there are those who have considered the whole range of issues, have compared and contrasted the positions taken by the government with the Constitution, find the government's policies wanting, and then have the courage to speak out against those policies, so that there is informed consent when we send those other patriots, those young men and women who honor us by wearing the uniform, abroad to fight and die for a cause. It's patriotic to make sure that the cause we ask them to sacrifice for is worth it.

JE: Let's shift to the ideological and philosophical underpinnings of American foreign policy in the wake of 9/11, the so-called neoconservative influence on this administration. Are you familiar with groups like the Project for the New American Century, a neoconservative think tank that called for—in very clear, stark terms, well before 9/11—massive increases in military spending and for a new, proactive and interventionist use of military force around the world?

The Project for the New American Century is comprised of a number of people derived from the years of Ronald Reagan, and they have as their fundamental tenets the concept of smaller government and a powerful America. They felt that the United States had a moral obligation to confront the evil empire of the Soviet Union. They also felt that the government of the United States had a moral obligation to confront the "communism" and economics of Roosevelt's New Deal. And there's been this war that these neoconservatives have been waging on two fronts: a war against entitlement systems here at home and a concept of expanding this American morality abroad.

When the Soviet Union collapsed, there was a vacuum that was difficult to fill. You don't want too much of a war dividend coming in if you're a neoconservative, because suddenly you have a lot of money.

What's the government going to do with that money? They're going to expand entitlement programs. Well, you don't want them to do that. You want them to get rid of the entitlement programs. So you need a new threat. You need something out there that can drive military budgets and military expenditures. You need a threat that will create an enemy who will take resources and enable people to say that it's the government's role to defend America abroad and therefore we need to pull resources from these entitlement programs. This is the fundamental ideology of these neoconservatives. They've been looking for a new threat. They've been looking for a new enemy since the collapse of the Soviet Union, and the residual elements of communism haven't been able to live up to that new threat.

Terrorism, however, has. Terrorism's something that doesn't need to be massive on the scale of a Soviet army, because it's massive in the minds of an ignorant and fearful audience. An act of terrorism can be minor, but it can be magnified tremendously through effective exploitation of the press and what you tell people. These neoconservatives who have hijacked the Bush administration are looking to work parallel policies of reducing government funds for programs like Social Security, welfare, Medicaid, and such, while finding ways to dramatically expand our defense expenditures. They needed an enabling moment. The Project for the New American Century predicted this enabling moment in their defining document on their vision for the new American military. They said that there will have to be some sort of trigger event, a new Pearl Harbor.

They got their new Pearl Harbor on September 11. And what did we see in the aftermath of September 11, 2001? Immediate action on all fronts. The Patriot Act was passed here in the United States without any debate by Congress; it just passed. It's a frontal assault on the Constitution. It's basically an empowerment tool to give law enforcement the anti-crime tools that they had been trying to get passed over the last decades but hadn't succeeded in doing because we are a democracy that believes in the Constitution and we felt that maybe it wouldn't be wise to give law enforcement certain powers without adequate supervision. That's the way America is. But in the aftermath of 9/11, because of the war on terror, because of the threat, we're suddenly told we have to give up certain elements of our security and of our freedom to be secure. And so the Patriot Act passed. And then, in the same breath, while the smoke's still rising from the ruins of the World Trade Center and the Pentagon, we're told: Iraq, the Middle East, the axis of evil. This has gone beyond simply nineteen men hijacking four airplanes; this has turned into a global conspiracy against the United States that must be confronted militarily. We have to act unilaterally; we have to break free of the multilateral constraints of the United Nations. So we create a perpetual war on terror. It's never going end.

What are terrorists? Who are these people? Where are they? They're just out there and they're bad; they're evil. They play on the fear and the ignorance of the American people, which is then exacerbated by a Department of Homeland Security that creates a color-coded mood ring that can be manipulated by the government at any time. Red, yellow, orange—we're afraid. Be afraid. The government can program that level of fear without any justification. We have an intelligence report that terrorists are about to attack. Who? We don't know. Where? We don't know. What? We don't know. But tell us and now we're afraid. And the more we're afraid, the more you ask us to give. Patriot Act II and enhancements to the Patriot Act. Now the budget's starting to be bankrupt—billions of dollars are flowing out of this country into a war on terror and more defense expenditures. But now we don't have money for what? Education, health care, infrastructure—all these entitlement programs are starting to be bled dry. And it's going to get worse.

This is what the Project for the New American Century is about. These are people who will use the horrific event of September 11 for their own political advantage. And the key to this is listening, for instance, to the words of Condoleezza Rice. When asked what September 11th was, she didn't say that it was a national tragedy, one of the most horrible days in American history. She said it was an historic opportunity. But an opportunity for whom?

JE: The argument in response to what you've just said from someone like Richard Perle, or Condi Rice, would be that it's one thing to look at the PNAC document and say, "Look, we needed a 'catalyzing and catastrophic event' to get what we want, and we got one." It's another thing to see 9/11 as an example of what will happen, and what does happen, when you fail to enact the vision they laid out well before 9/11. In other words, they might say, it's not that they've exploited 9/11, but that 9/11 was an indication of precisely why their policies are needed—to prevent future 9/11s and, in their words, "mushroom clouds." What's your response to that argument?

That's an absurd argument in the extreme. The argument that the threat posed by those who perpetrated 9/11 is in any way the equivalent of the threat, for instance, posed by communism in the aftermath of World War II is absurd. There was a time when this nation lived under the threat of nuclear annihilation. We had Russian nuclear missiles aimed at us, Chinese nuclear missiles aimed at us. Children practiced nuclear air raid drills. That was a tough time for America, a tough time for the world, and yet some pretty neat things were happening in the United States in the '50s and '60s, such as civil rights. You didn't see a suspension of the Constitution of the United States because the Russians were pointing nuclear missiles at us. Talk about mushroom clouds. We could have had an eruption of mushroom clouds across the country, but no, at that time this country was fighting some basic fights about what it means to be an American: civil rights, women's rights, human rights. We were in Vietnam with people dying, and yet we still went through the struggle as a nation to talk about who we are and what we are as a people. The threats that existed on the outside only magnified how important it was to be good Americans, how important it was to have a body of law that was consistent. 9/11 didn't change anything. 9/11 didn't change the Constitution. That Constitution was born from a revolutionary war that was so much more dangerous to this country than 9/11. Don't get me wrong. 9/11 was a tragedy. Those 3,000 lives that were lost that day is a tragedy. The billions of dollars that were lost because of the attack created economic catastrophe. But it doesn't change anything. It doesn't change the fundamental nature of this country. If anything, what it shows is that we have a lot further to go in terms of moving forward as a people.

9/11 should have prompted some soul-searching on the part of the American people to ask, "Why did this happen?" It wasn't an accident. This wasn't a freak of nature. Why did it happen? I'll tell you why it happened. It happened because there are people like Richard Perle and Condoleezza Rice and other neoconservatives who don't give a hoot for the rest of the world, who act as though the globe is their own backyard, and that the United States has an inherent right to gain access to resources at a price that's economical for the United States, but maybe not so economical for the people that we're gaining the resources from. Maybe we're trampling on their human rights. Maybe we're trampling on their society, their dreams, their hopes, their prayers for a better world. Suddenly people who were raised in that part of the world wake up and they say, "Why aren't I going anywhere? Why is there this brick wall holding me down? Who's responsible?" And fingers point to where? The United States. We become the enemy. They lash out. They attack us. I'm not condoning what happened on 9/11, but I'm telling you right now that we don't have to redefine who we are as a people in response to 9/11. We have to reexamine that maybe our society has drifted off course, and what's needed is for us to go back and re-embrace those values and ideals that define who we are as a people. You know, a love of mankind: "We the people of the United States of America. Life, liberty and the pursuit of happiness for all." Not just Americans, but for all. We should apply that globally. And I'll tell you what, if you do that, you'll start reducing the terrorist threat. I guarantee you this: what we've done post-9/11 has only made things worse. We haven't improved America's position in the world, we've made it ten times worse, and it will slide further down the path toward the abyss if we, the people, don't take control of what's happening in our name by those whom we elect to higher office.

JE: The name of your latest book is called Frontier Justice: Weapons of Mass Destruction and the Bushwhacking of America. *You talk quite a bit in there about the meaning of the frontier and the cultivation of Bush's image as a cowboy. Can you explain what you were trying to get across with that?*

I use two themes in the book that are attached to notions of the old American West. One reason why I pick on the old American West is that our president, George W. Bush, likens himself to some sort of old West character. Osama bin Laden attacks the United States, and he speaks of a wanted poster, dead or alive, with Osama bin Laden's picture up there.

The definition of frontier is that space that exists between civilized society and the wilderness. In our own experience as a nation, in terms of manifest destiny and moving out west, we had a frontier, a western frontier. And things happened on the western frontier. There was lawlessness, there were savages and such that needed to be tamed to bring "civilized society" forward. Oftentimes the towns that were on the edge of the frontier had a system of justice that wasn't quite rooted in Constitutional law. It was a well-meaning man who strapped on a 6-gun and ran the bad elements out of town. You didn't have the niceties of a court and jury. You had a guy who made a decision on the spot: you know what I'm gonna do? Pull the trigger and kill the bad guy. That's frontier justice. It's not legally correct, but sometimes it's the correct thing to do. Sometimes the situation dictates that style of justice. Of course, we've taken that concept and dramatized it in the form of *High Noon*: Gary Cooper, strapping on his guns and going down the middle of the street. He doesn't want do it, but he's gonna take on the bad guys in a big gun fight downtown and get rid of these bad elements so that civilized society can take over.

George Bush likens himself to a Gary Cooper kind of figure. Frontier justice. That's what's happening today. He claims that the United Nations, the system of law, "civilized society," is unable or unwilling to confront these evil elements: Saddam Hussein and his weapons of mass destruction, Osama bin Laden and his terror. The civilized world can't do it, so it's up to the United States to step forward into the frontier and bring justice, so that it can once again become civilized. That's why I talk about the second half of the equation. It's not just frontier justice; it's the bushwhacking of America.

In the old West, bushwhacking was the most cowardly form of combat. Bushwhacking isn't standing up face to face to the guys and pulling your 6-gun, and taking your chances on your speed and accuracy. It's shooting someone like a coward in the back. You ambush them. You let him run by and you shoot him in the back. You gun him down dead and never give him a chance. That's what Bush has done. He's not Gary Cooper. He's a coward who bushwhacked the American people by exploiting the fear and ignorance engendered in the post-9/11 environment to portray Iraq as a threat to our national security and Saddam Hussein as someone who possessed weapons of mass destruction that would destroy the very society that we live in. There is a need, therefore, for frontier justice to prevent mushroom clouds from popping up all over American cities. Bush lied to us. He bushwhacked us. He went to war on false pretenses. He shredded international law, not because there was a threat, but because it was an impediment to his own selfish goals and objectives. This is a man who went out to the prison—because we had Saddam in a prison, this bad guy named Saddam, the black bard of the Middle East, we had him in a prison. Sanctions were in place. Military forces had him contained. He wasn't going anywhere. And yet we pulled him out of the prison, accused him of rustling cattle, stealing horses, strung him up by the neck until he was dead, and while his feet were still twitching, you've got Bush desperately running around trying to find out where the cattle he rustled are. It turns out he didn't rustle any cattle. He wasn't a horse thief. There was no reason to hang him. And what's Sheriff Bush do? He runs around and says, well, he was a bad guy anyway, he deserved it. There's a reason why the United States gave up vigilante justice over

100 years ago, and that was to prevent the kind of abuse of power that took place there. George W. Bush is no practitioner of frontier justice; he's a bushwhacker who has ambushed the Constitution of the United States and the very values and principals we stand for as a nation.

JE: Bill O'Reilly, among others, has been talking a lot lately about views like yours as "internationalist." The implication, of course, is that people like you put the interests of the rest of the world before the interests of the United States. You believe in international law, you believe that Europe is civilized, and neocon intellectuals like Robert Kagan have a very different view. They think all of that is exactly what needs to be realigned. This is a different world now and we need to think, first and foremost, through the power of the United States, if there's to be any civilization globally in the future at all. What's your take on this skepticism about internationalism?

I don't view military service as a litmus test of your credentials as an American citizen, but I spent twelve years in the United States Marine Corps, not the marine corps of the international community. I wore the flag of the United States of America on my shoulder in combat defending my country. I continue to serve my country today in a number of ways, including as a citizen actively involved in holding my government accountable for its actions. The foundation that I fall back on in holding my government accountable isn't a system of international law, but the Constitution of the United States of America. I'm an American, first and foremost. I love my country more than anything. I'm willing to die for my country. Unlike Bill O'Reilly, I've gone into the military and put my life on the line for my country, so I'm a little bit insulted by anybody that would insinuate that somehow I'm not for America.

But I also understand that the United States is part of a global community and we have responsibilities as a member of this global community. The Constitution sets forth these responsibilities when it says in Article 6 that when we, the people of the United States of America, enter into a treaty or an agreement with a foreign entity that has been ratified by two-thirds of the United States Senate, it is the law of the land. It is not that I want others calling the shots on what we do as a people here in America, but we need to recognize that when we enter into an agreement, it is binding. We signed the United Nations Charter. We didn't do so with a gun to our head, compelled to do so after losing a war, kicking and screaming to sign a surrender document. No, we won

World War II. We were the victors. From that victory came the concept of the United Nations and the Charter of the United Nations. We put forward a concept that said we will reject war as a means of resolving disputes between nations, and that we should pursue non-violent means when we talk about fixing issues between countries.

Again, I know what it means to put on the uniform of an American service member. I know what it means to go war, and I know how it feels to have your life suddenly flash before your eyes as things happen around you, so I don't take this issue lightly. I believe that we have a duty and responsibility as Americans to ensure that every means possible short of war is exhausted before we go to war; that before we ask someone to give their life for our country we ensure that it's a cause worthy of that sacrifice. I like the United Nations and I like international law because it provides for a framework of discussion that enables us to come up with means short of war to resolve disputes. I don't put international law before the Constitution of the United States, but I recognize that the Constitution of the United States of America embraces international law through Article 6, and we are bound by that. So, I'm not putting old Europe in front of the United States. I'm not putting France and Germany in front of the United States. I put America first. But I hold America accountable for what it says it stands for and Bill O'Reilly or anyone else cannot go around and just unilaterally redefine what this country stands for. The Constitution can only be amended through a certain process. We need to have Constitutional gatherings in states and people have to vote on an amendment, and when you get a certain number of states agreeing to an amendment, then it becomes law. But Bill O'Reilly or any other talk show host sitting on their perch on TV can't suddenly redefine who we are as a people. I think that those people who would put an America-first policy blindly forward, with total disregard to the commitments that we, the people, have undertaken through the Constitution, through international law, through treaties, don't know what it means to be an American.

JE: Let's consider the political dimensions of what you're talking about. The fact of the matter is, if you look at polls, it seems that if you trash the French, your poll numbers go up; trash the UN, your poll numbers go up. We also know from recent polling about this phenomenon of the NASCAR dad, this demographic of white, working-class men who are identifying with Bush's foreign policy approach and the need for this war. Could you just weigh in on that dimension of things, the male side of the gender gap that's tilting Republican?

I deal with working-class, blue-collar guys all the time. One of the joys of my life right now is being a volunteer firefighter. And, you know, when you go to the firehouse, you meet these guys who are just the nuts and bolts of the community. They're the plumbers, the electricians, the UPS delivery men; they're lawyers, bankers, and doctors. They're every aspect of society coming together. It's a male-dominated society. We have women there, but it's a sort of macho society, too; a bunch of guys who like to believe they're real men doing manly things with other men in a manly way. It's pretty cool, but one of the things I have realized is that when men are confronted with real issues they tend to respond realistically. Ask a guy who's willing to run into a burning building what it means to put your life on the line and they don't take it lightly. Therefore, they don't take it lightly when you start talking about war and what it means to put you life on the line in a war. I would say that a man who is comfortable with being a man is somebody who's less inclined toward rushing off to war. Those who say that we have to go to war to prove something are really people that have an emptiness in themselves. They need to prove something to somebody. I don't know what. They live life vicariously. They watch NASCAR and think maybe they're the driver of number 3 getting ready to win the race and crash, but they don't have the courage to go out there and drive the cars themselves. They go to the WWF Smackdown, and watch these steroid-stuffed guys running around smashing chairs against each other and they fantasize about being out there doing the same thing, when in fact they're sitting in the stands with their beer belly and their high cholesterol, because they don't have what it takes to go out there and do that. There's a lot of frustration out there, I think, that's being exploited.

I'm not putting down NASCAR. A lot of guys like NASCAR who are legitimate, functioning citizens who just happen to like driving cars fast. I like golf, I like football, I like baseball, but that doesn't define who I am. If you like NASCAR, that doesn't define who you are unless you allow it to. When you speak of the "NASCAR dad," that's a discredit to NASCAR, and that's a discredit to most of the men who go out and watch NASCAR racing. But what it's identifying is that there is a segment of society that is vulnerable to this kind of exploitation. It's ironic that the person exploiting this vulnerability is probably the poster child for male deficit syndrome: George W. Bush.

Mr. Chickenhawk. A guy who didn't even have the courage to see through his tour of duty in the national guard. Maybe flying F102s over Houston, Texas was too dangerous, so he ran off to Alabama while millions of Americans were going to Vietnam. He has an administration chock-full of these so-called heroes, people who didn't have the courage to defend their country in a time of unpopular war, and yet today they've got us engaged in another unpopular war and they're asking other people to go out there and fight it for them.

Northampton, Massachusetts
October 22, 2003

VANDANA SHIVA

Dr. Vandana Shiva is a physicist, ecologist, activist, editor, and author of many books. In India she established Navdanya, a movement for biodiversity conservation and farmers' rights, and she directs the Research Foundation for Science, Technology, and Natural Resource Policy. Her books include *Biopiracy: The Plunder of Nature and Knowledge* (South End Press, 1997), *Stolen Harvest: The Hijacking of the Global Food Supply* (South End Press, 1999) and *Water Wars: Privatization, Pollution, and Profit* (South End Press, 2002).

JE: You've talked about globalization being a form of war by other means. What role does the US military play in the dynamics of globalization?

For countries like India it starts in 1988, at the beginning of this phase of a reorganization of the world order when the US trade laws were changed. Clauses were added—they were called Article 301—which basically allowed the US to engage, through foreign policy instruments and trade sanctions, against countries that were not opening their markets to US corporations. This was long before the World Trade Organization (WTO) came into force, long before the General Agreements on Tariffs and Trade (GATT) were ratified, long before this new phase of militarism. In a way, militaristic-style threats of trade wars were already used to open up the markets of the south for US agribusiness, the US pharmaceutical industry, the US entertainment industry, and so for us there has never been a separation between foreign policy, militarism, and trade. Usually the American Commerce Secretary travels to India in an Air Force jet. An Air Force jet was used by [Clinton Commerce Secretary] Ron Brown to come to India and threaten us with very severe action if we didn't give permission for Enron's polluting thermal power plant. At every step, our serenity and our democracy are undermined, and the repercussions of that are felt at the bottom, in terms of alienation of rights that are enshrined in our constitution. Since all this started, every element of our constitutional protections is being dismantled. It also means tearing up our societies along new polarizations under this pressure of globalization and the new opportunism created by fascist tendencies in societies across the world. I would call this convergence of forces that we are seeing similar to a global AIDS. It's an HIV epidemic and it is collapsing the immunity of societies and countries.

JE: One of the major claims the Bush administration surely will make is that they brought "democracy" to the people of Iraq. What's your reaction to that?

Well, democracy is supposed to be by the people, of the people, and for the people. The democracy that is being institutionalized under the threat of bombs and guns is by the corporations, for the corporations, of the corporations. And nothing makes this more evident than the fact that instead of rebuilding Iraq for the Iraqi people, the rebuilding of Iraq was made into an opportunity for returns to Bechtel, with a $680 million subsidy (of United States taxpayer money) to take over the assets, services, and resources while leaving the Iraqi people without water, without electricity, without schools, without security.

The fact that every second day you have some kind of a bombing—that you have more American soldiers being killed now than during the war—shows very clearly that the Iraqis are not feeling very liberated, otherwise they would not be taking the actions they are. Today Iraq would be at peace, schools would be running, water would be running, electricity would be running. Iraq continues to be in a state of war and the war today is even deeper. Today most Iraqis are against the invasion and you have Iraqis pitted against Iraqis—this is not an expression of democracy.

JE: For many Americans there is great mystery about why "they" hate "us." Can you talk about the dangers of that polarity, not only between states, but within societies themselves?

I think first of all there is no "us" and "them" in the world. Just the very construction of the "us" and the "them" is wrong. I think most people of the world relate to American citizens as other human beings. They do feel a little sorry for the very violent project that has been undertaken in their name. Nobody likes to have their freedoms hijacked in that way, and then be told that the Afghanis can't liberate themselves, that they need an invasion. The Iraqis can't liberate themselves; they need an invasion. The most important problem with this new polarization really is that the violence that's perpetuated against societies, the new colonizations that are put in place, do create an anger and an outrage and a resentment. Because systems that allowed people to live their ordinary daily lives are falling apart. Not only are systems falling apart, but people's abilities to live in peace, to live in harmony with all the diversity and plurality that our societies have been part of, are falling apart. That polarity does start to then create an "us" and "them" everywhere. For example, an "us" and "them" within Iraqi societies between the different sects of Islam. Within India we had healed the wounds of partition—which was what the last colonial legacy left us when the British tried to continue to rule us through force. When they couldn't succeed by force, they tried to create the divide and rule strategy of pitting Muslims and Hindus against each other that led to the formation of Pakistan. But India continued to be a society in which the Muslims, the Hindus, the Christians, the British, the hundreds of thousands of tribal communities were one pluralistic, diverse fabric. But in recent years, as globalization started to change our domestic structures and people are losing their jobs, unemployed people can be moved into thinking that their jobs were taken away because there are too many Muslims—rather than thinking that if we had less destruction of jobs we'd have more jobs, if we had livelihood protection at the center of economic policy, more people would have jobs.

So this baiting of the Other through xenophobic ethnic identity starts to become an absolutely natural offshoot. It is an inevitable side effect of economic policies, of globalization, that are designed to destroy jobs and livelihoods in order to increase corporate profits. That's the only agenda that globalization has: how to increase corporate opportunity by destroying people's sovereignty and destroying people's place in the economy. It is an economic arrangement without people. It's an economic arrangement for corporations.

We are locked into a three-level, totally discordant arrangement: economic globalization with so-called free trade, which is forced trade driven by corporations; militarism protecting the globalization that people don't want; and at the macro level, so-called representative democracy where there is this theater of elections every few years. But given that there is no security being offered to people, and everyone is experiencing insecurity, national representative democracy ends up being the ultimate playground for fundamentalism and fascism. Politicians can't offer a community a school, they cannot offer them a waterline, and they cannot offer them better jobs because that's not in their mandate anymore. That's in the trade rules of WTO and NAFTA, in the hands of corporations. It's been dropped from national parliaments. It's been dropped from provincial legislatures. So no one who goes around to ask for votes can say, "I'll get you a school. I'll make sure you have enough teachers." No, they say, "The reason your schools are running badly is there are too many immigrants. The reason your public systems are collapsing is because there are too many people of another religion, another race, another whatever." And fascism and fundamentalism then become the only recipe for a representative politics within the shadow of global militarism and global free trade.

JE: You have talked about the rise of various right-wing fundamentalisms around the world. How does the Bush administration fit into this?

In India we have seen the rise of the right after globalization took root. The right thrives on hatred, it thrives on fanaticism, it thrives on mutating every category within which our lives are organized. In the United States, the new intolerance and blindness are connected to this, because you can only have fanaticism in a society that has stopped being a reflective society, which has stopped being a society that looks at affairs, its own experience, its own changing situation, with some kind of depth of understanding. Fanaticism is literally the reflection of a lack of any kind of thinking. It's a reflection of unthinking societies. When fanaticism becomes the rule, it is nurturing those tendencies in societies that block people from participating in their own governance by taking them down a track of shutting out and suspending any intelligent reflection and engagement with world processes, national processes, and local processes. Fanaticism and fascism have always been reason for worry, because you can debate and dialogue with someone who is thinking. Difference in positions has never been a problem in society. Difference in positions has always had a resolution through dialogue. Fanaticism blocks the possibility of dialogue and feedback. You have a certain belief; it's not matching with the reality, and you have the possibility of feedback. Fanaticism blocks feedback. So you have constantly self-fulfilling prophecies. The problem becomes "a clash of civilizations" and you then engender a clash of civilizations. The problem is "people are lazy, otherwise we would have more employment" and you basically throw more and more people out of work. You constantly create the scenario that you predict is the basis of why you're assuming what you're assuming.

Globalization has been on the agenda of US administrations through both Republican and Democratic administrations. In fact, when we look at the United States in terms of economic policy, there isn't that much of a difference between the parties in terms of how the rest of the world is treated. After all, the imposition of Enron, the imposition of a Monsanto, all these impositions of the worst excesses of corporations were done during Democratic rule. The difference really is that, on the one hand, domestically the correction processes within American societies become less possible under the new tendencies of fascism in this society. And on the second hand, fascism here does give new support to fascist tendencies in other societies. That is where there is a huge difference in the political domain. But the economics of it are very, very similar between the two parties. And that's why we need a political shift through reclaiming economic democracy worldwide. I call this Earth Democracy. Earth Democracy because we need to re-link economics and politics once again, to re-link to people and de-link them from corporations. We need to de-link that amazing marriage of both our electoral processes and our economic processes in the hands of corporations, which is disenfranchising people both economically and politically and then creating the possibilities of all these horrible tendencies of violence and militarism and fascism to become the norm everywhere, with each fascism feeding the other fascism. That, I think, is the really worrying part that we need to shift out of.

JE: Given these continuities between the parties, do you think it makes a big difference to the rest of the world who wins the next US presidential election?

I think it definitely makes a difference to the rest of the world who wins the next election. Because corporate rule and corporate dictatorship are bad enough, but corporate rule and corporate dictatorship supported by fascism make a very toxic mixture. I think the Seattle demonstrations showed that citizens of the world are organized enough to deal with a resistance to corporate rule alone. It's the fascist tendencies that create such a dangerous situation because they leave no possibility for democratic dissent. They leave no possibility for political resistance. The only outcome is violence, which is why it's very, very important that in the United States that these fascist tendencies be brought to a halt.

JE: It's often claimed that the Iraq war is really about controlling Middle East oil? Do you think that's true?

The war in Iraq was very, very clearly about oil, as was the invasion of Afghanistan. The best security for the oil pipeline that was planned and not yet built was an occupation of Afghanistan. All predictions show that some of the biggest consumers of oil in the coming future will be Asian countries, because that is where production is being relocated. Resource-intensive production and labor-intensive production are moving to China and India. The result is the demand for oil is shifting there also. The war in Iraq was very, very much related to preventing any competitor from controlling the oil trade because all of Iraqi oil trade was shifting to the Euro. It was becoming extremely clear that before you knew it there was going to be a marginalization of the dollar-dominated economy of the United States. Saddam Hussein was a good excuse, but what was at stake was controlling the resources of the world. Tomorrow you could have a very democratic leader in a country, but if there's a vital resource there that needs to be controlled for global economic dictatorship, you'll still have the same phenomenon play out. That's why I spend so much of my time working on keeping vital resources like biodiversity and water in the public and common domain, because if we do not watch out, as biodiversity is converted into the green oil of the future, controlled by the five gene giants, or the water of the world starts to be controlled like the blue gold of the future and is bought and sold, we will have wars created around the control of these resources.

JE: Can you talk about how fear is used in the service of fanaticism?

Good societies have cultivated fearlessness and hope among their citizens. Good politics has always been about real courage, real fearlessness. Take Gandhi, whose ultimate weapon was fearlessness against one of the worst empires of our time. The very notion of not cooperating with that empire was based on fearlessness. When Martin Luther King walked in the Gandhian tradition, he walked in fearlessness. Every leader worth their name promotes fearlessness, promotes the ability to question illegitimate power, challenge injustice, and create real freedom for people. Bad leaders cultivate fear. They live on growing fear among people. Fear is bred by ignorance, and therefore they breed ignorance among their citizens. Fear, then, becomes a way to control people, to mislead people, to trap people into unfreedoms. Fear becomes a companion to unfreedom.

JE: The Bush administration is going to flood the American mass media with images of George Bush as a tough-talking, fearless, and steady cowboy. How does that fit into your analysis?

There are two forms of fearlessness. One is fearlessness that comes from within—the human strength of a clarity of vision, the clarity of experience, the clarity of knowing the difference between the good and the bad, the right and the wrong, the sustainable and the non-sustainable, the just and the unjust. But when George Bush, in total media hype, equipped with a flying helmet, doing a total pretend of riding a fighter jet, the fearlessness is not in George Bush. It is the aggression of militarized equipment that is actually being sold. That's part of the crisis that has occurred in US society—that the violence of militaristic arms, of bomber jets, is taken as pretend fearlessness, when it is really an instrument to create fear in the other. That is its only role. Your fearlessness, my fearlessness are not rooted in generating fear in the other by instruments of violence and instruments of militarism and instruments of threat. Fearlessness is the ability with no arms, no weapons, with nothing, to be able to say, "I will not let you abuse me. I will not let you violate my fundamental rights." That is fearlessness. Is George Bush as a human being—without that helmet, without the bomber, without that armed ship—able to deal with other human beings? That is the real equation of fearlessness, not with the intervention of militaristic display.

JE: The US has turned to the United Nations to try and rescue the disaster they find themselves in now in Iraq. How do you read the meaning of this shift?

The turning to the UN is in fact a recognition of the failure of US unilateralism. The original idea was, "We just don't have to go along with the rest of the world. We are smart enough, powerful enough, to be able to bomb anyone out of their senses." But having bombed people out of their senses, those tiny citizens of Iraq are organizing—not with Saddam Hussein's help—but just as very angry people who don't like occupation and don't like the deceit of an improved society not being brought to them. Now that there's a mess to be cleaned up in Iraq, you need more than military might from the United States. And the rest of the world will never join a US military, the rest of the world will never serve under a US military. My country was asked to supply forces to Iraq. The government nearly agreed, but the parliament absolutely refused. The condition being sent back from every part of the world is that if we have to help in the rebuilding of Iraq, it must happen under the United Nations, not under the US military. That is why the US is now turning to the United Nations, because they've created a mess, they're left with a mess, and their own military today is the target. The war is continuing in different ways and somehow they need to stop it. The United Nations is being brought in just like mama helps clean up after the mess young people leave.

JE: Are you hopeful that the massive rallies we saw around the world on February 15, 2003, can be the start of a movement that can help reverse the slide into fanaticism?

When the peace protests started and then culminated in that amazing coordinated expression on the 15th of February, two things became very, very clear. First, that citizens are ready globally to be the real alternative to corporate rule. Secondly, that they are organized on a world scale, that there is an organizing outside of the corporately controlled global marketplace, and that is the organizing of civil society on issues of justice and peace and sustainability. At no point in that peace movement was there a separation from the "anti-globalization" movement. The agenda of anti-globalization and the agenda of peace had become one, and of course it created tremendous hope to see that happen. I think what we in the anti-globalization movement need to do is build on that mobilization for peace.

I have been part of mobilizations in India against the WTO from before it came into being in 1993. I organized half a million farmers on the streets of India to tell our government that these treaties are going to destroy our lives. The way those governments could ignore the people and impose these treaties is the same as Mr. Blair and Mr. Bush trying to trivialize the democratic expression and democratic will of their people. Democracy is supposed to be a reflection of the popular will of the people. The day that popular will starts to get ignored, you have dictatorship. The experience of democracy is leaders reflecting what their people want. Any leader who abuses that cannot be called a leader of a democratic society. They can be called hijackers of power in the name of democracy.

Northampton, Massachusetts
September 23, 2003

JE: Can you talk about the media climate following September 11, and how it may or may not have been implicated in the rush to war with Iraq? Were there any patterns you saw contributing to public support for war and the Bush administration's ability to go to war?

9/11 was about people shutting down. It was about a lot of fear. The reality is that right after 9/11, the news media shut down and journalists, with few notable exceptions, basically scurried for cover. So you had this dynamic right after 9/11 where debate, narrow as it had been in the mass media, became very quickly much more constricted. I think the fear was contagious. It was in the air. Nobody in the mass media had to be told to quiet dissent about Bush. But when you think about it, in the first months of the administration he was being laughed at, he was being mocked, and he was being talked about as a basic incompetent who had risen way above his level of incompetence. Within a matter of days following 9/11 he was being elevated in the mass media as FDR reincarnated. All of a sudden, wow, he can read a teleprompter in front of the joint session of Congress. We underestimated this guy! He's really brilliant! And his stature from September 10 to September 20 just went into the media stratosphere.

JE: What's your evaluation of the media's performance since the war began? How would you evaluate the job they've done as journalists in a democracy?

Democracy is about what happens every day, not what's chiseled in stone or written in parchment about the First Amendment. I think the coverage of the war in Iraq in 2003 was really part of a pattern we've continually seen, where people such as Dan Rather, or Christiane Amanpour and others, who go along with the war agenda, later on after the fighting is over feel a little squeamish, a little embarrassed, and so they offer some kind of half-baked *mea culpas*. It's kind of like what

Mark Twain said about how easy it was to quit smoking. He said, "It's really easy; I've done it thousands of times." In a lot of ways the major network correspondents and anchors are in a similar place around becoming prostitutes to the war makers. When the missiles are flying, they prostitute themselves, and then later on it's easy for them to say, "Gee, you know, we should have been more independent." Then the next war comes along and they do the same thing.

JE: How do you account for this? Let's assume they're not terrible people, these journalists, and that they have a certain degree of professionalism. This could sound like conspiracy to a lot of people, that they're prostitutes to the war. How do you account for why something like that happens? What's going on that so many otherwise okay journalists, smart people, get caught up in this?

Well, how many people in their own work places, whatever their job happens to be, tell the boss to buzz off, rock the boat, and risk their employment? Journalists aren't any more or less courageous than people in other professions. They've got mortgages, they have kids, they want to pay college tuition, and they have a livelihood that they want to be able to depend on in the future. In a way, that's the point. You don't need to be a rocket scientist or a social scientist to know that if you're Tom Brokaw, and you're working for General Electric when you work for NBC, and General Electric is a military contractor, that if you launch an investigative series about war profiteering in the United States, it's not exactly going to enhance your career in that network. But Brokaw is not as good an example as many others who are not famous, or who have less income and less job security. In general, with a few exceptions, they're just not going to say, "Gee, I'm going to take this principled position, even though it means I'll probably lose my job or not be able to go up the media ladder any farther, in terms of advancement and income."

JE: Along those same lines, in your book, Target Iraq, *you say that the first Gulf War laid the groundwork for embedded journalists. That might seem counter-intuitive to a lot of people who think, "Hey, finally we're on the ground. We learned from those Pentagon pools in the first Gulf War, and now journalists were actually on the ground showing us war like we never saw it before." Can you talk about the Gulf War laying the groundwork for embedded journalists?*

New permutations don't necessarily mean any basic changes, and the coverage of the war in Iraq in 2003 was stylistically somewhat different from the coverage of the Gulf War a dozen years earlier. But the embedding of journalists was really about going to bed with the military. That's what journalists basically did. They traveled with military units that they were depending on for their food, their shelter, their health care, their livelihood, their survival during the time they were on the job. I know from watching CNN or MSNBC or FOX that you had this real sense of camaraderie between the reporters covering those units and the troops themselves. I heard one journalist, for instance, say, "These soldiers, we've gotten to know each other. They trust me." Well, that's not a good relationship in terms of journalism, when the people you're covering trust you not to report things they don't want you to report. That's a warning flag that there is something wrong with the arrangement. In retrospect, if you look at the coverage of the war in Iraq in 2003, you find that with rare exceptions those journalists who were embedded basically reported in ways that the Pentagon didn't mind too much. The better reporting came from the unattached, unembedded reporters. As one journalist covering the war for ABC pointed out, the unembedded reporters could cover what happened after the troops moved on—the carnage, the suffering, the mourning, the funerals, the rage, the injuries, the wounded children. The embedded reporters were like internalized warriors; they were hot shots moving along with the victorious troops. War is not just about winning; it's also about suffering.

JE: Can you talk a little bit more about the coverage here in the US of casualties during this war compared to other outlets—not just outlets like Al-Jazeera, but the European media?

If you're going to have US journalists embedded with the American troops, then you should also have journalists embedded with the Iraqi civilians. If you had had just as many American reporters embedded with the families in Iraq who were dealing with 2,000-pound bombs and cruise missiles exploding in their neighborhoods, then you might have had a much more balanced perspective as a TV viewer or reader or listener. The British press just did a much better job of covering what the war meant in human terms. What did it mean to be under those bombs? What happened in the emergency rooms of those hospitals? I'm generalizing here, because there were some instances of good, vivid reporting in the US media. Anne Garrels was not embedded. She was in Baghdad during the war. She provided some graphic reporting for National Public Radio, but the exception is not the essence of propaganda, because propaganda is about repetition, as any ad executive knows. It's not only the code words and the catch phrases that are repeated, but the images that are put forward. What is put into the coverage and what's left out? That's why even the supposedly better mass media coverage in the United States really didn't displease the Pentagon. With rare exceptions, NPR often seemed to stand for National Pentagon Radio. It was just a kind of tone, an overall balance or imbalance, that conveyed explicitly and implicitly that some people's lives matter a lot and some people's don't matter too much. There are worthy victims and unworthy victims. We take our cues from the Pentagon. We mourn the Americans who die. The Iraqis who die, well that's unfortunate but, you know, that's the way war is.

JE: Can you say more about these catch phrases and patterns you've noticed in these repetitions you're speaking about?

"War on Terror" is perhaps the most demagogic term that has come into fashion in politics and media in the United States in the last couple of years. And I think it's notable that at first after 9/11 it was a "War on Terrorism" and that got shortened both by the Bush administration and by the mass media journalists. When you stop and think about it, "War on Terror" is a very bizarre phrase. Terror is an emotion, an experience; it is a human disaster at an experiential level. It's not something that you can make war on. That is like saying we're going to have a war on fear. Calling this a "War on Terror" even elevated it from simply a "War on Terrorism." It made a kind of universality out of the demagoguery. So first there is a War on Terrorism: there are those bad people out there, and we're going to fight them, we're going to make war on them and what they do. Then it was almost an existential declaration of combat: wherever terror exists we're going to fight it. The hypocrisy is just so extreme that you can just flat out call it Orwellian.

I visited Baghdad in September of 2002, December of 2002, and January of 2003, and I would walk along the street and imagine what it would be like to have the cruise missiles landing on that block or in that area. I went to a children's hospital in Baghdad. I went there twice. I remember the second time, I went with Sean Penn, and we walked through the hospital and saw the children suffering from leukemia and cancer. It was a horrible situation with very inadequate access to drugs, which is one of the results of the US-led embargo. Chemotherapy is being basically disrupted or denied as a result of the US-led sanctions. And something Sean Penn said to me was very poignant. We left the hospital and he said, "You're in that place and you don't want a door to slam, let alone have bombs exploding." And I imagined what it would be like for the children there or their parents taking care of them in the hospital, or for that matter anybody in the area, when that war was to happen. Terror is a good description.

So we're in a realm where in the name of waging war against terror, the US government terrorizes, and it does so against civilians on a very large scale. You could argue that the terrorism of the United States continues, because the cruise missiles and the other weapons that were utilized were only part of what took place. Then you had the cluster munitions by the US Air Force in Afghanistan, then by the US Army in Iraq in the spring of 2003, and a lot of those cluster bombs were still left around the city of Baghdad and elsewhere, where children could pick them up; sometimes they had yet to detonate and you had these sharp shards of metal ripping into the bodies of these little children, maiming and killing them in many instances. That is also about terrorizing people. So the phrase "War on Terror" becomes this kind of projection that all evil resides elsewhere and that by definition everything that the Pentagon does, the White House orders, and Congress agrees to, is about challenging terror when in fact it causes terror for many people as well.

JE: What about "Shock and Awe"?

"Shock and Awe" was a kind of cutsie phrase, ostensibly to describe this massive display of firepower, which is just to say an unprecedented intensity of bombs dropping on Baghdad. It was talked about for weeks and weeks. I first saw it in the British press and it was talked about in the US media as well before March 20, 2003, and there was this drumbeat. Perhaps it was partly psychological warfare against the Saddam Hussein regime, but it really took hold and it became a kind of media fashion to echo that phraseology. That particular phrase is a glass through which we see the corruption of language as part of the corruption of citizenship, of public morality, of democratic discourse. Where we must be numbed and desensitized, words and images are utilized. Don't feel, don't think too much, go along with the prevailing agenda. The war makers, if they decide it's time to go to war, don't think too much or too closely about what that entails for human beings.

The contradictions for many people are more extreme now as we look at the war in Iraq, because the war was built on flagrant, extreme lies from beginning to end. So whether one is a pacifist or not, the fact that the war was built on lies really is something that punches up the contradictions to a great extent. We're left with the fact that the usual means by which the news media encourage people to try and feel good about a war were greatly magnified; they were exponentially increased. That's really important, too, because the real message from the war makers in Washington and the news media is not only that you should accept this war, but you should realize that it's necessary and therefore make peace with it. But you should also feel good about it—a war that will blow the limbs of children. When the war is based on lies, it is presented as something that you should actually be proud of; it should make you proud of being an American.

There was an enormous amount of prewar idolatry of the weapons. After all, there wasn't a war yet to cover, so the weapons weren't being used. In *USA Today* and in the major network coverage and so forth, you had this very elaborate, computer-generated graphic sort of coverage of the different air force and army planes and gun ships and helicopters and very snazzy weapons of all descriptions, and then the minute details were described. There was an idolatry there, a kind of gods of metal worship that, again, is an extreme perversion in human terms. It's not enough for us to be told to accept this war; we're really encouraged to gain some kind of vicarious pleasure from it.

JE: A moment ago you said that perspective guides the outlook and the rhetoric, and in one of your columns you talked about Susan Sontag— about how the way we look at pictures is also guided in some way by who we are, what we're used to, etc. Can you talk about what you were trying to get across in your commentary on Susan Sontag about how perspective works, how different people see pictures differently?

We really bring to the pictures our sense of context and there's a tendency, I'm afraid, among anti-war people for instance, to project their own reactions onto other people who may have a very different sense of the context of a war or an image from the war. There's a tendency, really, to project the meaning of the picture, and as Susan

Sontag points out, one person can look at the picture of a GI in the middle of a battle situation and say war is terrible, this war is wrong, and somebody else can look at the same photo and say, how admirable that in the face of so many dangers and so much unpleasantness and risk, these soldiers are willing to fight for what's right. While I think that the human dimensions of war need to be conveyed in terms of descriptions by words and photographic images and video and so forth, that does not really solve a whole heck of a lot. As a matter of fact, there is often a vicarious pleasure that a lot of people who are primed to see the value of a war take from the news coverage that might convey some of that. In a kind of peculiar inversion of reality, some people can look at real TV footage of a war and say, "This is so real, it seems like a movie I saw at the cineplex." So what's the referent?

I think it was Mark Crispin Miller who said, "Nobody seems to really die on TV because nobody really seems to live there either." Miller makes a very good point about the myth that television brings when it brings war into your living room. He says, can we think of anything more unlike war than watching this piece of furniture in the room? You get up, you go to the kitchen, you go to the bathroom; there's nothing's exploding around you, nothing's falling. It's a kind of conceit that we've had in this country since the Vietnam War, the cliché that television brought the Vietnam War into our living rooms. That's nonsense. Again, it depends on what representation, what interpretation we bring to what we see, but televisions don't blow up and they tend to be very confined and confining and defined, and often simply don't convey much of anything other than entertainment, reinforcing people's preconceptions.

JE: What about media coverage of 9/11 in this context?

I think the 9/11 coverage was a new low and an extremely dangerous one. The US mythos has often been about being the Mr. Fix It. Uncle Sam is the guy who is going to go in and make things right in Vietnam or wherever. That has been the mythology that propelled a lot of justifications for wars in recent decades. But from the get-go, 9/11 introduced another element as well into the media coverage and political discourse, such as it was, in the partisan arena in the United States—and that is the US as victim. Now we're not only the world's leading military power, we're not only the world' s only superpower, we, the American people, are the world's leading victims.

I think this is what Noam Chomsky was getting at. You had very opportunistic people like Christopher Hitchens and others, those avowedly on the right, who would attack, for instance, Noam Chomsky, when actually Chomsky was making a very simple point— that all lives are of equal value and that if you're going to bring a single standard of human rights and an authentic commitment to human life to the table as you discuss these things, you don't elevate the deaths of some as being way more important than the deaths of others.

Ed Herman and Noam Chomsky have written about what they call worthy and unworthy victims. They're talking about the capacity of the president and the mass media to convey explicitly and otherwise that these victims are worthy of our tears and these other victims, not only are they unworthy of our tears but we may actually feel pretty good about victimizing them, because after all, we're in a holy pursuit. The so-called collateral damage, well, it's unfortunate, but this is part of a great and noble effort.

As soon as we decide that there are worthy and unworthy victims, and that when an American dies, or even somebody in the United States who's not an "American" dies, that that is just so much more profoundly important than when other people die even if, or especially if, we killed them—as people in the United States who with our silence and our tax dollars enabled the Pentagon to do what it does—I refer to this as asking for whom the bell tolls. When you ask for whom the bell tolls, you're asking what is the rationale for an atrocity. Once you get into that, then all bets are off and all kinds of justifications can take place.

I did a search on the Nexus Media database for the first few months of 2003 for the word Nuremberg. I looked at National Public Radio and I searched for any discussion in just the huge numbers of hours that were devoted to the lead up to the war and then into the war on Iraq itself on NPR news programs. Was there a mention of the Nuremberg trials and the principles that were affirmed and established there? Nuremberg was mentioned four times on NPR in the first few months of 2003, and not on any one of those occasions was it in the context of the Nuremberg trials and concerns that some people had about the US War on Iraq, which, after all, was incontrovertibly a war of aggression. Robert Jackson, the justice from the US Supreme Court who went to Nuremberg in 1945, made it very clear that the Nazi leaders were being put on trial not because they lost, but because they launched an aggressive war. He described it as a crime against humanity that had no possible justification. So it's a reasonable question to ask:

wasn't George W. Bush guilty of some of the same crimes that people in the dock were convicted for at Nuremberg? How about Dick Cheney? Colin Powell? Donald Rumsfeld?

In a nutshell, when certain thoughts are off limits, when glaring hypocrisies and inconsistencies can't even be talked about in any depth in the mass media, you have a stultified media environment. In a very real sense, intellectually there is an infantilization of the US public, especially in war time. We're not supposed to notice. After 9/11 there was talk about the end of irony, but of course irony can't be killed. You can't drive a stick through its heart. People notice ironies, but in the mass media in this country there is almost a taboo against unauthorized ironies. When you talk about George W. Bush and the war on Iraq, you're just not supposed to talk about Nuremberg.

JE: With regard to this interplay between defensiveness and aggressiveness, on the one hand, the American people would likely not have supported a war of aggression, which is why we needed a pretext; we needed weapons of mass destruction. At the same time, once we're there, it seems Americans love their war. A lot of people love the cowboy stuff here, the Rambo stuff. But it's never quite seen as bullying, even though it might look like it to the rest of the world. This interplay between defending and being aggressive, defending yourself as a pretext for aggression, can you comment on this?

In the United States, the war on Iraq was sold largely as a defensive war. That notion was pervading the rhetoric from the Bush administration and their enablers in the US news media. We're defending ourselves. There could be nuclear weapons, all this stuff that couldn't stand scrutiny. I'm not that bright that I could see through this more than anybody really could. I just looked at it. It made no sense that Iraq would have a nuclear weapons program. I came out with the book *Target Iraq* a few months before the war started and the book says, point blank, that there is no nuclear weapons program. It defies logic, yet the Bush administration was saying things that defied logic, and the news media basically bought into the paradigm that one way or another, this is a defensive war. As long as a lot of people believe that a war is defensive, they're going to support it. In this case, as in so many others, it has just been a preposterous assertion. Usually when one makes a claim, one needs evidence first, before the claim can be made convincing. However, this is a very different situation; it's kind of like in Through the Looking-Glass: first the verdict and then the evidence.

That's very much the way the Bush administration played it and while they got some media flak along the way, they were able to make the sale. They basically said, this is defensive war. If we don't attack Iraq, there will be a mushroom cloud. And it worked, but I think that's really a testament to the power of media manipulation to convince people about things that have no factual basis.

JE: Fear, defensiveness, paranoia, being scared—those things don't seem very American. They seem out of synch with the American mythology and how we Americans like to see ourselves. This seems more in line with what Robert Kagan and other neoconservative intellectuals have been saying about "old Europe," how they don't quite have the fortitude we do. Can you anticipate how Karl Rove and Bush's other media handlers are likely to position Bush as strong, while questioning the weakness of the Democratic candidate, regardless of who it is?

In October 2003 George Bush said that the national news media were filtering some messages and that he needed to go around them to go to regional media outlets. That was quite ironic because the Bush administration has greatly benefited from the filtration function of mass media in the US, which basically allows certain messages to permeate the media environment while excluding, with few exceptions, contrary messages. If you look at, say, FDR saying that the only thing you have to fear is fear itself, the kind of tacit counterpoint to that from the Bush administration after 9/11 is the only thing you have to fear is not enough fear. That really is the ace card of those who have been looking for any and all rationales to ramp up the Pentagon budget— now we're at over a billion dollars a day—and to engage in what the former CIA agent John Stockwell called the process of being in search of enemies.

They have a long enemies list in terms of other countries, and fear is the only way to make it work because, all things being equal, most people in the United States don't want to have a war. They have loved ones or friends who will be somewhere killing and being killed, and it's a drain on economic well-being. But it's possible for the propagandists to make this sale based on fear: that if you don't do X, then the United States will suffer Y and Z horrendous actions. I mean, that's really the tipping point for public support, and 9/11 was a godsend for the politics of fear writ large. Essentially what Rice and Powell and Bush and Cheney were saying is, don't you worry about the details. We need to strike first and we'll worry about the details of the evidence later. It's kind of a policy wonk version of the tee shirt: "Kill 'em all and let God sort them out."

JE: Let's shift gears a little bit. Can you talk about the media process by which Saddam Hussein came to replace Osama bin Laden as the face of terror after 9/11?

We have a kind of counterpoint between human rights violations, our violations, and arch villains of the US government. The capacity, the power, of the president, or secretary of state, or secretary of defense, to hold up a report and say these human rights violations are horrible because we care so much about these particular people and this foreign leader is so horrible and we must oppose him and take military action against him, that's an enormous power. It takes power to highlight and define what purported reality is and what it isn't, what matters and what doesn't. By turning over to US government officials the power to define who matters and who doesn't, the journalists who cover Washington and so-called national security on the whole are led by the nose.

We have had a succession of arch-villains who are defined by the administration in Washington. I mean, think back: you had Ho Chi Minh, Qadafi in Libya, Manuel Noriega in Panama, Morris Bishop in Grenada, this tiny country in the Caribbean with what—less than 200,000 people. That tiny country was a threat to the United States? It seems preposterous in retrospect, but that was the designated enemy of the year, the month, whatever. And then, like shuffling the playing cards, they'll come up with somebody else.

Few of us had heard much of anything about Saddam Hussein before he crossed his CIA benefactors and invaded Kuwait. Then he's the bad guy and he's the great villain. That capacity is enormously powerful for the officials in Washington. I have to say, at a kind of psychological level there is a projection involved here. After all, take Manuel Noriega in 1989. Colin Powell became the chair of the Joint Chiefs of Staff and he spearheaded the idea that Panama, through Noriega's leadership, was a threat to US security and we had to go in and invade. Noriega had been on the CIA payroll. Saddam Hussein was a favorite of the CIA for a while, until he crossed the US and invaded Kuwait in August of 1990. So we have these dynamics: he's the good guy, he's the bad guy. Saddam was torturing when he was a good guy and he's still torturing now when he's a bad guy. We don't know what's going on inside of someone like Colin Powell or Donald Rumsfeld, but at a political level there is this massive projection going on.

In January of 2003 I was in a meeting in Baghdad with Tariq Aziz, ostensibly second in command of the Iraqi government under Saddam Hussein. My companion, who happened to be Dennis Halliday, a former head of the UN Oil for Food Program in Baghdad, brought a copy of *Time* magazine that had Donald Rumsfeld on the cover. Tariq Aziz took the magazine and said, "Oh yes, I'll be very interested in this." He looked at the cover with Donald Rumsfeld on it, and he said, "Oh yes, Rumsfeld, he is quite a warmonger. He didn't seem that way when he came to visit us in the 1980s." Of course, there is a picture available of Donald Rumsfeld, an emissary of the Reagan administration in 1983, shaking hands with Saddam Hussein in Baghdad. They had a lot to talk about. They had a lot of common interests to discuss. I sat there looking at Tariq Aziz in his well-tailored suit, his well-conjugated verbs, his erudite language, and I thought about what I came to describe as the "urbanity of evil." The guy was very charming and he was able to engage in very straightforward, witty discourse. You might like to go out and have dinner with the guy. Yet the take-home message about him from the US news media is that he's a totally different animal than the US leaders. He's cut from a very different cloth than the American leadership. Him bad, us good, never the twain shall meet.

Well, the urbanity of evil existed in Baghdad under Saddam Hussein and it exists in Washington under George W. Bush. As a matter of fact, the complicity with evil, with killing for political purposes, is in some ways more understandable under Saddam Hussein in Baghdad than under George W. Bush in Washington. Note that I say understandable, not justifiable. But if Tariq Aziz steps out of line under those circumstances, he's got to think about his relatives who could be tortured or killed by Saddam Hussein if Hussein feels crossed. What do the senators in Washington, the cabinet officials, and others in the government have to fear? They have to worry about not getting reelected, not being reappointed, and they certainly are urbane as well. But whether we're talking about bombing Hanoi, or bombing Baghdad, a lot of civilians die as a result of a failure to make a basic ethical position known and to speak out.

JE: What do you make of the kind of persona George W. Bush has put on the neoconservative agenda?

This is Howdy Doody becomes FDR. I mean, the guy is clearly vacuous. If you look at the history of Ronald Reagan, George W. Bush, and Arnold Schwarzenegger, who's a kind of Reagan on steroids, it is at first incomprehensible that these people could be governor of California, let alone president of the United States. But we're acculturated to accept this. These folks are truly figureheads. They have a personal role that they play, but they're serving a function and there's that interplay between personalities. They're really products and they're obviously serving huge multibillion-dollar corporate agendas. So it's fascinating to talk about the persona and the individual of George W. Bush. Yet at the end of the very dire day that we find ourselves in the midst of, we're really talking about an entire system that's cranked up for war and profiteering. That's our challenge: to go beyond the personalities and see that we have Reaganism without Reagan and Bushism without Bush when he goes on his merry way. I think of it as a symbolic Mr. McGoo presidency. It's the happy face put on the death machine, the smiley sticker that is plastered onto the missiles and the bombs, as the American flag was used.

What were the big positive visual images put on after 9/11? George W. Bush and the American flag. There was kind of a bait and switch operation that was enacted at that point. You had Bush as kind of the guardian of the flag. But the flag itself was utilized, I believe very sincerely, by many people who hung it from their windows and put it in front of their homes and their workplaces. Then within a matter of weeks, rather than embodying and symbolizing solidarity, caring, and grief for the victims of 9/11, the American flag as a symbol was plastered on the missiles that were going to kill civilians in Afghanistan, just as innocent as the 9/11 victims. So I see Bush as a kind of symbol of putting a personable face on a murderous policy.

JE: There are people on the left, and in the center, who say, oh, there's no difference between Democratic and Republican candidates. They're all the same. How important is this election, in your view?

This is not a garden variety Republican administration. This is the furthest right presidency that we've ever had. To conflate the Republican regime now in power with the Democratic Party is a misjudgment. There are elements of near-fascism in the first George W. Bush administration. Some of the policies, such as the Patriot Act, the suspension of habeas corpus, the kind of confluence of militarism and corporatism and jingoism, the erosion of civil liberties and so forth, the idea that it's okay to attack basically any country in the world at the say-so of the US president—there are some policies with proximity to elements of fascism already in place. I don't think we should wait to see how fascist a second term of George W. Bush could turn out to be. Sometimes people may say that's a risk we have to take. I wonder who the "we" is. Is it the people in this country and around the world who will bear the brunt of the economic priorities and militarism of the Bush administration? It is very easy to say, well, heck, the Democrats are bad, the Republicans may be worse, but it's not a big enough distinction. I think it's an important distinction. And I think it's a responsibility of progressive people to fight the right. If we don't do that, there's going to be even more hell to pay in the future.

New Haven, Connecticut
October 22, 2003

GREG SPEETER

Greg Speeter is Executive Director of the National Priorities Project, which he founded in 1982 as a way for community groups and the public to understand and participate in critical federal budget decisions. He has been a featured speaker at both policy conferences and training sessions for community organizers, has held a number of budget briefings on Capitol Hill, and is frequently sought out by the media for analysis of budget policies. Before founding the National Priorities Project, he worked for six years at the Citizen Involvement Training Project in Amherst, Massachusetts, where he authored books on community organizing and access to the political process.

JE: What does your research tell you about the current economic needs of this country versus its spending priorities?

We've got incredible economic needs, and they're just not being addressed by the federal government. We've lost three million jobs in the last three years. We have 43 million people who don't have health insurance. We have one out of every three schools that needs to be either totally rebuilt or significantly renovated. We have 31 million people who are hungry. We have a child poverty rate of almost twenty percent. And yet, when you take a look at where our federal tax dollar goes, you see that the money people pay back to Washington doesn't really address these needs. Over this past year, 49 cents out of every tax dollar has either gone to the military or to interest on the debt, and the interest on the debt is paying back for what we weren't able to spend in the past. It's largely due to the tax cuts that have been enacted over the last few years. We've spent three cents on federal education, two and a half cents on food and nutrition, two cents on housing, less than half a cent on job training. So when you take a look at the needs we have in this country, we ought to be spending a lot more money to address them. When you look at where your tax dollar goes, it's clearly going in the other direction.

JE: When people talk about federal budget priorities, they often talk about "guns and butter." Can you explain what that means, exactly, and how that relates to what you've just said about debt related to defense spending?

Throughout history there's been tension between the amount of money that countries are willing to spend on social programs versus what they spend on the military, and so people have traditionally considered guns versus butter one of the big debates in economic and social policy making. Certainly it's been a central issue for us over the last 30 to 40 years. In the '60s, the Vietnam War substantially cut back our ability to address the war on poverty. In the '80s, the Reagan military budget led to significant cutbacks in social spending. Really, when you look at the numbers, you see that over the past 20 years we have cut back a trillion dollars in housing, in education, in job training, in many other kinds of spending. People felt that once the cold war was over, we'd be able to put more money into butter, into social services and programs. In fact, mayors throughout the country have asked for an economic Marshall Plan, a peace dividend, to address our community needs. That really never happened. We cut back a little bit in military spending, but really ended up putting that money into dealing with the national debt. Then came the Bush budget. George W. Bush increased military spending from about 312 billion dollars to 400 billion dollars in roughly three years. That immediately began once again to make it very difficult to put any money into social spending, because we were putting all of our money into the Pentagon and preparing for war. So the big argument has always been guns versus butter, and at this point, given the amount of money that the Bush administration wants to spend on the military, there's really no money that we can spend to address some of our most pressing needs. Take health insurance, for example. In the '90s, people were talking about providing health insurance for everybody, but the fact is that 43 million people are now uninsured. We've already gone from 41 million people to 43 million people uninsured in just the last two years. At the same time, poverty's increased, and talking about providing health insurance or addressing educational needs is now really off the radar screen. What people are now talking about is addressing terrorism or addressing war.

JE: One of Bush's major campaign issues is tax cuts. And he frames tax cuts, of course, as putting more money in people's pockets, giving them their money back. Can you talk about this logic within the context of Grover Norquist, the influential conservative tax-cut advocate, and the larger neoconservative view of social spending?

Basically, what's happening with tax cuts is that some people are getting immense tax cuts and many other people are getting a little bit of a tax break. I think they're saying that this little break is helpful to them, but they're not looking at the bigger picture of who's really getting the tax cuts. It's important to take a step back and understand what's happened with income and wealth over the last 20 years. Most people have not seen their income increase very much at all. Poor people have actually seen their income decline from $12,000 to $10,000 over the last 20 years. Middle-income people have seen their incomes increase slightly from, say, $53,000 to about $55,000. The richest one percent have seen their incomes increase from $400,000 a year to a $1 million in 20 years. And when you take a look at the latest tax break, the tax break enacted in May of 2003, the lowest 60 percent of the population received less than 100 dollars a year in tax breaks. The richest one percent are averaging $25,000 dollars a year in tax breaks. So these tax policies are really designed to exacerbate this shift in income and this shift in wealth. The other thing that's happened with tax breaks is that as we cut taxes, it becomes very difficult for the country to be able to address community needs. In fact, Grover Norquist, one of the most prominent of the neoconservative tax policy experts, has said that he'd like to see the federal government shrink to the size where he could flush it down the toilet. Well, I think that's what's beginning to happen. We aren't able to address health care, we aren't able to address education, we aren't able to address many of these needs because the money just isn't there. We're increasing a deficit that's already out of sight, even though we managed to get it under control throughout the '90s. Now we're seeing that deficit go to levels we've never seen been before, and we know what the result will be. The federal government will say we just don't have the money to deal with some of our basic needs.

JE: How would you counter the argument that tax cuts are merely shrinking a federal government that's already bloated and could use some dramatic trimming? Do you think the administration's repeated rhetoric about the size of the federal government takes focus off of other negative repercussions of these policies?

This country, as I've said, is facing severe economic needs. Cities and towns just don't have the money that they used to have. State governments have said that they are in the worst fiscal crisis that they've experienced in the last 50 years. So the entities that are really receiving the brunt of these economic policies are our communities. You're seeing, in city after city, local governments cutting back in fire and police, basic security, cutting back in education, cutting back in other basic services that we used to take for granted. What's really big government is the military. Just look at where our tax dollar really goes. Forty-nine cents out of every tax dollar is either going to the Pentagon or to interest on the debt. Very little money is really going back into our communities, much less than what was going back in the '60s and the '70s.

JE: Let's turn to a neoconservative think tank called the Project for the New American Century, because I think they do a good job laying out in very clear terms some of the philosophies at work in the current administration. When people look at this group, they usually see it purely in terms of the aggressive, neo-Reaganite foreign policy agenda it has called for. Can you say something about the domestic implications of this characteristically neoconservative foreign policy agenda, much of which is currently being implemented?

The Project for the New American Century is clearly focused on military spending and foreign policy, but it's part of a much larger attempt by neoconservatives to take over and attempt to decimate the role of government for most people. There are some very real implications when we increase military spending, which is precisely what they called for prior to September 11. In the most general terms, it means we have fewer dollars to address other needs. I think it's important for people to understand just how big our military budget is, to make that the context for understanding their demand for increasing it further. One indicator of the size of our military budget is to compare it to what other countries spend. The United States spends, at $400 billion this year, about as much as much as the rest of the world combined. There is no doubt that we have the most fire-power, our soldiers are far superior to any other soldiers, our military is far more sophisticated than any other in the world. This was true in 2000, when the Project for the New American Century called for increasing defense spending by $20 billion a year. Well, we've done that. We've done better than that, so they've done very well in seeing their vision realized as the military budget has gone up almost $100 billion in three years. But it's important to take a look at how much we spend on the military compared to other things. In fact, if you add up the amount that the federal government is now spending on education, how much we spend on job training, food and nutrition programs, a variety of other programs important to communities, and you multiply that by 2 times, that's as much as we're spending on the Pentagon. And then there is the war. The war effort is another $141 billion just in the year 2003 alone. The military budget is one thing, that's the Pentagon, but we have to pay extra to pay for a war. So in fact we've had two payments for this war so far that have added up to $141 billion, and that's an incredible amount of money. We could provide health insurance for each of the 12 million children that don't have health insurance for the next seven years with that $141 billion. We could provide 1.4 million affordable housing units and totally address our affordable housing crisis. We could provide 3 million jobs with that kind of money, rebuild every school in this country that needs to be rebuilt, and provide jobs for 60,000 teachers for the next four years.

So that's an incredible amount of money, and what we try to do with the National Priorities Project is to bring these numbers down to a local level so that ordinary people can understand what they mean to them. So we've crunched the numbers to help people understand how much their communities are paying for the military and the war. Just to give you an example, the citizens of New York are paying $4.4 billion just for the war effort, Cincinnati is paying $111 million just for the war effort, Dallas is paying $550 million just for the war effort.

There's one community that we've been working in, a very low-income community with a child poverty rate of 41 percent, and it's spending $15 million for this war. But if you added the amount of money the city is also paying in federal taxes that go to the Pentagon budget, the amount comes to $60 million. That's in a little city of about 35,000 people, a city with an operating budget of $110 million. So in fact people are paying half of what they would to operate their whole city to the Pentagon and this war effort.

JE: Based on the number trends you're talking about here, trends over the past two or three years, how would you describe this administration's view of the overall value and contribution of the New Deal and the Great Society?

The neoconservative movement really represents a very radical approach to the role of the federal government. It's basically trying to cut back the ability of the federal government to address many of its community needs by increasing the military budget. When you look at their policy proposals, I think it's clear they want to cut back on the very positive things that have happened since the '30s, since FDR and the New Deal. My experience has been working in communities through the war on poverty, and I have seen the benefits of providing adequate job training, of providing Head Start, of putting money into self-help housing programs so that people are able to own their own homes. Those kinds of programs, very popular programs, by the way, were cut back in the '80s and have never been replaced. In fact, most cities have lost an awful lot of money for programs to address those kinds of needs.

Now what the neocons want to do is cut that back even further. They want to cut back in job training, to cut back on a variety of other housing and health care programs. At the same time, you see things like this big battle around Medicare. If they get their way, the people who are really going to benefit from Medicare are not going to be seniors so much as the major pharmaceuticals that have guaranteed monies coming. So I really think that there's this incredible battle that's been going on. A lot of the more conservative members of Congress like to talk about problems with social spending, but other people take a look at the very positive things that have happened when the federal government provides basic services to people. Federal spending did an awful lot to reduce the poverty rate. It cut the poverty rate in half in the '60s and '70s, in part due to the very positive benefits of Medicaid, Medicare, and other social programs. I don't think a lot of people recognize just how incredibly important those programs have been in transforming the lives of huge segments of the population. In the same way, as we've cut housing programs to a third of what they were in '80s, we've seen homelessness skyrocket. That's a direct result of cutting benefits for low-income people, and yet at the same time we've increased benefits for homeowners and for very wealthy homeowners. We've provided tax breaks for very wealthy people, but we've cut back the ability of low-income people to meet their most basic needs.

JE: The counter to what you're saying might be that we need to make sacrifices right now. It's a dangerous world, and 9/11 showed us just how dangerous. We need to sacrifice and build up our defenses, even if it means running up deficits and cutting spending in other areas.

First of all, some people aren't making sacrifices. When somebody benefits by getting a $25,000 per year tax break, they need to do some suffering as well. It's really important that we begin to redefine national security. We're the only industrialized country in the world that doesn't provide health insurance for its people. We have 43 million people who don't have health insurance. We are not doing as well as many industrialized countries in terms of education. We need to rebuild our schools. We need to make sure that people who are looking for jobs have jobs. We've lost 3 million jobs in the last three years, and if people don't have jobs, if people can't provide education for their children, if people are going hungry, if people don't have health insurance, then they're insecure. We need to be able to address that level of insecurity in this country. The federal government is not addressing those needs because we're pouring all of this money into unilateral war and providing tax breaks for very wealthy people.

JE: What do you expect to see if Bush wins a second term?

Over the next few years, if the neocons get their way, we're going to see increased money for the Pentagon, increased tax breaks for very wealthy people and fewer dollars going to education, housing, health care and other basic needs.

JE: What would you say to poor and disenfranchised people who are understandably frustrated with the system, who are too alienated or too distrustful of those in power to believe that voting in a presidential election actually means anything?

I'd say people really need to vote and that voting can make a real difference. We saw how close the election was in 2000. Yet in 2000, 100 million people did not vote. It's important that our representatives and leaders go after those people. It's also important that people recognize that federal policies mean something to their lives. They're paying taxes, and policies that determine how those taxes are spent mean something to their communities. We're talking about health care, we're talking about access to higher education, and if people really want to make a difference, they've got to recognize that the federal government does play a role in their lives. It's also important that people raise some of these questions to candidates running for office. I think candidates should be asked why we're spending so much money on a unilateral war and basically turning off the rest of the world. We've got to ask why it is, exactly and specifically, that we can't provide health insurance for people in this country when every other industrialized country is able to do this. We have to ask why we have a child poverty rate of 20 percent when many other industrialized countries have child poverty rates a quarter of that size. I think it's time we stop playing global cop and begin to cut a balance between addressing needs around the world, encouraging other countries to help us in fighting terrorism, while also assuring that we've got money left over to be able to address our own needs and our own communities.

JE: You've talked throughout here about how much taxpayer money is going to the Department of Defense budget. Where is that money actually going? Is most of it going to the troops? Couldn't someone rightly argue that by calling for cuts in the military you're not supporting our troops?

If you take a look at where most of the $400 billion goes, you'll see that about $100 billion is going to personnel, about $75 billion to buying more weaponry, and $30 to 40 billion to research and development. We claim that we're concerned about the troops, and yet 4 billion dollars, or 1 percent of the military budget, goes to family housing, and that money is scheduled to be cut over the next few years. So there are things we can do to really begin to protect our soldiers, but, if you take a look at where the budget goes, the big increases in the budget since Bush took office are primarily dedicated to buying more weaponry and providing research and development for even more weaponry. So that's really the direction that we're headed in. Buying more weapons and buying more sophisticated weapons.

JE: What do you make of the way Bush himself has framed his calls for increasing the military budget as a form of supporting the troops—given who actually fights in our military?

The people who are fighting this war are disproportionately young people of color who are poor. The people who are creating, designing, and benefiting from the wars are the generals and their higher-ups in the military, and some of the corporations who are receiving incredible benefits from this war. What you'll find is that the people who are being recruited for this war, the people who are fighting this war, are coming from the very communities that have lost money and job training. They are coming from schools that are falling apart, from families who don't have health care, who have been working two and three jobs in order to survive. So this itself is an economic issue.

JE: What concerns you the most, in real terms, about the possibility of this president getting re-elected?

What this election is all about is asking some very basic questions about the general direction of this federal government. Do we want to continue to see communities that are falling apart, that don't have affordable housing, whose schools need to be repaired? Do we want to continue to be the only industrialized country that doesn't provide health care for its citizens? This president has absolutely no regard for what ordinary citizens need and deserve in this country, doesn't care about providing everybody with decent schools, with decent health care. The budgets don't reflect that. He doesn't have any regard for our role in the world. He certainly has no regard for what other countries think of us. If he's trying to bring people together to address terrorism, then you don't get the rest of the world angry with you. So the bottom line is that I'm really concerned about our leadership in the world, and I'm concerned about what all this means to ordinary people here in the United States.

Northampton, Massachusetts
December 9, 2003

IMMANUEL WALLERSTEIN

Immanuel Wallerstein is Senior Research Scholar at Yale University and has been a seminal figure in the development of world-systems analysis. Among his books are *The Modern World System* (Academic Press, 1980), *Utopistics, or Historical Choices for the 21st Century* (New Press, 1990), and *Unthinking Social Science: The Limits of 19th-Century Paradigms* (Temple University Press, 2001). His most recent work is *The Decline of American Power: The US in a Chaotic World* (Norton 2003).

JE: I wanted to start with something that you talk about in The Eagle Has Crash Landed, *where you said that the economic, political, and military factors that contributed to American hegemony are the same factors that will inexorably produce the coming US decline. Could you talk about that contradiction?*

Sure, but it's not the "coming US decline." The US has been declining for 30 years. Take the three factors you talk about. Economics was the overwhelming basis of US hegemony as of 1945. The US was the only power that emerged from World War II that was undestroyed and it had already been in good shape before then. In 1945 it could out-compete anybody anywhere in the whole market, so this was just overwhelming. On the base of that it could build a whole series of things. It built a series of military alliances in a couple of years with Western Europe and Japan, which made those countries at that time basically into satellites of the US. It came to a deal with the Soviet Union, which amounted to a kind of status quo truce in the world, and of course it had the atomic weapons too. The US was extremely strong and really the US could get its way on anything that mattered for about 25 years. That's what we call hegemony.

Now that all begins to decline as of the late '60s and early '70s. First of all, economically the recovery of Western Europe and Japan, which the US endorsed and supported wholeheartedly because they needed people to buy their goods, turned them into powers that were basically economically competitive with the United States. There was very little difference after about 1970 in terms of the degree of efficiency of production in Western Europe, Japan, and the United States, so the whole basis of that overwhelming superiority disappeared, and that begins to undermine the ability of the US to get Western Europe and Japan to do whatever they wanted. They hold on to it for a while, basically brandishing the Soviet menace and their common interest vis a vis the Third World, but of course the collapse of the Soviet Union from this point of view is an absolute catastrophe for the United States, because it removes the major political weapon that they have for controlling Western Europe and Japan.

Today militarily the US edge is enormous, obviously. But anybody with two atomic bombs can hold the US a bit at bay, which is what North Korea is demonstrating. The US tried in every possible way to slow down nuclear proliferation, is still trying, but of course we went from one to eight, eight officially, another five or six who can do it fairly quickly and another fifteen or twenty who can do it fairly soon. Basically that overwhelming military superiority enables them to knock out armies, but it doesn't enable them to prevent a return atomic weapon, so that constrains enormously as we're discovering in the world today.

The US is not doing very well in Iraq against a guerrilla movement partially because it doesn't have enough troops. Partially because it really doesn't have the readiness of the American people to lose lives all over the place. And partially because the US is terribly unpopular despite the fact that it overthrew Saddam Hussein. They certainly can't move on Iran or North Korea while that's going on. So the US is overwhelmingly superior militarily in the sense that nobody is going to invade the United States and in an open battle the US is way ahead. But you can't really translate that into effective policy, which is what the US is discovering in the Middle East today.

JE: You mentioned that it was a catastrophe, the fall of communism, for US policy—

A political catastrophe—not for the people in that part of the world— just for the United States.

JE: Right, and that's something I think has relevance here. One of the things we're going to be looking at is the Project for the New American Century and the Wolfowitz Doctrine—and that's precisely what they said; they said they're going to need a "catalyzing and catastrophic event" to build up the military. Could you try to clarify what you see as the assumptions guiding their thinking?

They absolutely are the only people who agree with me that the US has been declining; they think they have a solution for it. Since 1970, more or less, there's been a single American foreign policy that every president from Nixon through Clinton, through George Bush for the first year of his administration, continued, including Reagan, everyone. I call it soft multilateralism. It's multilateralism that doesn't really mean it because it says, "Come along with us or else we do it our way." But there was a constant effort to try to assuage the allies and bring them along; this was element number one in soft multilateralism. The second element was try to persuade—half persuade, half intimidate—countries not to proliferate nuclear weapons. It was a partially successful policy. Now it's a question of whether you see this as a glass half full or a glass half empty. I think they did as well as could have been expected given the cards the US had to play. The people who are behind PNAC, Wolfowitz, Cheney, etc., they think it's a glass half empty. They think that this kind of policy was allowing the whole thing to slip away and that it could be reversed by a different kind of US policy: aggressive unilateralism. Unilateral policy on their part is not a sort of second best, it isn't because France and Germany and Russia and I don't know who else didn't go along with the US. They didn't want them to go along, they wanted to show that the US could do it all by itself. They thought that would do two things. They thought first of all that the old Europe and anybody like them across the world would collapse and say "Oh my God, there's nothing we can do now, so we better give into the US and we better support them." And they thought that countries like Iran and North Korea—not to speak of all the others that are possibly starting projects of nuclear weapons—would be so intimidated by this that they would all give in.

This was their reasoning. It's a thought-through policy. What they did was quite deliberate. They're just wrong. They're wrong in their reading of Western Europe, their reading of East Asia, their reading of the Middle East. They don't understand really how people think there and how they will react. Of course they have made the situation far worse than it was three years ago in terms of the attitudes in Western Europe, in East Asia, in Latin America and of course in the Middle East, vis a vis the United States. But it isn't that they were irrational—they knew what they were doing. They were coming out against the policy of every American president from Nixon to Clinton to even George Bush in his first year. In fact, I think you can't go back again. Many critics are saying, can't we go back to the old policy of what I call soft multilateralism. The thing is, it's too late now, because now people are so upset and angered and aware of what the US was doing in all of these countries that they're not going to buy that kind of policy anymore. So the administration has got itself in a deep hole and the US is going to have a very hard job getting out of it, in terms of having any impact on world affairs in the next 25 years.

JE: Within that, I hear an emphasis on military force and aggressive unilateralism, but where does empire or imperialism fit into this?

Of course that's underneath it in the sense that there are economic interests that are pushing these people. The US today is economically much weaker than it says and thinks it is, and this is not merely the fact that factories are disappearing and jobs are being lost, but that the dollar is in real trouble. The basis of US economic strength today is the fact that the dollar is the reserve currency all over the world. That's a political phenomenon. That's a willingness of other countries to accept the dollar as the reserve currency because they think the US is economically strong enough. This enables the Bush administration to cut back taxes enormously, to spend incredible amounts of money on the military, run up a half-trillion dollar deficit and have the Chinese and the Japanese (those two countries in particular, but many others), keep buying American bonds, which keeps our government afloat. Now, if tomorrow—and I think it will occur tomorrow or the next day—these countries decide that that makes no economic sense for them—it never made political sense, but if it starts to make no economic sense for them—then the US goes down the drain; I mean it really goes down the drain in terms of a real reduction of the standard of living and so forth.

These people want to stop all that, of course; they want to preserve the advantages that US capitalism has in the world today. If you want to call that imperialist, of course it's imperialist, but it's not their immediate goal. It's their middle-run goal. Their immediate goal is intimidation. So when people say, for example, very frequently "It's all about oil," of course oil is important and of course we want control of oil, but oil isn't enough to explain a war on Iraq. For one thing we weren't doing so badly in terms of oil before that, and we now are risking a lot more because we're risking a collapse of Saudi Arabia and we might lose much more on the oil fronts. So, yes, they're interested in oil, but that's a middle-run interest. The short-run interest was machismo. It would sustain the dollar; it would allow us to stop nuclear proliferation and so forth. It isn't working, but that was their reasoning.

JE: You talk about this administration's arrogance in one of your pieces. Can you explain what you mean when you point to their machismo and how it doesn't seem to be translating politically the way they thought it would? Are they really this naïve, or is there something behind their assumptions not seen on the surface?

The Greeks had the word for it—it was hubris. Pride goeth before the fall. We've been running the world for 50 years. We ran it easily for 25, and then for another 25 we've been running it with greater difficulty. We're used to it now. It isn't that these people in the Bush administration don't know the rest of the world—a lot them are quite sophisticated; they travel and they speak other languages and so forth—but they really have come to expect that people will defer to them. They really think that they have a lot to teach and nothing to learn. Nobody has nothing to learn and that's what's so hard to understand culturally when you've been on top. And that's it. After World War II there was a lot of talk about how the US had to learn how to assume its responsibility in the world, and it was difficult because we'd come out of an isolationist tradition. In fact, that was an apt expression because in terms of the social psychology of the American people and the American elites, that's what happened from about '45 to '70. They learned how to assume their responsibilities in the world. And just as they learned it, US hegemony began to decline. They should have started learning then how to live with less power.

I see '72 to 2000 as a sort of waste of thirty years, of what could have been a re-learning. Now we've got to do it, and these people are saying "no, no, no, the last thing you want to do is re-learn how you fit in the world." But, look, every American president without exception probably makes a speech sometime in which he says, "The US is the greatest country in the world." That's nice hype; it gets everybody to applaud. But an awful lot of people think their country is the greatest country in the world; they think it's a lot better than the US. So the US has got to live in a world in which its view of itself is not other people's view of it. It's got to learn to live in a world in which it's a strong, very important power with a long tradition. But it's not the only one there. And it's got to learn to talk to people, converse with people, dialogue with people. It's not that they're always wrong; it's also true that we're not always right.

This is very hard psychologically. It's probably going to take a great defeat to get the American people ready for it. When we eventually pull out from Iraq in not too glorious circumstances, and when the dollar collapses, as I expect it will, and when we have a multi-currency world, it's going to be a big shock. The shock can go in two directions. The shock can lead to a kind of right-wing, very inward looking anger, or it can open up new possibilities, a new frame of mind. That's the great internal debate in the United States and it's getting very intense. I find that the antagonisms between the two sides of American political life are much deeper, stronger, more passionate then they've ever been in my lifetime and I think that's because we're playing for very high stakes.

JE: You say that "it may require a shock to the system," and a lot of people have been saying that 9/11 was that shock. Can you talk about how 9/11 functions in all of this?

It was an enormous shock because it broke a myth, and the myth was that we were invulnerable at home. In fact, it was a remarkable event. Here we have a bunch—not a state—a group of miscellaneous people who are fanatics, yes, but just a miscellaneous group of people, and they are able to pull off a highly sophisticated operation that does an enormous amount of damage right inside the United States, in New York City and at the Pentagon. It's astonishing and the American people were astonished. And what the Bush administration did immediately was to try not to have the American people think about that.

Think about all they've turned it into: "Let's get the bad guys." Well, sure, let's get the bad guys. But how come the bad guys could do this? How come the bad guys have so much support? And how come the bad guys risked their own lives to do this? We didn't want to discuss it; in fact it was deemed unpatriotic to discuss that, so the shock was diverted strongly into a kind of patriotic, knee-jerk response that allowed the administration to pull off this fiasco in Iraq.

But it's wearing off. The body bags are coming back. You look on TV and when the helicopter is shot down you see little kids doing V signals. I saw that just the other day. Other people see that and they begin to wonder. It's beginning to sink in to maybe half the American people. The other half is in a narrow box. That's what this internal cultural struggle is about.

JE: You've just talked about body bags, and you made several comparisons on several different levels to Vietnam. Before this war started that was one of your fears, that we might return to another Vietnam. You mentioned how LBJ was taken down by that and that this war had the potential to do the same for Bush. I'm just wondering how you think your prewar comparison has held up?

Of course in Vietnam we were facing an opponent that was militarily somewhat stronger than Iraq. On the other hand, Vietnam channeled Vietnamese nationalism, and the Iraqi struggle is beginning to channel Iraqi nationalism against the US. The difference between Vietnam and Iraq for the administration is at the time of Vietnam there was a draft. And the draft meant that lots of people got pulled into the armed forces who didn't want to be pulled into the armed forces and that created the growing unpopularity of that war for a number of years. On the other hand, Vietnam was in the heyday of anti-communism, of the danger of the spread of communism, and that was a very strong force; so it took a long time. We entered Vietnam in a big way in '65; we didn't get out until '73. I would say it took at least three years to get an anti-war movement going, and only in about '68 did it really begin to get going and pull down Johnson, along with the Tet Offensive. This time it's all going faster, but of course there aren't as many body bags as there were in Vietnam. Still, everyday in every way, another soldier gets killed; it's very wearing, especially when you don't see the plus side. That's what the administration keeps saying, nobody's showing us the plus side of all the good things we're doing, but we are not quite sure what all those good things are. We still don't have full electricity in Baghdad, and I'm absolutely astonished by that. One would think with all our engineering skills we could restore full-time, 24-hour electricity to Baghdad.

The fact is we don't have enough troops there. We can't send in more troops because that's going to be politically, terribly unpopular. Nobody wants to give us any troops, no other country, really. No one except Britain is giving us any serious amount of troops, so there's not much hope that they will. As I read the newspapers, they say that we can't even keep up our present troop level without calling out more reserves and that's very unpopular. We're already calling up more reserves than the American people like, for longer times than they like. These reservists are in for two years and they don't have to renew, and lots of them are not going to renew because they didn't sign up for being in Iraq and being shot at daily in a very nasty way. So the US government is in a bind. They can't pull out because that would really hurt politically. I don't say that Bush will lose the next election, because there are too many things that can happen between now and then, but he's not in very good shape.

JE: People often say that politicians are all the same—what would four years more of Bush really do or mean if things are already this bad anyway? Are the global, structural forces you're describing so huge that it really doesn't make much of a difference if he's reelected?

Well, what can I say? I think he's plowing the United States under and he'll plow it further. He's certainly plowed the world further under. We're in a chaotic situation in the world and he's throwing fuel on the fire—so that's what I think another four years of Bush would do.

JE: When Bush ran for office in 2000, in virtually every stump speech he talked about the military, and how Clinton weakened the military—how he was basically an effeminate president and we need the "guys" to come in there and restore not only dignity but American power. Can you talk about that rhetoric?

You know, that is classic Republican rhetoric since World War II and particularly since Nixon, so it's nothing special. Every Republican candidate against the Democratic candidate has always argued that the Democrats were weakening the military, that the Democrats are weak, and they have a certain audience for that, so they were playing the usual card. I don't think there was anything special in George Bush saying that about Clinton. George Bush's father said that about Dukakis and certainly Reagan said that about Carter, and Nixon about McGovern, and so forth, so I think that is just standard stuff. Of course, they mean it in the sense that usually Republican presidents increase expenditures in the military.

When George Bush became president all this was up in the air. I think that there were two factions in his administration. There was one that wanted to continue the old policy—that's basically Colin Powell. And then there were the PNAC people. The moment George Bush becomes president, nobody has the upper hand because he appoints both of them. The first foreign policy crisis that he runs into is the half-downing of an American plane over China. At that time there was a fight within the administration and the Colin Powell camp wins out and they handle it the way they've traditionally handled such things. 9/11 is what tips the balance in favor of these other guys, to the dismay of not only Colin Powell but of the so-called "old Bushes."

The only reason George Bush went to the UN at all over Iraq was that he was publicly criticized by all of the closest associates of his father—James Baker, Scowcroft, etc. Everybody assumed his father's hand was behind it, and I assumed that too. They put a lot of pressure on George Bush to pull back from full unilateralism, against the warnings of people like Rumsfeld. They went that way, and fortunately for Rumsfeld that policy basically fails. Now they say, "You see, go to the UN and that's what you get, you get into trouble." In a certain sense, they're right, because they've created a situation in which they can't win in that milieu. It's a self-fulfilling prophesy: if you act the way the neocons act, then in fact, their statement that you can't act in any other way becomes more and more true. Unless you change it really radically, you can't go home again to the old foreign policy and expect it to work. It won't work anymore. So the Bush policy won't work and the old policy won't work. We need something radically, radically new.

New Haven, Connecticut
November 5, 2003

JODY WILLIAMS

Jody Williams won the Nobel Peace Prize in 1997 for her work to eliminate landmines. Prior to her work on banning landmines, she worked for eleven years to enhance public awareness of US policy in Central America. From 1986 to 1992, she developed and directed humanitarian relief projects as the deputy director of the Los Angeles-based Medical Aid for El Salvador. From 1984 to 1986, she was co-coordinator of the Nicaragua–Honduras Education Project, leading fact-finding delegations to the region. Previously, she taught English as a Second Language (ESL) in Mexico, the United Kingdom, and Washington, DC.

JE: Why did you protest the war before it started? Why were you one of the demonstrators early on?

The Bush administration is the most dangerous administration in the history of our country, and I started saying that almost immediately after September 11. It was unclear until September 11 how radical this man would be. I think the question we all ponder is where this administration would be today if September 11 hadn't happened. I'm sure you've heard the comment that Bush needed Osama bin Laden just as much as Osama bin Laden needed Bush, in order to define the mission of his administration. I don't know what he'd be doing if he didn't have his found war on terrorism to define himself. From my perspective, the most chilling moment was within the 48 hours or so after he finally landed on Air Force 1. I remember seeing him on the television and he's looking up and he says, "We have found our moment, we have found our mission." It was totally chilling to me. It seemed like he was actually expressing to the nation that he believed that he was chosen by his God to save us all from terrorism. I think it unfortunately neatly dovetailed with the serious political agenda of the people that surround him in the White House. I believe, along with many others, that September 11 gave him the opportunity to carry out an agenda that they had been planning for a decade or so.

JE: Richard Perle said something the other night that contradicts what you've just said. And he's not the only one. It's been said a lot by neoconservatives who've won favor with this administration. What he said is that this notion that September 11 gave them an opportunity to push through their agenda is completely naïve and disingenuous. What they've been saying is that it's not that they had this agenda and September 11 came along and allowed them to push it through. It's that September 11 was a wake-up call to liberals and pacifists and foreign policy realists who believed that the old strategy of containment would be enough to prevent such a nightmare from occurring.

I understand that they want the American public to believe that the invasion of Iraq was a response to September 11, but I think it is a lie. I believe that it is part of a neoconservative agenda to assert and make certain that American hegemony is untouchable. This thinking started after the end of the cold war, after Ronnie Reagan won that war for us. Cheney challenged the people around him under the first Bush administration to think big. The people he challenged—the two primary poles in the challenge that I remember were Wolfowitz and Powell—he challenged them to think grandly about a post-cold war world in which the US was supreme. How could the US use its unequaled power, wealth, military, technology, etc. to make sure that it controlled the world? Unfortunately, the Wolfowitzian model, which was much more aggressive, is the one that Cheney and his friends thought was the way to go. September 11 gave them the opportunity to put in play plans they had been considering since the first Bush administration. I understand his spin, but to me it parallels the spin of Bush and all of the people around him when they keep implying that somehow Saddam Hussein was connected to September 11. A blatant lie. Bush himself, caught off guard in a press conference, even said that there was no definitive connection between Saddam Hussein and September 11. Yet, how many times do you continue to hear them make that implication or claim? It is a spin. It's a lie.

JE: Did you see the Diane Sawyer interview where she kept pressing him on that connection, between Iraq and September 11? His response was, essentially, that it doesn't matter. That it's not the issue. And there seem to be a lot of Americans who feel the same way. A lot of people who now know there were no weapons there will turn around and say, "Well, it doesn't matter. He was a brutal dictator. We got rid of a bad man."

Saddam Hussein is a bad man. Nobody would dispute that. My question to my students at the University of Houston whenever I speak is, if George W. Bush had gone to the American public and said, "I want to invade Iraq because Saddam Hussein is a bad man, I want to invade Iraq because I think the Iraqi people deserve democracy and we can bring it to them," if he had gone to the US Congress and said the same thing, would the American people have stood by and supported that position? Why aren't we invading Burma? It has been controlled by a military dictatorship since the late '80s. Why aren't we overthrowing Musharraf in Pakistan, who took over the country by coup, who refuses to give the democracy that he said he was going to give to the government? Why are we in bed with all of the -stans, you know, Tajikistan, Turkmenistan, our latest new friends, who are horrific dictators that do not allow freedom of expression, human rights, etc., etc., in their countries?

We support democracy when it is convenient to the interests of the United States. Maybe I'm an idealist to believe that there should be some sort of standard for determining how we conduct our foreign policy, but I believe there should be a standard. We are seen in the world as hypocrites, we are seen as liars, we are seen as an imperialist power. It is tragic that Americans for the most part don't really understand how much the United States government is hated around the world. If you go outside of the country—and not just to the resorts in Mexico or places like that where you can stay in a Hilton like the one you would stay in in America—if you go talk to people around the world, they are terrified of the United States government. That is really sad to me. I have the privilege and dismay of interacting with government and military types all over the world on the landmine issue. Obviously, we talk extensively about the current situation in the world. Almost everybody I talk to from Turkish diplomats to Canadian military to Thai people, almost every one of them has said that they are terrified of the United States government under George Bush. They are terrified of the US military under Rumsfeld. That is really scary.

JE: You were fighting to get the United States to respond to the landmine issue during the Clinton administration. At that point, you were mixing with a lot of people. Do you see a difference between how people were responding to the US government in those circles then, and what you see and hear now? Is there a difference between how they talk about the United States, or have they always seen the United States as an imperial power, perhaps just with different kinds of personalities selling it?

People always recognize a great power to have its self-interests at the forefront of its policymaking. When it was the cold war, when it was the Soviet Union and the United States, those two blocks put their self-interests first. But from my experience, people see a radical change between the US pre-Bush administration and now. There was a belief that even though the US did want to assert itself and its dominance in the now unipolar world, there was the belief that you could talk to Clinton administration people, that he was a globalist in a certain sense, and that he did have an understanding that even if the US was going to assert its dominance, it still had to kind of fit into a puzzle somehow. It might be the biggest piece in the puzzle, but it kind of had to fit into the puzzle. The Bush administration in my view—from what I have experienced in my work around them, not with them for sure, on the landmine campaign and my support for the International Criminal Court—the Bush administration really does operate on an "it's my way or the highway" framework. People say that sort of tongue-in-cheek, but it is the truth. Some of the administration, the people from other governments that I have talked to about this, have been very clear about it, that when the administration sends its minions to talk to them, it's not a discussion about how X government and the United States can work together on X issue. It is the United States going in and saying "This is what we want, this is what we want you to do." Not how can we work together to deal with the issue of terrorism, or how can we work together to deal with global warming or whatever the issue is. The US goes and tells them what to do.

It is really easy to hide behind the fear here in the United States and believe they hate us for our freedoms. "They"—the amorphous "they." I was on an airplane and a woman said that to me: "Isn't it terrible how they hate us for our freedoms?" I said, "Well, who are they?" Of course, "they" are radical Arabs. I said, "Well, if you look at the recent surveys in the world of countries with freedoms equal to or greater than those we have in the United States, the populations of those countries overwhelmingly dislike us as well. So do they hate us for our freedoms, too?" They do not hate us because we are free. They hate us because they are afraid of the military power of the United States and its willingness to use it at any cost, with blatant disregard for the feelings of the international community.

JE: So when you say that this administration is the most dangerous you've seen—

I think that. I do. I have fought with my husband over this from almost the day after September 11. I started calling them the most dangerous administration in our lifetime. I joked and said I'd almost like to see Reagan again. I'm sure you've seen that written. It's sort of tongue-in-cheek, but at least… I don't know, he was sort of contained. So my husband and I got into it a bit. He said, "How can you say that? Some of these people are the same people who were in the Reagan administration and then in the first Bush administration." I said, yes, exactly. And during those years while they were in power they were designing their agenda for the future. Clinton knocked them out for a few years, but now they're back and they are back unopposed. At least under Reagan they were still fighting the Soviet Union. Under Bush there was confusion as to how the world was going to shake out. Now there's no confusion. These people have unrivaled power. They have a total willingness to use it. That is terrifying. And they don't care about what the rest of the world thinks—anybody. I find that terrifying. They're talking about using nukes. They're talking about developing little nukes to use like any old weapon. That's not terrifying to you? I think it's unbelievable. Then we wonder why there is a proliferation of weapons of mass destruction? We wonder why other nations want to speed up the development of weapons of mass destruction? It's insane. Are we going to take them all out? That's Perle's point of view. There was an interesting piece in London's *Daily Telegraph* the other day talking about the Perle agenda. You know, Perle arguing, go in and take out Syria. Take out Iran. Go in and take out North Korea. Are we going to take everybody out? And when do we stop taking them out? We take out Pakistan of course if Musharraf is assassinated…do we take them out? Then do we take out India because it's got a nuke too? I mean, where does it stop? Another question I keep asking myself is, why do people in the US think that if we have bigger weapons and more weapons it's going to make us safe from terrorists? We have the most advanced military in the world. We have the most sophisticated weapons in the world. We have more nuclear weapons that anybody in the world. Did that stop September 11? It didn't stop it. If we get more nukes, if we get mini-nukes, if we get this, that, and the other, how is that going to stop a terrorist attack? It isn't.

JE: Do you think it's easier to say the things you're saying now than it was right after September 11?

Well, I've always talked about it. I have every right to say what I believe. That's what makes us still have something of a democracy in America.

People are increasingly aware that they have to speak. They were terrified of speaking in the beginning and people are still afraid to speak. It's pretty amazing. When I speak about these people, it just makes me want to go take a nap sometimes. You know what I mean? You wake up and hope they'll be gone. But they're not going to be gone.

Since the fall of 2003 I have been a visiting professor at the University of Houston. We were discussing a number of global issues and one of the students on one of the chat boards wrote that she had been talking with other students and they were afraid to give their opinion on the computer because they believe that in John Ashcroft's America they were under surveillance. Then she had the presence of mind to say, "How ridiculous for me to think that, as a student at the University of Houston, Ashcroft would worry about what I have to say." Yet, she self-censored because she was afraid in today's America that what she had to say would be observed. I don't know what she thought they would do with it.

Right after that I was in Denver. I was speaking with an organization I work with called Peace Jam, which tries to educate young people that working for peace is hard work, it's not a utopian dream. It's something that you actually develop a plan for, some activity you want to carry out to contribute to building peace. It's not a miracle. It's not utopian. It's hard work. One of the teachers involved with the students in the Peace Jam program came up to me and said, "I don't dare talk in America anymore. I don't dare state my opposition to Bush." She was protesting the war under the banner of Not in Our Name and people actually tried to drive their car at her and her young son. Not to run them over but to scare them. She said that it scared her enough that she feels very isolated and afraid to speak her mind in America today.

Two weeks later I'm in San Francisco and another teacher comes up to me and says that she teaches debate and she wants the students and teachers debating about American values in Bush's America, but she doesn't dare. She's afraid of what might happen to her, and also what it might do to her students if she educates them about what's happening in America if they have no outlet to bring about change. So she self-censors.

If you self-censor, you do 90 percent of the work for them. They don't have to do anything. If they scare you so much you don't dare say what you think… that's the beginning of totalitarianism, for God's sake. I found that incredibly frightening. And it made me absolutely determined never to self-censor. I don't care.

JE: How would you describe the worldview of the major players in this administration?

I found one recent article on Wolfowitz hilarious. It called him a utopian dreamer. It called him an academic intellectual. I wanted to throw up, quite frankly. It's what people out of power do. They either go to academia or they go to think tanks. It's not like he was some great intellectual who was plucked out of the ivory tower to assist in building the ideology of the Bush administration. He's an ideologue. And he's been in power in how many different administrations in the United States? There's this article talking about him as this great dreamer who's trying to bring democracy to Iraq. Perhaps there's some filament of the man that believes something in democracy, but his administration is certainly suppressing civil liberties in America today. I don't believe you can bring democracy to a country the way they are doing it, through an invasion, through an occupation, with absolute ignorance of the culture, ethnicity, and political culture of that country. It's unbelievable to me. Unbelievable. They are driven by their own egos and their own vision of the world. They develop their own vision of the world sitting in a little group talking to each other. There was also a very interesting article about Mr. Bush commenting that he doesn't bother with the news because he has objective input from people like Condoleezza Rice, Wolfowitz, Perle. If I had the same three people telling me what was happening in the world, and they have basically identical points of view, how would I be getting objective information? But obviously he doesn't want objective information. He doesn't want his worldview shattered or shaken. None of them do.

JE: Are you a pacifist?

No. Winning the Nobel Peace Prize does not necessarily make you a pacifist, as we know from Henry Kissinger, whom I believe is a war criminal. I am not a pacifist. I think sometimes you need to have police and military action. Of course you do. If someone is breaking into your house you call the police, they come and take the criminal way. They go to jail. When the terrorists attacked the United States I fully supported working with the international community to share intelligence to capture them and bring them to trial, and put them in jail for life. But you don't invade another country just because you don't like the guy. That is breaking international law. The Bush administration may scoff at international law, but if you act with impunity at that level it filters down through all levels of society. If people believe that those in power can do whatever they want and not have to pay for it, it affects all of the fabric of society. I worked in Central America during the wars of the '80s, during the Reagan-Bush wars, as I like to refer to them. I was not a pacifist then either. I saw what happened to the fabric of those societies when the military and the politicians could impose their will with impunity, kill people with impunity—it destroys the fabric of society. Why do people believe any law matters? It's horrifying.

JE: On the one hand these guys are unilateralists. As you say, their agenda seems to be to move away from the UN. They have problems with France; they want to restructure Europe, etc. But isn't it also true that it was politically viable to do that? Because the minute they started beating up on the French and the UN, their base of support here solidified and grew. So they didn't have to hide that. So what does this say about Americans' view of the UN and our alliances?

I don't hold the UN in high esteem, frankly. I support the need for a United Nations. I think it needs a significant overhaul. But I don't think you overhaul it by doing what the Bush administration did to it. You work with it to bring about change. It was so irritating to watch him try to go back to the United Nations to cover his butt after they started to fail in their occupation. You don't want to use them when it's to your disadvantage, but you want to use them when it's to your advantage. Again, I think the American public is woefully ignorant when it comes to things outside the United States. I think we're an incredibly parochial, provincial country. I would have to look this up, but recently I saw a statistic on the percentage of people who read the newspaper. It's phenomenal. The percentage of people who have passports, who have been anywhere—I mean, how can they have any kind of perspective when they've never been anywhere?

It's human nature to want to believe our leaders. You want to believe all the mythologies that you're taught. I'm actually working on a book right now that has come out of two years of listening to people express their ignorance about American foreign policy. Trying to give people just a basic primer to understand the huge gap between the mythology of American values and how the values really play out in foreign policy. It's that gap in the foreign policy that makes the rest of the world hate us and see us as imperialist hypocrites. But Americans are just fairly ignorant of the history of this country and so they are unaware. They want to believe that we really stand for democracy everywhere. That we really stand for freedom of expression and a strong, viable free press and the right to dissent, and it's ridiculous. Sometimes we do; often we don't. People really have to know that, to understand why this country is so disliked right now. It's not pleasant to learn the truth. It's very unpleasant. Ignorance really is bliss. I wish I were ignorant. Unfortunately, I'm not.

JE: Should people be scared as a result of 9/11?

Should they be afraid of our administration or should they be afraid of terrorism or both? I think they should be afraid of both. I'm afraid of the Bush administration. I'm afraid of what they're doing to the United States internally and in the world. I'm afraid of how they have alienated so many governments. I hate to use the words 'war on terrorism' and dealing with the terrorist threat, I think it's obvious that the terrorist threat is real. What blew me away is that people acted like September 11 was the first. The Twin Towers had been attacked in 1993, for God's sake. What about the embassies in Africa? It's not the first time there's been terrorism in the United States or against US interests. I recognize the scale is much bigger, but it's not a new phenomenon. It's just been dramatically manipulated.

JE: Is there some basic connection between the work you've done, your experience with landmines in particular, what you've seen, and how you feel about this administration?

Look, one of the wonderful things about the landmine issue is how it was carried out. How the world worked together to bring about this treaty. It was radical. It was different. We stepped outside of the UN, not to insult the UN but because we recognized that the ossified structure was not going to produce what we needed, which was very simply a treaty that immediately banned the production, the trade, and the stockpiling of the weapon because the weapon was killing and maiming people all over the world, in seventy, eighty countries. We were able to galvanize public opinion to such a degree that we stimulated governments to take a risk. I recognize they took a risk. They took a diplomatic risk to address this problem differently from how other problems have been addressed. They stepped outside the UN; they made a stand-alone system to negotiate the treaty in which a majority ruled. In the UN any one nation can stop a negotiation. You can have a hundred countries in one room negotiating something and if one country disagrees, it's halted. Is that democracy? I mean, what is that? It's dictatorship of the one. I think it's hideous. We were able to make a different system in the negotiation of the landmine treaty. We worked in open partnership with governments. It was governments, civil society as expressed through the international campaign to ban landmines, which is 1,400 different organizations in countries around the world working together on this issue. Agencies of the UN were involved; the international Red Cross was involved. We all worked together for a common cause. We had a goal: to find a way to ban the weapon. We worked together to ban the weapon, and we have worked together since to make sure that the treaty is obeyed—which is a huge difference, and one of the reasons we are very successful. We didn't clap our hands and walk away when the treaty was negotiated. We recognized that it was merely the beginning, the possibility of the end of landmines. But if we couldn't get the governments to actually ratify the treaty and obey it and implement it, who cared? So what? You've got a nice document. We wanted to make sure that it was viable. And we have made it viable. We also showed the world that there are different ways to deal with problems.

Other issues have been addressed through the model of cooperation that we sort of established with the landmine campaign. The formation of the international criminal court, for example. A very strong coalition of non-governmental organizations working with governments to make that happen in spite of US opposition, vehement opposition, much stronger opposition than we had on the landmine issue. I think the world is in a horrible place, but it's also in a place where governments are recognizing that if they want the world to be different, they have to stand up and make it different. You can't just sit back and say, "Oh, the US is horrible…" If you don't want the US to dominate the world, work together to make it different in a positive way. It's not easy, but what's the alternative? Giving into the hegemony? Not in my book.

JE: One of Bill O'Reilly's favorite criticisms recently of those who oppose the conduct of this war is to label them "internationalists." He'll say he's an American first. Then you have neocons, guys like Robert Kagan, who have said France is hypocritical in its opposition to this war because they're not dealing with the reality that without our guns protecting them, they wouldn't have the luxury to sit around and philosophize about our militaristic streak.

I'm an American. I would wager that French people don't feel protected by our guns. I don't feel safer since we invaded Iraq with no provocation. I don't believe the rest of the world feels safer that the United States of America invaded Iraq unprovoked. Does that make the world feel safe? Does that make the world suddenly think that America is out there defending us all? It makes the world think that this administration has run amuck. That's a very different image from the wonderful America intervening and helping defeat Hitler and Japan. That is not the same as what we're seeing today and they twist history to make it seem the same. It is not the same. I, as an American, do not feel safe with this administration running around unilaterally invading countries. I'm talking as an American who wants to be safe in my country. I don't feel safe here with these people. It's not just because I run around loving the rest of the world. I see absurdities in other countries, believe me. I've worked with them. But they're not invading everybody at the drop of a hat. I don't have to worry about what France is doing. I worry about what this country is doing. This is my country and my country is invading countries unprovoked. Hello? I have every right to stand up and protest. I don't feel safe with this administration. I don't believe the invasion of Iraq made me safer and I'm going to say it.

JE: What would you say to people like my uncle—a good guy. A smart guy. A working-class guy. And a conservative, who supports Bush and the war.

I would ask him about Mr. Bush admitting in October or November in 2003 that there was no link between Saddam Hussein and the attacks on New York on September 11. Admitted it in public at a press conference. If there was no link, why does his administration continue to lie to the American public and imply that there was? If Mr. Bush had wanted us to support his policy of invading Iraq to bring down Saddam Hussein, to bring democracy to Iraq, in some sort of reverse domino theory through which we can get democracy just brewing throughout the region, why did he not state that openly and honestly to the American people and to the Congress? A president who lied to the people of America and to the Congress to further his policy objectives, is in my view worthy of at least a Congressional investigation, if not impeachment. I believe that a president should speak the truth to the people of the country. He lied to the people of America. Why did people get so upset about Bill Clinton's lie? Bill Clinton's lie cost nobody's life. Bill Clinton's lie merely affected his reputation and his relationship with his wife, right? It didn't do anything to American security. This man lied to Congress and the American public and we're supposed to say that's okay? We're supposed to applaud his war? It's Bush's war. It's Mr. Bush's war. It is not a war that makes us safer from terrorism. I don't care how many times he says it. It does not make us safer from terrorists. We will be attacked again.

Fredericksburg, Virginia
January 6, 2004

MAX WOLFF

Max Fraad Wolff is a doctoral candidate in economics at the University of Massachusetts, Amherst. He has written widely on finance and international political economy.

JE: How do you view the Bush administration's economic record?

First and foremost, I would split up my critique of this administration's policy into two separate tracks. One is that I don't favor many of their basic ideological assumptions and guiding principles. In other words, I believe there are significant and serious issues regarding the espoused worldview. Market fundamentalist rhetoric has reached a fever pitch in the US broadly and in the corporatist wing of the Republican Party particularly. The other indictment I would have centers on the actual policies undertaken. These need to be separated because, frankly, they are almost entirely unrelated. Rhetoric and policy are never identical. This administration has stretched the gap to a near breaking point. They are very fortunate to have been granted a free ride from much of the media—present company excluded. Minimal analysis would reveal a yawning gap between word and deed. If you accept their stated worldview, as most in my profession do, you immediately face a serious problem with administration action. From steel to textiles and beyond, free market speeches are directly contradicted by electoral needs for protection and the restriction of trade. The oft-touted fiscal restraint of the Republican Party has been shredded by Bush. Thus, we are told to fear and despise tax-and-spend liberals and to love cut-taxes-and-spend Bush—as long as the spending goes to leading firms and foreign and domestic military and monitoring spending. I suppose that is how federal surplus became record-breaking deficits as economic weakness—particularly in labor markets—drags on and on.

To be fair, economic times were hard across their early years in office. To be factual, they were heavy-handed, long-term irresponsible, and often unsuccessful in their responses. In response to the bursting of the stock market bubble they produced housing and bond market bubbles. In response to growing inequality they passed ruinous rounds of tax cuts targeted and delivered to the most fortunate. In response to trade deficits they have created downward wage pressures and subsidized profits that leave the masses no choice but to chase the cheapest foreign imports, while the increasingly wealthy purchase foreign luxury goods. Surprise, surprise: this produced growing inequality, soaring trade deficits, and lasting instability. As we meet today, the last big shoe—the housing market bubble—is yet to drop. Some of the deregulatory moves are ideologically consistent. However, many major policies look obviously to be based on rewarding contributors, enriching friends, and using the public purse to empower friends, allies, and select groups of swing voters and states. A stunning lack of competence and an inability to pull off even basic and simple advances that should come from the employment of their worldview means that more or less they're undertaking a set of actions that I don't think are prudent. And they are doing this so poorly that perhaps you have to look to their foreign policy track record to see as unmitigated and abysmal a set of failures.

The federal budget is a disaster. The trade deficit is ballooning out of control. The dollar has fallen. Poverty levels have risen. China is passing the US as a destination of foreign direct investment. We have the most unequal distribution of wealth in the developed world and growing, tens of millions without health insurance. I don't like the way they're going about things, and they're not doing a very good job of what it is they're trying to do. Dubious policies poorly executed—that would be the fast summary. I would ask people who watch or read this interview to ask themselves if this is acceptable. Is this the best they think America can do? I don't. I don't think economic theory or history supports or will look kindly on the actions and results of this administration.

JE: What do you see as their economic worldview?

There's the espoused worldview and then there's the economic policy. The idea is that the private market does things more efficiently, less expensively, and overall better than the public sector, so the public sector should be reduced, the private market should be deregulated to pursue highly efficient, highly profitable remedies to problems economic. This is and always has been a faith-based initiative. Reality—as is always the case—is more complex. There are not pure forces of good and evil at work in an economy. Free markets don't exist outside of theory books. Real markets, like all institutions, have real strengths and terrible weaknesses. Markets are one of many ways societies have developed to distribute goods, services, and wealth. They are as strong, efficient, and egalitarian as the broader societies that produce, host, influence, and support them. Markets are not natural or inevitable. Sites of exchange are created and maintained by particular societies and modified and influenced by their context. All of this is denied by the timeless, contextless, wisdom of naturally occurring and efficient markets celebrated in a quasi-religious worship by many in the administration. This is nothing other than a modern, scientific sales pitch for deregulation and the dismantling of the New Deal and Great Depression-era welfare state.

The problem is that the American middle class is, in no small way, the product of the policies they are trying to dismantle. They need to push a new ideology to convince a significant portion of the American middle class to vote for its extinction and to hate anything that stands in the way of this project. This worldview is an odd mixture of market worship and traditional values rhetoric. It involves a strange brew of family values, corporatism, anti-taxation policy, and reverence for military interventions and police power. Bush administration policy is a Frankenstein of crudely stitched initiatives defined by a confused mix of hatred for ideological opponents, preference for martial solutions, fraudulent traditional family values, and free marketeering. I don't think there's much to support their initiatives in terms of hard economic fact. It has fared terribly when employed. Perceptions of policy success are achieved despite the Bush team's efforts, yet they're splattered across headlines. I am sure this helps. Sooner or later the basic realities of strapped consumers sinking ever deeper into debt, facing stagnant wages, will emerge. In the past, the inability of unfettered private markets to deliver on vaunted claims has resulted in interventions to patch real problems produced by theoretically perfect markets. In such moments free market rhetoric often proves as popular as Herbert Hoover did in 1932.

JE: If that's their worldview, how have they been trying to implement it? What are the key moves they've made?

Waves of major cuts in progressive, capital gains, and estate taxes. We have already had two and we may be looking at a third to secure reelection. Imagine massive tax cuts in the midst of nearly $500 billion deficits. Oh wait, you can just read about that in the papers. Progressive income taxation is the most targeted. This form of taxation hits harder as your income rises. You don't just pay more money; you pay a higher percentage of your income. These and other income equalizing taxes are in the cross hairs. All of the above delivers vast sums to the wealthy.

This is nothing short of purposeful upward wealth redistribution. There is no serious economic debate on what this is and has been producing—rising inequality. There's been intentional reduction in the equity of the system. In other words, we're rewarding the highest income groups more than ever before in terms of our tax models, at least more than since the era of managed capitalism began in the '30s. State finances are squeezed and services are cut—redistributing wealth from the many to the few. You target the highest income people for the largest tax cuts for one of two reasons: either you are corrupt and paying back people who donated to your campaign, or you honestly believe that trickle-down works. Assuming you are not corrupt, you would seek to return wealth disproportionately to the wealthiest people hoping they spend it, creating an economy built around meeting elite needs and desires. A vast service class catering to whims for luxury goods, private professional services, vacations homes, resorts and spas, and private doctors will be built up around private decisions to spend. Sound familiar?

In addition you need to crush union movements, limit corporate oversight and the ability to file lawsuits. You would want to limit environmental standards, state regulatory authority, and corporate taxation. Much of this has been done, and so attention is coming to center on directly subsidizing private firms with public monies. Cost plus contracting and privatizing would then be favored. Wars are a popular way to transfer wealth and silence criticism at the same time. I would assume you'd have to believe the trickle-down theory, or that it's just a smash-and-grab gangsterism.

JE: Can you put these tax cuts into historical context?

A way to look at how radical this government is—they have cut taxes twice, à la Ronald Reagan, and their response is to cut them again. Keep in mind, all of Reagan and Bush I's policies are now law. Thus, they heap their doses of privatization, deficit spending, state service cuts, and regressive taxation atop a mountain of similar programs under their predecessors—including Clinton. All of this while spending billions a week on military adventures. Having seen the same kind of results that made Reagan's people sign on to raising taxes— exploding government deficits, soaring inequality and the social and political warning signs that come along with that—this administration steps on the gas. Their response has been, "We made a mess, let's make the mess bigger, so we can really change things." One might find a parallel with Iraq. Once started, the misadventure takes on urgency as it fails. Bush may become famous for ruinously finishing his father's war on Iraq and Reagan's wars on the welfare state and theAmerican middle class. So much unfinished business and so little restraint— internal or external—is a combustible mix. The only real question is the extent of the damage.

JE: Why are the exploding deficits we're seeing something that the average American should be concerned about, in your view?

Deficits are a contested issue because they're rarely explained and often politically exploited. In the simplest form, a deficit is when the federal government's tax revenues do not cover spending. If Uncle Sam is spending more than he is receiving, he is running deficits. If, as an individual, you are presently spending more than you are receiving, which most Americans are, you are running a deficit. Throughout history governments run deficits. The most common reason is that they want to stimulate the economy. Wars, disasters, huge public projects, and major economic downturns suddenly leave the state with insufficient funds to undertake planned or desired programs. Recessions have driven many large increases in America's recent national debt. The national debt is the sum of our past deficits and surpluses. Private businesses, allowed to make their own spending decisions—that's what free enterprise means— become concerned about near or long term economic prospects. They then begin to save, and what does that mean? They spend less on new machines, develop fewer new products, and lay off workers.

Firms need to make these adjustments to survive real or perceived coming economic weaknesses. This creates a problem in the economy; there's money missing from the circular flow; it's missing from the system. This creates recession. This is what happened beginning in the spring of 2000. Scared, the government tried to step in and solve this problem by cutting taxes and raising government spending. The federal government reduces its income, cuts taxes, and increases government spending. The state is getting less money and spending more. Many notice the government spending more than it is getting in tax revenue and borrowing to make up the difference. Before long there's a discussion about deficits. What people should know enough to care about is what they are getting and what they are losing. What taxes are cut, which taxes are not cut, what are their tax dollars spent on, what is not spent on? That is where all the action is for the individual

American. If they cut your taxes, you're that much better off. If they cut taxes, but not your taxes, you get nothing, and your government has less money to spend on things you might need or want. You may lose from a tax cut; you may gain from a tax cut. It all depends on which taxes are cut and how you and your community are affected. Likewise, if the state responds to recession by increasing government spending, the question is, on what? If they spend on something that benefits you, you're better off. If they spend on something that hurts you, you are worse off.

JE: What are the implications of these economic policies for middle-class Americans?

Millions of people who think of themselves as middle class are already poor. They've refinanced their homes several times, have huge credit card balances, and are unsustainably in debt. Wages have not kept up with spending for many years. We can and do continue to purchase and live the way middle-class people do. However, that prosperity has already slipped outside the reach of many, many millions of our fellow Americans. They are already not middle class, and their numbers are growing. With the first stumble in the credit stream, or in home refinancing, or when that essential service is cut by a strapped government, they will begin to realize they have been left behind. There is growing awareness already that the dream is slipping away.

I would guess that already a third of that vast middle, as defined by economists—not self-defined—is already actually poor. They are hard working people, but because they've taken on so much debt, sent every member of the house out to work longer and longer hours, they can live as though they are middle class. The longer this regime continues, the larger that number will become, and the more rapidly the day will come when they can no longer call themselves middle class. The political future of the country rests on how they respond to a) the fact that they're a growing group, and b) who they blame when that other shoe drops. That is where the action is to determine the economic future and probably a lot of the political future of this country. The growing rage of these people and their desperate attempt to identify the cause of their suffering are already a driving force in this society. When they get mentioned at all in popular discourse, they are called soccer moms and NASCAR dads. They are victims of one of the greatest upward wealth redistributions in the modern world.

JE: How do you respond to the administration's claim that 9/11 is one of the reasons the economy went hard and deep into recession?

The attacks alone would have certainly rattled the country. It was a horrible tragedy and it shook people up and was a terrible, devastating event to witness again and again and again on television. This exacerbated preexisting economic conditions. It did not create the recession, nor the stock market and macroeconomic downturn, which were already clearly occurring prior to the attacks.

The idea that the Bush plans are somehow a response to September 11, I think is totally ridiculous. If you want a stark example, right after September 11, invoking the attacks, Bush pushed the exact tax plan that he ran on in 1999. The tax plan he ran on became a unique response to September 11? I think it's hard to pin that on any particular ideology. It's pure Machiavellian, political opportunism. I don't think their plans had much to do with September 11, other than creating space for policy. The attacks turned an administration that lacked the credibility of winning the popular vote into valiant defenders of a nation under siege. No opportunity was squandered in the rush through a wish list of unpopular legislation as the nation grieved.

JE: Do you see any connections between these economic theories and policies and the administration's foreign policy, specifically the political ideology that emerged after 9/11?

Foreign policy and economics are intimately intertwined. This is an insecure time for corporations and the administration, which are essentially one and the same. If you want a good example of the revolving door, look no further than the Bush administration. You can hear the doors swinging. It's a frightening world. If we saw the Clinton era being defined by a pro-market free trade in which the United States used its influence in the WTO, IMF, World Bank, BIS, OECD, UN, etc., Bush's people are much bigger at pushing smaller bilateral trade deals with the armed forces. They ran against extended foreign engagements, over-stretched militaries, and nation-building—all the things they are now doing. In the process, they have failed royally to win friends and allies and make progress in the free trade stream. They are driving a basic systemic shift in the global economy that really picked up steam and urgency after September 11.

This administration is switching the world system to one in which a dominant military becomes the basis of economic success. Contracts will be brow-beaten or invaded into being, resources snatched or pressured. You can see that with the "Coalition of the Willing." States' allegiances are bought or pressured. Governments are pressured out of ICC [International Criminal Court] membership because they need US military aid. Spheres of influence are developing, the US pitted against those it is undermining, attacking or out-maneuvering. The idea that runs throughout the Bush Departments of State and Defense is that this is a new economic period; it is not one of corporate battles, although that's the rhetoric. It's one in which the power of the US central state will be systematically brought to bear at great cost in lives, both American and foreign, at great cost in resources, both American and foreign, to secure for American firms, and for America, a dominant position in the next century.

JE: One of the key ways this administration has justified its economic policies in the wake of 9/11 is to tie them to the national interest...

The whole patriotism thing has an analogy in economics. Neoclassicals are fond of the saying credited to Margaret Thatcher called TINA: There Is No Alternative. You may or may not like this free market that we're pushing—the United States, the WTO, IMF, the World Bank—but it doesn't really matter because there is no alternative. It's our game or backwardness, poverty, wretchedness, and unscientific wallowing in discredited ideology. The same thing is done in the political realm. The menu of choices lists excited obedience, patriotism, resistance, enemy combatant, or weasel. This series of false choices is sold by the Bush administration and bought by a subset of the American public. That is, don't question the government, send your child off to whatever the war of the month is, pay your taxes, push for tax reductions across the board for your charity-case local billionaire, and keep your mouth closed. You'll be rewarded with whatever we don't finish from the table. The scraps will go to you first and the rest of the people simply won't eat.

This is the new global and local version of TINA, made harsher and meaner for the new post-boom war economy. Now that the country is legitimately imperiled—although I would argue largely by foreign policy decisions made by this administration—people have a sense of insecurity; it may come from working long hours, from having a government that provides fewer and fewer second chances and basic services, from watching those around you who don't have any money live a worse and worse life, from the fact that there are almost 50 million people in this country with no health insurance, from the fact that millions of jobs have been lost under Bush's watch—but there's a basic feeling of insecurity. For many it is about the viability of the family, the viability of the job, the viability of the country, the security of your retirement, your relationship with your children, the schools to which you send them, etc. That is exploited. The idea is root for a winner; America and the American military are winners. But it's so fragile that some guy on the street corner with a paper sign who criticizes this agenda could cause the whole thing to fall apart. Many confused, frightened people find a choice-less, paranoid vision of the future viable because they want and need to be able to look to their leaders in these trying times. They have been taught that only elites dare to talk back and disagree, and have been encouraged to identify opponents of administration policy as wealthy, whiny people who don't do their part to help. Criticism, like loose lips, sinks ships. When you have a nude emperor, that's always true. You can't have clothing discussion hour. So in a nude emperor time, discussing the clothes is always off the list. This emperor is particularly nude, to the collective horror of many of us. The specter of this nude emperor in these terrifying times has led millions to imagine clothing, fine and flowing robes. But if you don't see the robes, then you have a different vision and it's less appetizing.

JE: A lot of people would suggest that the increased military spending we've had under this administration will actually benefit the economy. What's your view of this?

Increased military spending benefits the economy because any spending would. If the government bought textbooks, that would also benefit the economy, only we'd be left with more kids with high school and college degrees instead of more unexploded ordinances in Third World countries. Both are spending; they both inject money into the economy. All expenditures fund the purchase and sale of goods and services that benefit the overall economy. But if you build up a giant arsenal, the temptation to use it is higher and it means that money is channeled to the four or five large defense contractors who reap the profits.

The other issue is that if you overspend—which in 2003 we did to the tune of more than $400 billion, with everyone's guess at about $500 billion in 2004—that money must be paid back. That means, somewhere down the road, Americans will pay taxes and get nothing. Future generations' taxes will go to pay back those who loaned the government money in the form of buying government Treasuries. Among the groups and individuals who buy a lot of Treasuries are foreigners and foreigner institutions, who hold over a third of our debt, with the rest held by banks, insurance companies, and wealthy individuals. Amidst the bold declarations, the America-rides-alone talk, and the military ticker tape parades, they have sold the future tax receipts of the federal government to the rest of the world. While we can go it alone and we're mighty tough, whatever we do we had damn well better pay the rest of the world a third of our future tax revenues. That's not so macho. We lose the cowboy image. The cowboy occasionally stopping the horse, getting off the saddle and going to the Western Union to wire money to the rest of the world is not in a lot of Western films. It doesn't seem super cool. But that would be the new American debt cowboy. Our cowboy is going to have to hop off that horse periodically—by the way, the horse that he won't own—and make payments to whoever does own the horse and the saddle and the gun and the boots and the hat. You'll still see the cowboy riding around, but this messes with the image.

JE: One of the ways that people neutralize the kind of criticism you're wielding against this administration's economic philosophy is to label and dismiss it as class warfare. Your response?

Class warfare? As if there's an option. I mean there are different classes of income, which is usually what people mean by class: wealthier or less wealthy. Different classes of income in this country have different interests. There are other theories of class as well. One such theory divides the economy according to positions relative to the production, appropriation, and distribution of value and surplus value (crudely similar to profit). This theory offers very powerful insights but is rarely discussed in American politics, so I won't discuss it much further in this interview. However, I think people would understand your question differently if they used this theory of class. It's a nice story that everyone has the same interests and we can go skipping off together into the sunset. But like most nice stories, by the time you're 10, when you're confronting the reality that the tooth fairy didn't put the money under your pillow and that no fat man in red pajamas—you better hope—is coming down the chimney to slug that milk and cookies, it is time to grow up and move on. It's time to confront that everyone doesn't have the same interests, shock of all shocks.

JE: What about the fact that the administration tells us daily that our economy's in recovery, and that key indicators are proving that Bush's economic plan was right all along?

Who recovered? Who didn't? Well, the millions of people who don't have jobs didn't recover. They lost. So too did millions more who are underemployed, without health care, unable to afford childcare, hopelessly indebted, and so on. The people whose unemployment benefits ran out didn't recover. They lost. The people whose cars were repossessed last year didn't recover. They lost. The record-breaking numbers of people who will default on their home payments and their credit card payments—they didn't win either. They lost. The overall economy has done better, and that is a good thing. It has done better than it did two years ago, when it did really, really badly. If I were to give an analogy: if you have a child who gets straight Ds and they come home the next year with straight Cs, that's good. It's a serious improvement and it should be acknowledged. However, this is not the dean's list, okay—that has to be kept in perspective. And the overall economy, because it's a giant aggregate, over thirteen trillion dollars involved, all different sectors, all different levels of income, can obscure the reality for many of the people.

We've had a job-loss recovery, in which we haven't created enough new jobs. We're down millions from where we should be. That is, millions of American families are touched by prolonged and perhaps serious unemployment. Millions of people have left the work force all together, so they are not counted as unemployed. However, since they earn no income, at least none legally, they might well be considered to be in trouble. Likewise, the average work week has fallen, so we know a lot of people are involuntarily part time. In other words, they may be working 20, 30, 35 hours a week when they want at least 40. We know the labor force participation rate—how many people are in the labor force—has fallen to a multi-decade low of about 66 percent. So we know fewer people are working because a lot of them have given up. We also see staggering rates of personal indebtedness, heavy overuse of public services—homeless shelters packed like never before, food banks stretched to the breaking point in many cases. The recovery has missed tens of millions of people and there's no telling how long it will last. There is an awful lot of unsustainable stimulus in our weak economy; the federal government is pumping cash into the economy, as is the rest of the world, by loaning us money at unsustainably low interest rates. Interest rates are at 40-year lows, making it cheap to borrow money, and everybody is. The debt goes up, and you have stagnant wages, so people aren't earning more. The federal government is taking in historically low percentage levels of tax revenue. People are buying cheap foreign imports and they can barely make it. That calls into question how robust the recovery is and how many people have really recovered. To which you could add the 40+ million with no health insurance and the millions of people whose retirements have been called into question or decimated.

These things tend to sort of tell a nerve-wracking story about the potential future. Could the economy do well for a while? Yes. I hope it does. But, again, it's on a very tenuous foundation, this economy— unsustainable government support, unsustainable debt, home refinancing. These are things you can't do forever. That's what we've done to ride out the recession to the extent that we have. It's been very painful for a lot of people over the last three years.

JE: For middle- and lower-income Americans, what are the implications of a second Bush term?

I think millions and millions of Americans have had—or thought they had—the luxury of feeling like they would survive, that their middle-class status would survive come the better governments and worse. That delusion is certainly dead now. Whether it was the Republicans or the Democrats, whether it was this candidate or that, many people felt they could relax and little was at stake. That luxury is now over. Given the pain, the increased debt, the loss of job stability, the outsourcing of employment, the enormous financial fragility of the modern American economy that has developed over the recent past and gone into hyper drive in the last three years, there is no fat left to cut, the saws are on the bone. It is my personal opinion that a significant portion of the American middle class may not survive another four-year term of this administration. There is only so much more to refinance, there will be rising interest rates on accumulated debt, there will be continued weakness in the job market that you simply cannot afford. So, like 2000, and what happened there, in 2004 there will be a referendum on your future—called the presidential election. And this time, it won't be more or less the same. An enormous number of people, whether they realize it or not, cannot survive, even with the delusion of middle-class status, with four more years like the past four.

Northampton, Massachusetts
April 7, 2003